FRANK R. KRAMER

Voices in the Valley

MYTHMAKING AND FOLK BELIEF IN THE SHAPING OF THE MIDDLE WEST

THE UNIVERSITY OF WISCONSIN PRESS

Published by the University of Wisconsin Press
430 Sterling Court, Madison 6, Wisconsin

Printed in the United States of America by
Vail-Ballou Press, Inc., Binghamton, New York

Library of Congress Catalog Card Number 64–10923

TO MY MOTHER *Mabel Shaw Kramer*

ACKNOWLEDGMENTS

I am deeply indebted in the preparation of this book to the librarians of the Wisconsin Historical Society Library, the Public Archives of Canada, the Newberry Library, and the Iowa Historical Society Library. Special gratitude is due the Wisconsin Committee on the Study of American Civilization for grants which made possible two leaves of absence and in particular to Miss Alice E. Smith, Chief of Research of the Committee, Dr. Vernon Carstenson, Dr. Merrill Jensen, and Dr. Clifford L. Lord, whose insights and encouragement contributed fundamentally to the progress of this study. Further financial aid was provided by the Social Science Research Council.

For preparing the map for my book I am grateful to the Cartographic Laboratory of the University of Wisconsin.

My colleagues, Dr. Forrest M. Keen and Dr. John I. Kolehmainen, brought their special skills to the examination of various chapters; Mr. and Mrs. Frank Lucas of Friendship, Wisconsin, Mrs. Eva (Chyda) Bock, and Eleanor Ledbetter generously supplied materials for Czechoslovakian lore; for aspects of the work of the Jesuits in Canada, Mr. Wilfred Jury of the University of Western Ontario was most helpful. I owe a particular debt of gratitude to my wife Hetty for her help in every phase of the manuscript.

The chapter "The Devil and Champlain" is reprinted by permission from *Inland Seas,* Quarterly Journal of the Great Lakes Historical Society, Vol. VII (Fall, 1951).

F. R. K.

Heidelberg College
July, 1963

CONTENTS

ILLUSTRATIONS

[Myth is] the universal instinct of any human group, large or small, to invest, almost always unconsciously, certain stories or events or places or persons, real or fictional, with an uncommon significance; to turn them into instinctive centres of reference. . . . Made thus typical, the story becomes a communal possession. . . .

E. M. W. TILLYARD

The civilization of an epoch is its myth in action.

HERMANN BROCH

Myth is wisdom's last word.

BRUNO SNELL

INTRODUCTION

*I*nto the great interior of America came waves of immigrants—not like the slow thrust of glaciers but tumbling swiftly, from foreign lands and from states near by, one upon the other. Yet like the ice that gouged out the Great Lakes and changed the course of rivers flowing into the Mississippi, these massive movements left records anonymous and sweeping but none the less vivid—the basins and ramifications of folk beliefs.

It is of such beliefs that this book is written. They emerge in dramas staged in Canadian forests and Kentucky farms, where Huron rituals and Methodist revivals renewed the awful sense of intimacy with the sources of natural and spiritual power. They are the colors of the spectrum that arched over Champlain's dream of fresh water empires and the terrestrial paradise of the Jesuit missions. They are crystallized in symbols of bank barns and homesteads, symbols that sum up the little family worlds of Pennsylvania Germans and settlers in the Middle West and image their differing ideals of progress—the taproot of enrichment for soul and soil, the spreading runners that promised a luxuriant growth of the interior. They are frozen in the charts and maps, the figures and credits from which Yankees built railroads and lithographic cities with straight thoroughfares and sinuous byways of finance. They materialize in workingmen's myths of a new social faith—of trade unions that would soon, it seemed, be centers of democracy and "harbingers of universal happiness." And they flourish today in the myths of the American way that industry transformed from the folk idylls of farmer and laborer into a national cult.

These richly variant expressions of folk belief are fascinating in themselves, not as exhibits in a historical museum but as vivid reminders that folk logic grows as lush in fields tamed by a tractor as in those worked by oxen, that mirages glow wherever "the lone and level sands" of human life stretch far away. But in this book we are concerned rather with the way in which people's beliefs affect their actions—the way in which they lead us to folk assumptions so implicitly accepted that people are seldom aware that they have them and so deeply imbedded that they continually color and shape their behavior.

If these assumptions have value for the historian, it is just at this point; for the folklore, symbols, and myths that embody them reveal, like outcroppings of rock, the substratum of reality on which people build their beliefs. Settlers of the early Middle West would have thought the Huron festival summoning all the spirits of the forest to a three-day revelry was a piece of primitive nonsense; but their own lore is one long conversation with mysterious natural powers, and a Presence spoke to them, as to the Indians, through the earthquake, wind, and fire. Pennsylvania Germans, too, were steeped in a tradition that saw mind and purpose in nature, but they reversed the pattern of the Indians' great cosmic family: like the cattle and Conestoga horses, the celestial Furies were domesticated, were a part of the *Heimat*, the home-center of a larger family circle.

How, then, must a measure like the Homestead Bill have looked when it was translated into Pennsylvania German? What a different kind of reality from the homesteaders', who construed it as a title to the garden of democracy, or from the Yankee industrialists', who interpreted it as a blueprint for larger factories and cities! And the engineers of these cities, men whose world

was erected on the girders of abstract, anonymous symbols—
what would they make of the reality of the Mississippi Valley,
where a century ago all things were reduced to the human equation, to metaphors of humanity? The same landscape is framed
by folk symbols and folklore into very different realities; and it
is these separate little worlds that people really live in, worlds
in which they find the sources of power and the myths to justify
and maintain it.

While we were on the trail of these realities, it became increasingly clear that wherever we happened to be—whether in
Huronia or Jasper County, Iowa; in Reading, Pennsylvania, or
Ohio's Western Reserve—we were following a strangely familiar
network, a pattern of folk "logic" that recurred again and again.
It was not simply that traditional lore cropped up in different
dress and dialect; in each area folk belief moved along well-
charted ways of "reasoning," guided by the same ancient as-
tronomy to similar havens.

But is it strange that men should interpret their different
worlds by the same processes of folk logic—by the analogies, contrasts, and reciprocities with which they reduce everything to
their own understanding, by the one magic formula exalted to an
absolute? No stranger, perhaps, than that they should idealize
women from Pretty Polly to Juliet in similar ways. "Two of
the fairest stars . . . her eyes in heaven would through the airy
region stream so bright that birds would sing," chants Romeo,
making a reciprocal metaphor of their celestial gleam. But all is
not serene: Romeo is a Montague and she a Capulet; what
cannot be ignored must be explained away. So "what's a
Montague?" reasons Juliet; "it is nor hand, nor foot." The world
is narrowed to Juliet, and then—"Heaven is here where Juliet
lives; there is no world without Verona's walls but . . . hell itself."

So was it when French missionaries and explorers were cap-
tivated by the tribal harmony of the Hurons, likened their own
settlements on the St. Lawrence to the Christian communities

of early Palestine, and contrasted them with the corrupting civilization of Louis XIV; when they equated the Indian's apparent simplicity with the noble artlessness of "natural man" and made their qualities reciprocal; and when they exalted the intensity, harmony, and serenity of their life to a terrestrial paradise. So was it too when the Middle Western homesteader made of the Mississippi Valley a "garden of the world," and when a Yankee promoter sang: "Plymouth Rock is only the doorstep of a house that reaches to the Golden Gate." So it is with all the Middle West and with the folk everywhere, for analogy, contrast, the reciprocal exchange of qualities, the narrowing of everything to a single factor and the magnifying of that factor to an absolute are fundamental processes of folk logic.

In this way each folk * fashions its myth. As in the lore of the Hurons, myth *creates* its world—the psychological focusing of a complex physical and social universe into an organic, intelligible whole. As it was among the Jesuit missionaries, prairie farmers, and workingmen, myth is a picture and a prayer—an image of reality and an aspiration to achieve it. As in the minds of Scotch-Irish settlers in the lower Middle West or, more recently, of industrial leaders, myth is also the response to the challenge of "heresy"—to whatever appears to distort the vision of reality or disrupt it. Certain facets of myth are revealed better, perhaps, in some myths than in others; but in varying degrees the characteristic patterns are found in all.

Yet behind these myth patterns—implicit in every body of folk belief—there appears a certain insistently recurring relationship of ideas. There is, first of all, a prevailing view of *reality*—a forest filled with spirit life; a private world that one can enter only through emotion or intuition; a land teeming with material things like ore, machines, money, oil; a rational universe ultimately reducible to abstract symbols. Believers in these realities derive

* A "folk" may be any group (e.g., ethnic or occupational) which has developed mutually recognizable symbols and patterns of group thinking and behavior.

from each the special kind of *power* presumed to be inherent in it (how else could power be genuine or lasting?). The awful authority of the medicine man rested on the spirit voices of the wilderness; from the Presence pervading Kentucky hills was lit the inner fire that would bring the millennium to being. The seed-force that sprouted farms upon the prairie was nurtured in the "garden of the world"—the virgin Truth of agrarian democracy; the abstract symbols of scientific reality supplied the energy for the dynamos of industrial growth. And finally in this recurring relationship of ideas, there emerges *myth,* which embodies reality in canonical form and naturalizes the notions of power that stem from it.

These basic components of folk belief—reality, power, myth —seldom appear in such logical sequence. To a Henry Ford, expanding power may be the all-absorbing fact; later—when it has grown big enough, perhaps, to jostle other power elements in society—he begins to look for roots in reality, for a way of fitting his pattern of power into the natural, inevitable order of things. To a crusading knight of labor like Terence Powderly, myth may itself be the doorway to reality, the matrix of power. But folk belief is an organic thing: these vital components are all there whether we start with flower or seed.

But why, if mythmaking processes and the elements of folk belief are alike everywhere, is it of particular interest to examine their configuration in the Middle West? It is because the migrations of common people from many nations into the great interior of America was truly a *folk* movement. It is because the interior moved so rapidly from the wilderness frontiers of the nation to the industrial frontiers of the world that we have an unparalleled opportunity to see how the myths of one folk shouldered those of another and were fused and transformed under the impact of historical forces. And it is because it was in the Middle West that industry adapted agrarian and labor myths to its own myth of the American way.

Frenchman and Huron

*F*rench explorers and missionaries in Canada in the seventeenth century discovered a land of forests and Indian villages, of rapids and myth. It was a world molded as much by prolific mythmaking as by prodigal nature: spirits had fashioned the land and the rivers (an island-world that fitted well the assumptions of explorers looking for the Northwest Passage); they governed the behavior of the earth and of the skies above it. Man and nature were of one order of being, and so their attributes were mutually interchangeable: nature, like man, had a mind and a soul; and men might share in the extraordinary powers of a spirit-invested universe. Like the medicine men, Champlain, Nicolet, and the Jesuit missionary Brébeuf had (in the eyes of the Indians) something of the supernatural, the demonic, that linked them with the spirits; and it was this regard for them as men endowed with powers beyond the ordinary that was to aid them immeasurably in their explorations into the waterways, the communal society, and the souls of the Indians.

In the wholeness of this animistic universe, in this communal reality, the French found the wellspring of social and spiritual dynamic in tribal life. Huron ceremonies like the *Ononhwaroia*, a ritualistic abandonment to demonic powers, renewed the partnership men had with the spirits and—in that oneness—the very integrity of their being. The Feast of the Dead, the burial in a common pit of bodies exhumed from graves in various villages and covered over with layers of furs and other valued possessions for the poor to salvage, preached powerfully to the French of innate selflessness and spiritual fervor. As the Indians had reduced their physical and social world to an intelligible whole by analogy, by the cosmic equation of man and nature, so the French by the same processes of folk logic likened the stoic nobility and harmony of Indian life to the primitive communities of Rome and Palestine and contrasted them with the cynical, sophisticated civilization of Louis XIV. In vivid memoirs and annals they shaped the myth of an organic community of "noble savages" in which France might find the pattern of a reality that would provide a new and vital power.

1 · A DREAM OF FAIR WATERS

*What dost thou believe, then, if thou
dost not believe in thy dream?*

*W*hen in the summer of 1671 St. Lusson,
the royal agent of France, stood near the falls of St. Mary's in
upper Michigan and intoned the ritualistic formula annexing in
the name of Louis XIV the Sault and Lakes Superior and Huron,
he was claiming for his king a land long hallowed in the lore of
the representatives of most of the fourteen Indian peoples assembled for the ceremony. This was the traditional meeting place
of the tribes. It was the legendary home of Hiawatha. On the
nearby island of Michilimackinac the great Algonquin culture
hero Manabozho had been born, had with giant footstep crushed
the beaver-built falls of St. Mary's to their present drop and reduced the cataracts above into rapids, had hunted the beaver
with eight-league strides in Lake Superior, and had by one account created the world and taught his people to make fire and
fish nets.

It was a memorable occasion. Within a half century after they
had begun serious exploration of the Great Lakes region the
French were now erecting the cross and the royal emblem at the
strategic point linking the upper lakes with the lower. Within
a few years after St. Lusson had taken verbal possession of the
lakes and "all countries, rivers, lakes, and streams contiguous and
adjacent thereunto . . . bounded on the one side by the seas of
the North and of the West, and on the other by the South Sea,"

Father Marquette, who had arrived from Chequamegon Bay too late for the ceremony, and Louis Joliet, now listening with personal interest as St. Lusson spoke, would be placing the stamp of authenticity on his words by the exploration of the Mississippi. Yet the real significance of the occasion lay not in the dubious claim to the waterways stretching from the Atlantic to mid-continent and from there somewhere south to the ocean. The pageant was remarkable rather for the symbolism implicit in the gathering together of the tribes through the influence of an inimitable group of diplomat-traders and missionary-explorers who must now have been deriving ironic satisfaction in challenging the Algonquin Creator in the heart of his creation and matching wits with the Trickster.

There was, first of all, Nicolas Perrot. He had threaded the lakes and rapids from the St. Lawrence to the Mississippi and the more unpredictable eddies in the minds of the Indians. Thoroughly familiar with their folkways and folklore, Perrot had been able almost alone to persuade the chieftains of the Wisconsin tribes—the Potawatomi, Menomini, Sauk, Fox, Mascouten, and Miami—to assemble at the Sault to acknowledge (at least formally) the sovereignty of the French king.

There was Louis Joliet, who had two years earlier, on the advice of an Iroquois captive, forsaken the northern canoe route from the Sault to Montreal in favor of the Iroquois-infested trail through Lake Erie—the first recorded visit by a white man to this last-discovered lake. On the north shore of Lake Ontario he had met La Salle and had told him of his discovery, and La Salle was soon to sail his famous *Griffin* westward over the same route.

Conspicuous among the nearly naked Indians and the resplendent uniforms of the king's representatives were the *robes noires* —the Jesuit missionaries Allouez, Dablon, and André. They knew, no less than the traders, the bitter physical fatigue of portaging through swamps and underbrush. Far better than the traders they understood the spiritual weariness of carrying the burden of the faith through the tangled growth of Indian social and religious legend.

These were the men on whom the King of France relied to maintain his empire in the New World—these and a few that had come before them, never more than a handful at any mission or post. But how were so few, almost wholly dependent upon the resources they found at hand, able to extend their explorations and influence into the heart of the continent? As divergent as trader, explorer, and missionary were in their motives, they were agreed upon this point: that they must know and understand the Indian in order to get his beaver skins, to penetrate his land, or to effect his conversion to Christianity. They mastered the difficult languages, sat on the floors of smoke-saturated cabins, cramped themselves into canoes for trips of hundreds of miles into the wilderness, and listened to tales of demons and spirits and of dreams that decided wars. Until, finally, the Indian became less strange, less savage, as the Frenchmen came to know him, and emerged as a human being.

What the explorers and missionaries learned about the Indian and his land was enough to accomplish in great part the aims they set for themselves. But the vast new country and the folkways of tribal peoples were working slow changes in the Frenchmen—incalculable changes that carried far beyond their aims and remained long after the beavers and the Indians had retreated. These developments did not spend themselves, in fact, until they had modified the social philosophy of Europe and left enduring patterns in the culture of midwestern America.

*F*ew of the magnificently mad explorers of the sixteenth and seventeenth centuries who naively supposed that they could reach the riches of the Orient more quickly across the American continent than by digging straight through the center of the earth were better prepared for their mission than Samuel de Champlain. The smell of gunpowder was as familiar to his nostrils as the perfumed wiggery of Paris; as Royal Geographer in the court of Henry IV, he knew with equal thoroughness the minutely measured distances of map-making and the long sea miles between the French coast and the Mexican Indians. To well-filled sails of experience he added the stout rigging of character: courage, perseverance, tact, piety, and vision —all were his. As he sailed into the Gulf of the St. Lawrence in 1603, one thing alone was lacking to the success of his exploratory venture into the Canadian wilderness—an area manual on the history and culture of devils.

Hardly had he rounded the cliffs of the Gaspé Peninsula when he came to grips with the first of the demons that held the New World in fief. It was a portent of what was to come, of the hosts of devils that would contest his passing the rapids and portaging the falls, until finally he overcame them and became, in the eyes of the savages, himself a benevolent spirit.

"There is still one strange thing," wrote Champlain, "worthy of an account, which many savages have assured me was true";

that is, that near the Bay of Heat, toward the south, there is an island where a frightful monster makes his home, which the savages call Gougou, and which they told me had the form of a woman, but very terrible, and of such a size that they told me the tops of the masts of our vessel would not reach to his (sic!) waist, so great do they represent him; and they say that he has often eaten up and still continues to eat up many savages; these he puts, when he can catch them, into a great pocket, and afterward he eats them; and those who had escaped the danger of this awful beast said that its pocket was so great that it could have put our vessel into it. This monster makes horrible noises in this island, which the savages call the Gougou; and when they speak of it, it is with unutterable fear, and several have assured me that they have seen him. Even . . . Sieur Prevert from St. Malo told me that, while going in search of mines . . . he passed so near the haunt of this terrible beast, that he and all those on board his vessel heard strange hissings from the noise she made, and that the savages with him told him it was the same creature, and that they were so afraid that they hid themselves wherever they could, for fear that she would come and carry them off.

And then this sober, seasoned explorer makes a candid admission.

What makes me believe what they say is the fact that all the savages in general fear her, and tell such strange things of her that, if I were to record all they say of her, it would be considered as idle tales, but I hold that this is the dwelling-place of some devil that torments them in the manner described. This is what I have learned about this Gougou.[1]

Sailing up the St. Lawrence in a ship of more than ten tons, Champlain could afford to dismiss the Gougou: the sturdy vessel and the narrative of Jacques Cartier, who almost a century before had ascended the river to the site of Montreal, made the odds reasonably safe. But it was another matter when, ten years later, Champlain reached the rapids that boiled in disheartening succession near Montreal and on up the Ottawa River—long the highway of the Algonquins and Hurons and after Champlain the route of French missionaries, explorers, and traders to the western Great Lakes for almost two hundred years:

He that would passe them, must fit himself with the Canoas of the Sauages, which one may easily carrie . . . . And beside this first Sault (rapid), there are ten Saults more, the most part hard to passe . . . . They [the Indians] told us, that beyond the first Sault that we had seene, they trauelled some ten or fifteene leagues with their Canoas in the Riuer where there is a riuer [the Ottawa] which runneth to the dwelling of the Algoumequins [Algonquins] . . . and then they passed fiue Saults [the Cascades, Split Rock, Cedar and Coteau rapids], which may containe from the first to the last eight leagues, whereof there are two where they carrie their Canoas to passe them: euery Sault may containe halfe a quarter or a quarter of a league at the most.[2]

Such was the highway to the Orient—enough to turn back any but the most intrepid explorer, the most incurable dreamer. Being both, Champlain would not be discouraged. "The strong love which I have always cherished for the exploration of New France," he once testified in the tone of a credo, "has made me desirous of extending more and more my travels over the country, in order, by means of its numerous rivers, lakes, and streams, to obtain at last a complete knowledge of it, and also to become acquainted with the inhabitants . . . to learn the language, and form relations and friendships with the leading men of the villages and tribes, in order to lay the foundations of a permanent edifice, as well for the glory of God as for the renown of the French." [3]

Now if ever the time was ripe for furthering these high-sounding aims. Ten years of forthright diplomacy had earned him the respect of the Indians and the ear of such men as Jeannin, the royal superintendent of finance. And last year he had secured a commission from Louis XIII with such sweeping powers as to make him—on paper at least—the actual ruler of New France. But prestige and powers must have seemed feeble and far away when, on May 27, 1613, he reached the great Montreal rapids.

Here two years earlier his "hair stood on end to see such an awful place"; here he had run the rapids to prove to the Indians that he was not afraid and then admitted candidly: "Even the bravest people in the world who have not seen nor passed this place in small boats such as theirs, could not do so without great apprehension." [4] He was perhaps the first European to shoot these rapids; in 1535 Jacques Cartier, though he had laughed down Chief Donnaconna's dire warning not to flaunt the wrath of Coudouagni, god of the rapids, had turned back. More than half a century from now the veteran Louis Joliet, returning from his epochal tour of the Mississippi, would capsize here, losing his maps and papers, in sight of the city now rising on the shore.

Once again, at the entrance of this American Avernus, Champlain with four Frenchmen (including the young Nicolas du Vignau, who had promised to lead him to Hudson Bay) and one Indian guide found himself trespassing on the domain of aboriginal demons—twelve miles of whirling, weaving waters known as the Long Sault. "The rapidity of the current is so great," Champlain reported, "that it makes a terrible noise, and in pouring down from one layer of rock to another it makes so much white foam everywhere that the water cannot be seen at all." [5] Caught in another white hell on the Gatineau River not far to the west, the Récollet brother Gabriel Sagard had asked his guides how such things could be. "They replied that it was the devil's doing or the devil himself." [6] The trees on the bank stood trunk to trunk; portaging was impossible. Champlain was forced to drag his canoe with a rope wound around his hand. "As I was drawing mine," he continued,

I thought I was lost, because it swerved into one of the whirlpools, and if I had not, fortunately, fallen between two rocks, the canoe would have dragged me in . . . . In this danger I cried to God, and began to pull my canoe, which was returned to me by a back current, such as is found in these rapids. Having escaped, I praised God, begging Him to preserve us . . . . As for our Frenchmen, they did not have any better luck, and several times they expected to lose their lives, but the Divine Goodness kept us all safe.⁷

And this was only the first of the rapids. The Northwest Passage was a grim carnival—now a roller coaster, jerking the canoe suddenly ahead and shooting it breathlessly over and between the rocks, now a tunnel of horrors in which spirit hands reached up to grasp the canoe and overturn Indian and Frenchman alike with Plutonic impartiality. It was the playground of the devil, was, in fact, created by Ta we' ska re (or Tawiscara) himself, the evil brother, as the Hurons (whom Champlain was soon to visit) spun the tale. The good brother Tse' sta', they said, had made the land smooth and rolling, the forests clear. He had added all kinds of trees with fruits convenient to the hand, blackberries, strawberries, raspberries in vast clusters, maple with syrup coming out when the tree was tapped. Fish he made without scales, and—the supreme gift in this Huron utopia— had arranged the river currents so that they flowed down with the downstream paddler and back when he returned. But when the evil twin Ta we' ska re saw what his brother had done, he flew into a rage. He threw up mountains on the rolling hills, spread barren wastes, shrivelled the berries and gave them thorns, coated the fish with flinty scales, and filled the rivers with falls and rapids.⁸

Safely past the first Stygian barrier, they fought their way to Chaudière Falls (a literal translation of Asticou, "the Boiler") in the present city of Ottawa—"the most wonderful, dangerous, and terrifying of all," says Sagard in awe; "for it is wider than a full three-eighths part of a league." ⁹ Dropping over wide flat ledges, it now roars with less ferocity than the traffic moving north over the bridge to the right of the rapids between Chaudière and Philemon Islands; but early nineteenth-century sketches reveal its original grandeur. Wherever else along the Ottawa the devil may have ranged, here in this fearful splendor he had his throne, and "these poor people are so superstitious that they would not believe it possible for them to make a prosperous journey without

the tribal world of spirits which his astonishing exploit
to warrant. We in this day have a way of doing the same
of regarding a saintly man, for example, as one apart
e rest of us, as a saint akin to the spirits.

much of all this did Champlain appreciate or take seri-
Did he recognize what it might mean to him in furthering
lorations, in smoothing the rapids and shortening the route
ay? Especially now, when he was striking out on his own?
iendly Hurons, who might have furnished him canoes and
, had not come down to the Lachine rapids this season to
He was dependent upon the tribes he visited for every-
e needed and could expect little from the Allumette tribe,
ere middlemen on the Ottawa and would not take kindly
prospect of his dealing directly with the tribes of the
r (on occasion they refused passage even to the Jesuit
naries). Champlain was no novice in Indian relations: in
years since he had turned westward over the St. Law-
he had learned that the impact of a man's extraordinary
ity in plunging confidently into perils terrifying to the
s themselves was an effective force—as effective as guns,
ses, and threats in winning their co-operation. Yet there is
nt in his memoirs that his reception was anything but a
g tribal tribute to his daring. He would not, of course,
er how closely he fitted the part of an *oki* until his visit
Hurons two years later. But if he entertained any thoughts
ver of reaching the North Sea on the wings of his reputa-
hey were suddenly interrupted by the dramatic disclosure
Vignau had grossly deceived him—a disclosure as challeng-
o his diplomatic adroitness as the rapids had been to his
ge.

nau's unmasking began innocently enough: Champlain set
e Chief Tessoüat his plan of finding a trade route to the
Sea (he neglected to mention the map Vignau had shown
n France on the strength of which he had spent a year of
aration and was now risking his life in the rapids) and

observing this ceremony at this place." Champlain watches the
savages with half-amused, half-understanding interest while

one of them takes up a collection with a wooden plate, into which
each one puts a bit of tobacco. The collection having been made,
the plate is passed in the midst of the troupe, and all dance about it,
singing after their style. Then one of the captains makes an harangue,
setting forth that for a long time they have been accustomed to make
this offering, by which means they are insured protection against
their enemies, that otherwise misfortune would befall them, as they
are convinced by the evil spirit . . . . This done, the maker of the
harangue takes the plate, and throws the tobacco into the midst of
the caldron, whereupon they all together raise a loud cry.[10]

Accumulating courage and agility for perhaps a hundred years
in this region, the Indians grappled with the devils of the Ottawa
rapids whenever there was a chance of success and learned to
save their lives by appeasement and portaging whenever there
was not. It was a matter of skill and sorcery—what they could
not win by the one they maneuvered by the other. And so when
Champlain, who apparently had neither, appeared miraculously
on the lovely waters of little Muskrat Lake a few miles east of
Allumette Lake, Chief Nibachis, "who came to visit us with his
followers, astonished that we could have passed the falls and
bad roads in order to reach them," was struck with awe at this
visitation. "After offering us tobacco, according to their custom,
he began to address his companions, saying, that we must have
fallen from the clouds, for he knew not how we could have made
the journey, and that they who lived in the country had much
trouble in traversing these bad ways: and he gave them to understand that I accomplished all that I set my mind upon; in
short, that he believed respecting me all that the other savages
had told him." And a little farther up the Ottawa at Allumette
Lake, Chief Tessoüat, whom Champlain had met at Tadoussac
in 1603 and again at Lachine rapids eight years later, "was
greatly amazed to see me, saying that he thought I was a dream,
and that he did not believe his eyes." [11]

Tessoüat might have been paddling through pools of meta-phor; the Indians loved nothing better than excursions into the metaphorical, and "unless you accustom yourself to it," said the Jesuit Father Jean de Brébeuf, "you will understand nothing in their councils, where they speak almost entirely in meta-phors." [12] But there was nothing figurative, as Champlain well knew, in the chief's exclamation. He had met up with the astonishing effect of dreams in this country four years ago when he had led a party of his Indian allies on a raid against the Iroquois near the lake that bears his name. As they approached the enemy camp, they became apprehensive about "how much of their undertakings would succeed" and repeatedly asked him whether he had dreamed. To each query he answered no.[13] But by this time he may have remembered what he had learned in the previous year at Quebec. "They believe also that all the dreams that they have are true; and, in fact, there are a great many of them who say that they have seen and dreamed things which have come to pass or will take place." [14] He had, at any rate, a providential visitation: he dreamed that he saw the Iroquois in a lake, drowning. "When I woke up they did not fail to ask me, as is their custom, if I had dreamed anything. I told them the substance of what I had dreamed. This gave them so much faith that they no longer doubted that good was to befall them." [15] The Jesuits were soon to think that dreams were "the master of their lives," "the God of the country." [16] Dreams, ac-cording to tribal lore, were inspired by demons—good and bad —and dreams were the media of their materialization. Cham-plain's materialization at Allumette Lake, like that of the demons, belonged to the world of dreams.

Would to heaven, Champlain must have thought, his unex-pected appearance among these far-off Algonquins had been as easy as taking shape from a dream, or as simple as dropping from the skies. He was quite ready, however, to agree with the Indians that there was a touch of the supernatural in his escape from so many diabolical whirlpools and not the least unwilling

to accept their awed esteem. Two ye
he would come to appreciate how
folk belief their credulity was. "Whe
something extraordinary," he learne
a rage as if out of his reason and se
as we should say, a great knowing
The man who had tamed the turb
Lawrence to Allumette Lake must b

The extraordinary skill, strength,
shape or appearance, the unexpec
works of the devil or manifestations
Indians, wrote Father Bressani forty
stitious regard for anything that sav
mon." [18] It was a conception permea
the familiar demons or good luck c
Aaskouandy) which everyone carried
the form of odd stones or eagle claw
seen powers that moved and regulate
in an old Huron maxim with a mir
practical humor "that skill, strength, a
powerful Aaskouandy that a man ca
man, as doctor and priest of the tribe
spect for the mysterious. "Ordained" ir
had entered his body, he maintaine
Champlain discovered, by healing th
events, "in short, by practicing all abt
Devil." [20] And finally, the vast, inexpl
powers over Huronia gave proof throu
were there.

And so when Chief Nibachis harang
miraculous appearance of this man wh
he set his mind upon, he was not merel
the village, or even conferring an hon
him. He was according his unexpected g

* Spelled also oki or uki.

tion in
seemed
thing—
from th
How
ously?
his exp
to Cat
The fr
guides
trade.
thing
who v
to the
interic
missic
the te
rence
audac
Indiar
promi
no hi
passin
disco
to th
what
tion,
that
ing
coura
Vi
befor
Nort
him
prep

asked for four canoes to continue his trip as far as the Lake Nipissing tribe. The chief, his one eye cocked on the threat to his own monopoly if this determined explorer should succeed in his plan, replied with a shrewd mixture of sound sense and superstition. He described "again the difficulty of the roads, the number of rapids, the wickedness of those tribes" [21] (the Nipissings had a widespread reputation as sorcerers). The story is an intriguing one, and Champlain tells it with deep relish: how he (Champlain) countered that he had Vignau's word that he had been in the country of the Nebicerini (Nipissing Indians); how Tessoüat, whose island was the northernmost point Vignau had reached, turned upon the young impostor: "If you have been among these people, it was while you were asleep . . . . You are a scoundrel, and he [Champlain] ought to put you to death more cruelly than we do our enemies"; how Thomas, the interpreter, came to the distracted Champlain shortly after this staccato by-play with the intelligence that Tessoüat had sent a canoe secretly to the Nebicerini to inform them of the Frenchman's coming.[22]

This was highly disturbing news. What further obstructions did the old chief have in mind? In a few days, Champlain felt, the whole atmosphere had changed: when he arrived, the chief had hailed him as a man of unusual—even supernatural—talents; now he was impugning Champlain's faith in his guide and trying to block his passage into the interior. But there was still a chance to save face and recover the advantage: he might coax or promise, bluff and threaten, or indulge the vagaries of savage superstition. Few historians can bring themselves to mention his choice—the dream superstition. "Thereupon," he says, "in order to profit by the opportunity, I went to the savages to tell them, that I had dreamed the past night that they purposed to send a canoe to the Nebicerini without notifying me of it, at which I was greatly surprised, since they knew that I was desirous of going there." [23]

It was Tessoüat's turn to pull himself out of the rapids of intrigue. He may have had his suspicions; but a dream was too subjective, too much a part of his own beliefs, for him to question it. Instead, he denounced Vignau's malicious deception so vehemently that the Indians were ready to "tear him in pieces." [24] Champlain was now convinced (his early doubts about Vignau's veracity had grown greater as he had led him—against the Indians' advice—into more and more rock-choked channels), but he wanted to hear the confession from the lips of "our liar" [25] himself. He took him aside and threatened to hang and strangle him if he persisted in his hoax. Vignau confessed.

What now should he do with the impostor? To release him to the fury of the savages was unthinkable; no Frenchman, himself included, would be safe in the future. Years later Duluth, already launched on a trip into the unknown regions west of Lake Superior, turned back when he heard that a party of La Salle's men (his rivals for the glory of opening the West) was in the hands of the Sioux and paddled down the Mississippi to rescue them. And Champlain could scarcely jeopardize his reputation by delegating his responsibilities to Tessoüat. Characteristically, he moved promptly but with cautious restraint—with something of the same qualities that had brought him so far up the Ottawa. He set loose the cowering Vignau not to the Indians who had been clamoring for him but to the wilderness he had falsely claimed to know.

Champlain had lost little by acknowledging the justice of Tessoüat's accusations—either of his own standing or of future French security. His explorations, of course, had run into a dead end. But he had had a more intimate glimpse of the streams of Indian behavior—currents as important to his purposes as the route to Hudson Bay. In grappling with the demons of the rapids and the demonic in men's minds, he learned that it was the unusual in a man's character that impressed these Indians most deeply, that drew from them an awed respect charged with the atmosphere of spirit worship. White men, too, respect character, but no such tribal lore lies beneath their feeling.

The discovery held interesting possibilities for Champlain's present plans; he found no difficulty, for instance, in exploiting his reputation to bring a trading flotilla of forty canoes back over the long route to the St. Lawrence. Moreover, the folk belief that set him among the *okis* might prove to be a useful formula—a formula for transmuting the base metal of dependency into a golden potential for assistance and negotiation. On his second ascent up the Ottawa River two years later, Chiefs Nibachis and Tessoüat received him with feasts, outfitted him with provisions, and set him on his way to the Nipissiriniens.

All the facets of his relations with the Indians glowed with the dominant hue of his personality, enhanced as it was by superstition. We see it when he is trading with them, exploring with their help, or leading them into skirmishes with the Iroquois. It is at its brightest when he is arbitrating their disputes, warbreeding disputes like the one he was called upon to settle between the Hurons and Algonquins during his stay in Huronia in the winter of 1615–16. Here he is no head of a great trading company, no captain of arquebusiers, no spokesman of the king. He is in the sorry plight of impatiently accepting the hospitality of the Hurons after having been carried back to Huronia with a wound suffered in the fiasco against the Iroquois a few months before. And yet his word commands respect because, as Morris Bishop says pregnantly, "of the recognizable integrity of his spirit." [26] And this, as the Indians recognized also in the Vignau affair, is the stuff that *okis* are made of.

What we are saying seems like a truism—until we become involved in explaining the success or failure of the French in America through the policies of statesmen and fur companies (how strange they must have seemed at times to native diplomats!) and forget that the Indians saw these policies only in the personalities of the men who tried to carry them out. In time the *compagnie des marchands* became popularly known in France as the *compagnie de Champlain;* to the Indians it had never been anything else. It was all very well to come to Canada armed with a gun and a commission from Louis XIII empowering the holder with the right to make treaties, propagate the faith, build forts. The next step was to make it mean something to the Indians, to deal with tribal behavior. It was better, in short, to be linked with the *okis* than with the king.

But we must say no more of Champlain and what he learned about *okis* and demons. After all, we can see the impact of the extraordinary more clearly in the events of a few years later than in Champlain's stray notes. We can trace it in the superstitious transformation of the Jesuit missionaries into gods and devils. We see it too in the story of Jean Nicolet, Champlain's young ambassador to the "Chinese" at Green Bay, Wisconsin, and of Nicolas Perrot, whose reception as "wonderful men," that is, as *okis,* helped to lay open to them the waterways of the western Great Lakes.

*I*n the late afternoon sun Jean Nicolet spotted a clearing along the western pine-fringed banks at the entrance of a deep inlet of Lake Michigan and gave the order to beach the canoe. He had come "about three hundred leagues Westward"; if his scattered bits of information and his seven Huron guides were correct, he must now, at the end of this inlet, be nearing the home of the mysterious "people of the sea," [1] the long-sought *Gens de Mer*, who might not be Indians at all but an eastern colony of the Chinese. It was time to pause for a few days, both to ready himself for the delicate task of appearing as Champlain's emissary before the tribes (or the Mandarin) with whom he was to make a treaty and to send on one of his Hurons with the word that he, a white man, would be coming.

As the Indians unpacked the large birchbark canoe, Nicolet took out two impressive items—a brace of pistols to awe the natives if they should be another tribe of Indians and a "grand robe of China damask, all strewn with flowers and birds of many colors" [2] to wear if the Mandarin himself should be waiting at the dock to greet him. But the rest of his equipment was far more impressive. It included:

> 15 yrs. intimate acquaintanceship with Indian mind & manners;

1 legend (variable) that the continent of North America was an island;

an undetermined no. of rumors that a "different" people dwelt in the West;

2 sturdy shoulders braced by years of paddling & portaging, the shoulders *d'un des plus robustes Sauvages*—of a man who had undergone "such fatigues as none but eye-witnesses can conceive"; [3]

100 yrs. belief by white men in the myth of a Northwest Passage;

1 measure of self-confidence born of the regard his Indians had for him as one of their chiefs & as akin to the *okis*.

Thus heavily laden with the weight of its dusky crew and bright destiny, his canoe in this spring and summer of 1634 had cut north and west past fabled Manitoulin Island, past the turtle-shaped rock where, two hundred years later, the Indians were still offering sacrifices of tobacco to insure their safe passage,[4] and had followed the pointing finger of the island to the rapids of what is now Sault Ste. Marie. Almost within sight of Lake Superior, Nicolet had turned back and headed west to Mackinac Island, the legendary birthplace of Manabozho, the Great Hare, or (as it was once more familiarly known) Michilimackinac, "The Great Turtle." We may wish Nicolet had recorded the ceremonies which his Hurons doubtless performed as they approached these Meccas of Indian folk belief; perhaps he was too familiar with such ceremonies to comment.

Dipping down the endless pine rim of northern Lake Michigan with the waters on his left reaching the sky before they reached land, Nicolet had reason to feel a lift of heart. He was perhaps the first white man to look upon this inland sea; this was the farthest into the continent that any explorer had yet probed. And although Lake Michigan's waters were not salt there was a good chance that he would at last be realizing the hundred-year-old dream of finding the Northwest Passage to the Orient.

There could be no doubt that there was one: fact and fancy, white man and Indian, concurred on this point. Of the great legacy which his chief Champlain had left him (including the broad, basic policy of living among the Indians to master their way of life, their lore, and their languages and to mold friendships with the leading men of the tribe) this dream was the richest portion. Champlain had himself inherited it, of course, from sixteenth-century map-makers like Abraham Ortelius and Gerardus Mercator, who show great inland lakes as an arm of the North Sea west of the sources of the Ottawa River, and from Sir Humphrey Gilbert and Richard Hakluyt, tireless journalist of North American exploration. It was one of the great germinating myths of the century, a bit of European folklore that opened up a continent, and it ranks with other myths down the years that underlie epochal economic and social changes like the myth of the "noble savage"—a vital if incipient factor in the so-called Romantic Movement.

But Nicolet knew nothing of Ortelius and his followers: he had picked up his clues from the Indians in the Nipissing country, where he learned of the Ouenibegoes (Winnebago)—a tantalizingly ambiguous Algonquin term meaning "ill-smelling" people (*Puants* to the French) or "sea water" people, whom his imagination clothed in Chinese robes. As a modern writer suggests: "The wish is evidently parent to the thought, for so keen was the desire to find a waterway that would bring the western sea within easy reach, that any hint or intimation of such a possibility would at once have brought the imagination into play and would have placed a favorable interpretation on the wildest rumors." [5]

And there were many such rumors or tales adding to the hypnotic power of the dream that Nicolet eagerly laid up from the stock of Indian lore. The Indians believed, for instance, that there was a different people living to the west "without hair or beards," [6] and they believed that the salt sea lay not many moons away. They thought so because of the rumors borne to them across the Big-Sea-Water; they believed it also because it was implicit in the cosmogonic legend that the continent was an island, a legend long familiar in the winter campfires of the Hurons and Algonquins.[7] Nicolet most probably heard the version recorded by Father Jean de Brébeuf, who accompanied him as far as Allumette Island on his way to Huronia.

They say [wrote Brébeuf] that the husband of Aataentsic (goddess of the moon), being very sick, dreamed that it was necessary to cut down a certain tree (in heaven) . . . and that, as soon as he ate of the fruit, he would be immediately healed. Aataentsic, knowing the desire of her husband, takes his axe and goes away with the resolution not to make two trips of it; but she had no sooner dealt the first blow than the tree at once split . . . and fell to this earth; whereupon she was so astonished that . . . she returned and threw herself after it.

Now, as she fell, the Turtle, happening to raise her head above water, perceived her; and, not knowing what to decide upon . . . , she called together the other aquatic animals to get their opinion. They immediately assembled; she points out to them what she saw, and asks them what they think it is fitting to do. The greater part refer the matter to the Beaver, who, through courtesy, hands over the whole to the judgment of the Turtle, whose final opinion was that they should . . . dive to the bottom of the water, bring up soil to her, and put it on her back. No sooner said than done, and the woman fell very gently on this Island.[8]

[And from a later Wyandot version of the creation legend] The Island grew to be a Great Land—all of North America, which to the Wyandots [Hurons] was all the land of the earth.[9]

In the light of Champlain's (and his predecessors') convictions, the legend made sense. But Nicolet would soon put it to the test, for his Huron had returned to tell him that the chiefs were assembling to await his arrival.

The Huron must have carried out his task with a fine sense of propaganda values: when Nicolet landed, pistol in each hand, at Mogarshogara or Mogacutc (presumably at Red Banks, a few miles above the present city of Green Bay), the site of the Winnebago village, "they dispatched several young men to meet the

Manitouiriniou—that is to say, 'the wonderful man.' They meet him; they escort him, and carry all his baggage." [10]

A truly royal reception for this damask-garbed dignitary, arriving in state in his birchbark canoe! To say nothing of the feasts held in his honor by each of the chiefs of the four or five thousand that had gathered quickly at the news. "At one of these banquets they served at least sixscore beavers." [11] Nicolet's subdued elation breaks through the straightforward account of Father Vimont, to whom he told his story; for all his elaborate pre-staging and his familiarity with the Indian practice of banqueting their guests, he must have been surprised at his magnificent welcome by these men who had never heard of him before, who did not know that he had lived as a chief in a separate cabin among the Nipissings, or that his own chief was the powerful and honored ruler of New France. His surprise would have been greater if he had been able to hear from Nicolas Perrot the impressions he gained some fifty years later of the Winnebago of Nicolet's own day. "In former times," said Perrot, "the Puants [Winnebago Indians] were the masters of this bay, and of a great extent of adjoining country. This nation was a populous one, very redoubtable, and spared no one . . . . If any stranger came among them, he was cooked in their kettles. The Malhominis [Menominis] were the only tribe who maintained relations with them, and they did not dare even to complain of their tyranny. These tribes believed themselves the most powerful in the universe." [12]

Hardly the kind of men to be awed by a stranger, even one from Europe wearing Oriental robes! There were, of course, the pistols, which Nicolet fired as he stepped on shore, and whose noise and flame ushered the Winnebago in a split second into the age of iron. Champlain's guns had made him thrice welcome as an ally of the Indians from the Gulf of the St. Lawrence to Huronia, once they had seen him fell the Iroquois at distances and with results impossible for bow and arrow. But no stray bird had fallen at the blast of Nicolet's pistols; the Winnebago fled at the noise because they believed that the Thunder-God himself stood in their midst.

The very ground on which he stood was sacred in the lore of the Winnebago: legend made it the original home of the tribe; here the war-bundle of the Thunderbirds was kept; on this spot the spirit chiefs of the Thunderbirds brought to earth the first men.

The Earthmaker, so the legend ran, had created four brothers —Kunaga, Henanga, Hagaga, and Nanyiga—and made them chiefs of the Thunderbirds. Then he created four earth-brothers, whom the four chiefs brought down to earth, in an oak tree at a place called Within-Lake on the southeast shore of Green Bay. According to other tribal accounts, the Thunder-people were Thunder-beings themselves, transformed into human shape at the general meeting of all the animals, near Red Banks. Molders of earth as well as winged escorts of mankind and patrons of their culture, the Thunder-people carved the valleys and smashed dents in the hills with their war clubs.[13]

Over much of the North American continent the Indians knew the Thunderbird. A wheel with its hub at Green Bay and its rim circling through Mexico and Hudson Bay would hardly cover his range. The savages watched him spread his enormous cumulo-cirro-stratus wings to blot out the sky; they saw the black monster devour the lightning-serpent and wage unceasing war with the god of waters. Like the Turtle clan among the later Hurons, the Thunderbirds headed the Winnebago hierarchy.

The crack of pistols, reverberating down these long valleys of legend, opened up for the stranger who held the thunder in his hands the powers of the Thunderbird tradition, made him destroyer, champion against evil, *Manitouiriniou.* If Nicolet was greeted as a god-king, it was not only (as we are told) because of his melodramatic entry with roaring guns and gorgeous robe. He owed his royal reception to the sacred shores on which he landed—the natural stage for such a drama—and to the long conditioning of legend that made the Winnebago mind receptive to the idea of his supraterrestrial status. How powerful such conditioning can be we know from a modern parallel, when—in the United States and later in Central America—supposedly mature people, their minds colored by lurid interstellar extravaganzas, swallowed in terror the broadcast of an imaginary invasion of the men from Mars.

Nicolet's remarkable exploration into mid-continent had begun with a hundred-year-old myth and had ended in folklore. It is a chapter out of Herodotus, who knew better than most of us how curiously the themes of lore make up the symphony of history, how inevitably the oboes and strings of legend supplement brass facts.

For Nicolet the golden myth of the Northwest Passage—though it would beckon others for another century—quickly changed to redskin reality. Despite intriguing reports that the "Great Water" lay but three days' journey away, he turned back to Quebec, apparently satisfied with his achievements. He had traced a rainbow-like trail five hundred miles into the wilderness beyond Champlain's western route—fifteen hundred miles from the Gulf of the St. Lawrence—and had discovered Lake Michigan. More important still for the moment, he had successfully completed the mission on which Champlain had sent him—to strike a pact with the Winnebago in the hope of laying the groundwork for the extension of trade to the Midwest. If no pot of Chinese gold glittered at the end of the rainbow, he had at least discovered, as Champlain had done before him, how effectively exploration and trade could be advanced along the byways of Indian superstition. He had confirmed the soundness of the Royal Geographer's experiments in human cartography, in marking the longitudes and latitudes of Indian behavior in the half-shadows of tribal custom and lore.

We need not doubt that Nicolet took full advantage of the Winnebago Indians' superstitious acclaim. He had begun his apprenticeship at Allumette Island, where daring men became *okis,* and he had lived for eight or nine years among those famous sorcerers the Nipissings, sharing in tribal deliberations, listening to tales of spirits and demons, and watching ceremonies of magic. Better than Champlain himself he knew the wellsprings of savage behavior; better than he realized he was equipped to play the role of Thunder-god in meeting and winning over the Winnebago. He had need of this more than of his other gifts, particularly since he was relying almost wholly upon the resources of the savages, whom, as Father Vimont said, "he could shape and bend . . . with a skill that can hardly be matched." [14]

It was no fault of Nicolet's that his thrust into the West was but an interlude in the story of exploration, that it gave no immediate impetus to discovery, trade, or settlement. On Christmas Day, 1635, his superior died, and it was over thirty years before another white man appeared in what is now Wisconsin. Nicolet's exploit received scant attention in the accounts of his own day, and contemporary historians do not greatly elaborate upon them. Yet his meeting with the Winnebago is one of the clearest instances we have of the effective use which the French made of Indian lore to further their interests, one of the most typical illustrations of the sympathetic understanding of Indian folkways which helped them to move, in the incredibly short space of thirty-one years, from the Atlantic coast to the heart of the Midwest.

*O*n August 5, 1634, the Jesuit missionary Jean de Brébeuf reached the southeast lobe of Georgian Bay and made his way to the Huron village of Ihonatiria. "What, Echon," * cried the astonished Indians (it had been five years since Captain Kirke's seizure of Quebec had forced him to leave Canada); "and so thou hast come back . . . ! We are indeed very glad; the crops will no longer fail; during thy absence we have had nothing but famine." [1]

Sunk deep in their memories was the miraculous downpour that broke the drought of 1628. The clouds had seemed to split and vanish as they reached the cross before Brébeuf's cabin— dramatic proof, claimed the medicine man Tehorenhaegnon, that this alien symbol was frightening the Thunderbird away. But Brébeuf had his Hurons kiss the cross and pray, and "in truth," he noted, "their fervent simplicity inspired me with devotion; briefly, they did so well that on the same day God gave them rain, and in the end a plentiful harvest, as well as a profound admiration for the divine Power." [2]

As if the miracle play of 1628 were but a dress rehearsal, drought descended again upon Huronia in the summer after Brébeuf's arrival. And again, when Tehorenhaegnon's incanta-

* The Huron name for Brébeuf (sometimes spelled "Echom"), perhaps from an attempt to pronounce "Jean."

tions, the dreams, the dances, the feasts had failed, he turned upon the cross, charging "that the house of the French was a house of Demons, or of ill-disposed people who had come into their country to make them die." [3] Perhaps Brébeuf understood the moods of this troubled people; perhaps he was only reacting humanly to the medicine man's accusations; at any rate, he reversed the charges. God, he suggested, was angry with Tehorenhaegnon and his followers, "who . . . perhaps had themselves caused the drought by their intercourse and pacts with the devil." [4] Once more the rain poured down, interrupting the Hurons' procession and their prayers to God and prompting them to believe, despite Brébeuf's protestations, that "nothing is impossible for us." [5]

It was becoming quite usual for the French to be looked upon as unusual beings. "These peoples," Brébeuf concluded, "admire and esteem highly those persons who have anything that elevates them above the crowd. Such persons they call *oki*, the same name as they give to demons." [6] Taken "at the same time . . . for Angels and for Devils," [7] the French found it impossible to be themselves—to be simply human beings. It was in general the natural consequence of their superior technical knowledge ("You are Manitous,* you Frenchmen," an Algonquin had once said; "you know the Sky and the earth"); [8] yet this turning of everything into supernatural superlatives etched the pattern of their relationships with the Indians, colored their own thinking in the very process of opposing it, and involved them deeply in tribal folklore. "You are responsible," said Brébeuf, "for the sterility or fecundity of the earth, under penalty of your life; you are the cause of droughts; if you cannot make rain, they speak of nothing less than making away with you." [9]

Brébeuf found himself balanced delicately between the roles of divine benefactor and diabolical fiend—the same roles, incidentally, which the Indians on occasion assigned to their own

* The Algonquin term for animistic tribal deity or spirit.

medicine men. To be fitted with masks of such supernatural characters was not altogether a disadvantage: they might, in fact, even enhance his hope of changing Huron beliefs "into true Religion . . . like spoils carried off from the enemy" and of resetting this pivot of spirit lore upon which "almost their whole life turns." [10] But the land had hardly turned green after the drought when an epidemic of smallpox struck, and the heat of tribal hysteria melted the mask of Providence and hardened that of the devil—just as it transformed Tehorenhaegnon (in Brébeuf's eyes) from the character of charlatan into the servant of the demon.[11]

Had Brébeuf been able to cure them, the balance might have swung to awed worship. But he could match Tehorenhaegnon's treatment of feasts, straw effigies, and dances [12] only with a few raisins and a bit of senna, and the epidemic spread swiftly. So different was it from anything the Indians had known before, so much more virulent, that they quite naturally conceived it "in the form of a powerful demon," perhaps, as the little sorcerer Tonneraouanant asserted, from the great lake (Lake Huron, whence incidentally the French had come).[13] But the belief gained ground that men who could "open or close the Heavens to them at discretion" [14] must also have the sinister power of brewing the red death, that the Algonquin captain was right who told them "that they were mistaken in thinking that the devils caused them to die,—that they should blame only the French for this." [15]

The transition from their own familiar demons to foreign devils was an easy one. The black robes, the crucifix, the sign of the cross, the mysterious magic writing—these were only the more obvious of the proofs that the Jesuits were "past masters in this (black) art, and have an understanding with devils." [16] Miasmal whispers shaped the myth. "They talked of nothing but an imaginary cloak, poisoned, it was said, by the French." [17] And neige de France—the sugar that persuaded Indian children to baptism—that was poisonous, too.[18] Like a monstrous genie that drought and epidemic had brought out of its bottle, tribal feeling endowed the Fathers with the powers, first of creator, and then of destroyer.

Taken for *démons incarnés* in a world of black and white, the Jesuits very naturally looked upon their adversaries through similar magnifying lenses. All spirits—good and bad—became demons, and the demons converged into devil. It was the devil himself who was deluding these poor barbarians; their medicine men were tools of Satan. They could hardly think otherwise, such was the character of religious thought—or rather of the highly developed myth of Satan—in seventeenth-century Europe.

On the streets of London or Paris, or of any continental city, hideous cripples writhed their way along with the strong-limbed; the half-witted and insane mingled with throngs at the marketplace. Society was midway, so to speak, between the primitive tribal practice of allowing nature to have its way with disposing of the helpless and unfit and the modern effort to correct mental and physical abnormalities. European economy sufficed to keep its anomalies alive—living exemplars to the superstitious of the devil and his works. It was an age that did not or could not, like the twentieth century, rid itself quietly of its freaks and closet its feeble-minded, that could not create the comfortable illusion that nothing ever happens to alter the "normal" operation of natural law. It lived daily—and in the open—with its demonic monstrosities.

But evil spirits possessed the universe as they possessed the bodies and the minds of men. They flung comets across the sky, darkened the sun in broad day, and maliciously mingled cloudburst and drought. They were, in Lecky's words, "untrammelled by the laws of matter, actually hovering around . . . watching every action with a deadly malignity, seeking with all the energies of superhuman power the misery of mankind." [19] And it is probable that at no time did men's misery give the devil and devil-dealings such increasingly frightful significance as in the days of Loyola and Luther and for more than a hundred years later.

We mark a rapid crescendo of horror through the chaos of the Thirty Years' War and the Massacre of St. Bartholomew—political and religious chaos that made men lash out blindly against their enemies, seen and unseen—to the holocausts of witches whose flames leaped highest in the seventeenth century.[20] Here are the final stages in the ontogeny of the devil—the swift channelling of observed horror and remembered folklore into the myth of Satan; for now madness in "all its forms was absorbed in the system of witchcraft," [21] and popular belief cloaked all spirits with the devil's mantle.[22]

From a France driven by hysterical superstition to pass decrees against witches in Brébeuf's Rouen as in Paris, St. Claude, Toulouse, and elsewhere; from an "invisible world" peopled with shapes of living light and darkness the Jesuits sailed to do battle with the Indian spirits. Certainly the dark immensity of forest and the tribal world in which they now found themselves—a world of supernatural absolutes and of the magic of medicine men—would make it easy for them to believe that the devil reigned here as he reigned in France. Yet they argued the case over the years in the tribunal of their minds until, like Aristophanes' Just and Unjust Reason, their testimonies seem to mount the witness stand: [23]

BELIEF (*Brébeuf*): There are among these People men who presume to command the rain and winds; others, to predict future events; others, to find things that are lost; and, lastly, others to restore health to the sick . . .

SCEPTICISM (*Paul le Jeune, Father Superior at Quebec*): I do not know whether the devil thrusts himself into this; but I do know well that, in examining these frauds a little closer, you will find that the first inventors of them are either dead or absent.

BELIEF: That they have these gifts from God, nobody in my

opinion will care to say; that all they do is deception or imagination, hardly accords with the reputation they have acquired, and the length of time they have followed this profession.

SCEPTICISM (*Le Jeune is beginning to change his mind*): I have believed until now that the devil deluded them, filling their understandings with error and their wills with malice, though I persuaded myself that he did not reveal himself visibly, and that all the things their Sorcerers did were only Deceptions they contrived, in order to derive therefrom some profit. I am now beginning to doubt, even to incline to the other side.[24]

BELIEF: How is it that their tricks have not been discovered during so many years, and their business has acquired so much reputation, and been always so well rewarded—if they have never succeeded except by sheer imagination? No one dares to contradict them. They are continually at feasts, which take place at their command. There is, therefore, some foundation for the belief that the devil occasionally gives them assistance, and reveals himself to them for some temporal profit, and for their eternal damnation.

If there were some doubts that the devil and not the medicine man shook the bark huts erected for the practice of magic,[25] the Fathers were nevertheless convinced that the "devil communicated with him by means of . . . throbbings in the breast." [26] As the epidemic grew more violent, the devil began "to whet some tongues against us" [27] and even prompted the medicine man Tonneraouanant to try his incantations on the ailing Father Le Mercier. Brébeuf, shocked at what he took for an attempt to involve the Fathers in tribal lore, exclaimed: "The prayer he offered availed nothing, and was only a compact with the Devil." [28] A chance remark? Not when we remember his comment on Tehorenhaegnon during the drought; not when we consider the awful meaning of the phrase in Europe. But these were as nothing in the face of the devil's full-dress appearance as master of ceremonies in folkways committing the entire tribe, when every member of the nation participated in the tribal feasts. For "as regards feasts, it is an endless subject; the Devil keeps them so strongly attached thereto that they could not possibly be more so." [29] And nowhere was he worshipped more fervently than in the *Ononhwaroia*, the feast of the "turning of the head."

The Ononhwaroia

At Ossossané, the capital of the Bear clan on the east shore of Nottawasaga Bay, the Huron captains were assembled in council. The village happened also—by an odd coincidence, "or rather the purpose of the devil to spite us"—to be the Jesuit outpost La Conception, considered in this year 1639 as the most promising of Huron missions,[30] and the Fathers were invited to attend. Deep urgency darkened the captains' faces; the affair, they said, "was one of those most important to the welfare of the country." [31] To Father Jerome Lalemant, who was in charge of the mission, this might have meant any of a number of crises—perhaps even the creeping shadow of fresh Iroquois assaults. But for all the Jesuits' five-year familiarity with Huron ways, it is unlikely that they were prepared for what the captains told them—that they had hurriedly summoned the council to consider the request of a sick woman of nearby Angoutenc that all the clans unite in a feast for her recovery.

The sick woman, they said, had seen a vision. One evening, with the revelry of a village feast in her ears, she had stepped out of her cabin carrying her daughter in her arms and had suddenly become aware that the moon, holding a little girl like her own, was drawing near and speaking to her.

"I am the immortal seignior general of these countries," said the specter, "and of those who inhabit them; in testimony whereof I desire and order that in all quarters of my domain, those who dwell therein shall offer thee presents which must be the product of their own country—from the . . . tobacco Nation, some tobacco; from the neutral Nation, some robes of outlay; from the Sorcerers, a belt and leggings, with their porcupine ornaments; from the . . . Islanders, a deer skin." [32] And the specter graciously included the French.

"The feast which is now being solemnized in the town," added the *oki* of the moon, "is very acceptable to me, and I desire that many like it be held in all the other quarters and villages of the country." [33]

Filled with the giddiness of the vision, the sick woman turned and re-entered her cabin, and immediately she sank to the floor, her head twisting and jerking in the unmistakable symptoms of the *Ononhwaroia,* the "turning of the head," or more accurately, "the upsetting of the brain." And then she fell asleep and dreamed that the whole village was dancing about her, "with goings and comings and outcries through her cabin" (in celebration of the *Ononhwaroia*). And when she awoke, she resolved "to demand in public that they should celebrate this feast for her." [34]

An incredible demand—that the people of her village and of the other Huron villages as well should drop the usual routine of living and put on a feast in her honor and for her cure that would temporarily impoverish the nation! Yet the captains had assembled immediately to consider it. It is not surprising that Brébeuf, after "the experience of five years, during which I have been studying the manners and usages of our Savages," [35] exclaimed:

They have a faith in dreams which surpasses all belief . . . . They look upon their dreams as ordinances and irrevocable decrees, the execution of which it is not permitted without crime to delay . . . .

The dream is the oracle that all these poor peoples consult and listen to, the Prophet which predicts to them future events, the usual Physician in their sicknesses, the Esculapius and Galen of the whole Country—the most absolute master they have. . . . They hold nothing so precious that they would not readily deprive themselves of it for the sake of a dream. . . . A Dream will take away from them sometimes their whole year's provisions. It prescribes their feasts, their dances, their songs, their games,—in a word the dream does everything and is in truth the principal God of the Hurons.[36]

This, then, is what the Fathers had been invited to hear; and now they were asked what they thought of it. "The substance of the response was, that they could not do a worse thing for the country . . . that they were continuing to render homage to evil spirits, whose empire, consequently, they were more and more confirming over themselves and over the country, and that only misfortune could happen to them if they continued to serve so bad a master." [37]

The head chief, "an adroit and crafty man, if ever the earth bore one," [38] smiled and addressed his followers. "This is the advice I gave to my nephews, the French, last Autumn. 'You will see this Winter,' I said to them, 'many things that will displease you,—the Ononhwaroia, the Outaerohi (fire-feast), and similar ceremonies . . . . Pretend not to see what shall take place; with time, it may change.'" [39] These studied, conciliatory tones were still in the ears of the council when deputies arrived to announce the presents that the woman of Angoutenc had requested—six dogs, fifty cakes of tobacco, a large canoe, and among other things a blue blanket, "but with this condition, that it must belong to a Frenchman." [40]

The force of this stipulation was not lost upon the Fathers. You are making sport of us, they answered; "the sick woman might as well return, if, without our contribution and our homage rendered to the devil and to his ordinances, she could not recover." [41] The feast, the Fathers suspected, was in their "honor," a demon-sent opportunity for the head chief to compromise and incriminate them with this deeply rooted ceremony. Perhaps they were right: the subtle strokes of tribal feeling were more obvious to them than to us. At this distance we see only the broader outlines—the captains' intuitively felt need on any pretext, in the face of a three-pronged invasion by the Iroquois, the epidemic, and the French, to retemper the national spirit in the heat of a ceremony honoring all the spirits in the country in a tribal All Saints' Day.[42]

It was a piece of high strategy—if indeed the chief intended, as he probably did—to use this occasion to involve the Fathers! For the most stubborn redoubt of Indian folkways, as well he knew, was the feast—any kind of feast, but especially the *Ononhwaroia*, when for three days the entire populace gave way to the mad intoxication of uninhibited revelry. "Father Le Jeune," the Algonquin medicine man Pigarouich had said at Quebec a few years before, "I will speak in my turn. Know, then, that whatever there may be in your belief, there are five things that I will not give up, —the love for women, the belief in our dreams, the eat-all feasts, the desire to kill the Hiroquois, the belief in sorcerers, and making feasts even to bursting. Those are the things that we will never abandon." [43] In a land where feast and famine rode as demonic a pendulum as boom and bust in modern times, where any day might serve a menu of disease and death, tribal psychiatry prescribed a full stomach and emotional release as the most efficacious remedy for driving out the nation's devils. The economic, psychological, social, and physical evils of the tribe responded to the feast treatment.[44] Lalemant confessed himself at a loss to do justice to the significance of feasts, and then, in Brébeuf's metaphorical style, made an excellent statement: "I do not know how to characterize feasts, as regards our Savages. They are the oil of their ointments, the honey of their medicines, the preparations for their hardships, a star for their guidance . . . the spring of their activities and of the Ascwandics (familiar demons),—in short, the general instrument or condition without which nothing is done." [45]

In short, the chief knew what he was doing.

Such, says Lalemant, to whom the whole ceremony was a vast and unreal drama, was the end of Act I. It was time now for the fires to be lighted throughout the village and for the sick woman of Angoutenc to be escorted through them—two or three hundred separate blazes. The masque crescendoed to a climax in

Act III, the mad extravaganza that gave its name to the feast. All that had happened before was a mere warming up for these "furies of Hell." Each person in the village set out to run the path the afflicted woman had taken through the fires, making "frightful contortions of their faces," and having full "liberty to do anything, and no one dares say a word to them. If they find kettles over the fire, they upset them; they break the earthen pots, knock down the dogs, throw fire and ashes everywhere, so thoroughly that often the cabins and entire villages burn down . . . . Each one kills himself to do worse than his companion . . . ." [46]

Nowhere had the Fathers seen so complete an abandonment in the name of religion to elemental emotional drives. The leaping fires, the grotesque dances, the wild singing, the destructive mania—a whole nation, to use Brébeuf's vivid image, with its "brain in a sling." [47] "I am no longer surprised," said Lalemant, "that Satan is so greatly pleased with this feast and solemnity . . . since in it all the internal and external faculties apparently strive to render him a sort of homage and acknowledgment. And it would seem that, of all the ceremonies of the feast, he especially values this one, where even the mind so labors in his behalf, as may be seen in what follows." [48]

What follows, in Acts IV and V, are the riddles. The moment has come for the revellers—but not yet for the woman of Angoutenc—to declare at each of the fires through which she has passed their own special desires as they were revealed in dreams, or rather to hint at them in riddles. Again the entire community throws itself into the game until all the riddles have been guessed and everyone has his desire, his *Ondinonc.* A strange and delightful paradise is Huronia, where (like Europe, we suspect, during the Crusades) everyone's dreams may come true, where the community does not rest until the desires of each of its citizens are satisfied.

But what of the poor woman for whom the feast supposedly was celebrated? On the third and last day, she begins her final walk through the village attended by several of the Indians, "all filing along, one by one, without saying a word, with the faces, appearance, and attitudes of persons afflicted and penitent . . . . Seeing them, then, walk as they do, it is impossible to form any other opinion than that they are persons who desire to inspire with compassion, and bend to mercy, some powerful sovereign whom they recognize as the origin and cause of the trouble of the person in question, and on whose will depends, in their opinion, its continuation or its cure; and, in fact, such is precisely the case." [49]

Now at last the woman of Angoutenc proposes her riddle. Immediately her people shower her with kettles, pots, skins, robes, blankets, cloaks, necklaces, belts, leggings, shoes, corn, and fish. All this for the patient? No, says Lalemant, they are trophies of Satan—or, rather, a thorough ceremony of faith and homage that these people render to him whom they recognize as their sovereign master and Lord, upon whom they consider that all their happiness or unhappiness depends.

Suddenly the village rings with a shout: the riddle is guessed! Everywhere the Indians are striking the bark walls of the cabins, congratulating her on the recovery of her health. And the curtain closes with a final present from the people, crowning her last desire.

"To eyes illuminated by the light of faith," [50] says Lalemant (in language which the prevailing European idea of the Prince of Darkness makes more literal than it would be today), the *Ononhwaroia* was a masterpiece of Satan's histrionic and directive talents. Satan wrote the play, according to Brébeuf and Lalemant,[51] directed its production through the medicine man or the chief, arranged its climax in the sorrowful scene designed to excite compassion in himself, the "sovereign master and Lord" who had brought sickness upon the people, and reaped his "trophies" in the denouement.[52]

But the *Ononhwaroia* was itself a climax, and not alone to the Fathers' belief that here, if anywhere, was the "donjon of Demons," [53] and that such feasts were but the dramatic flourish to signing Satan's pacts. Nor was it simply the latest and boldest attempt to involve the Fathers in tribal ritual by inviting them to the council, asking their opinion of the matter, and having "us solicited,[54] both at the Residence of Saint Joseph in a similar case, or here on certain other occasions . . . seeking from us homage and acknowledgment of his sovereignty in these countries."[55] More significantly still, the *Ononhwaroia*, the feast for all the spirits of the country, was the climax of those ceremonies and observances which the old men and the Captains called "*Onderha* . . . the prop and maintenance of their whole State."[56] For in this drama the emotions were periodically purged, fears of starvation and illness went up, at least for the moment, in the steam of the kettles and the smoke of the fires, and every Huron lost himself in the community and the community lost itself in the ceremony. So total and intuitive a surrender profoundly impressed Brébeuf; the conclusion he draws is revealing: "If our Christians were to put into execution all their divine inspirations with as much care as our Savages carry out their dreams, no doubt they would very soon become great saints."[57]

Huronia was a land of dense forests and brilliant clearings, a land where deep black shadows and blazing sunlight blotted out some details of the tribal landscape and threw others into bright relief. And in the process of suppressing here and magnifying there, old myths were strengthened, new myths were born.[58] In a setting of alternate light and shadow the Jesuits became alternately gods and devils, the medicine men demons and their people deluded innocents, the *Ononhwaroia* at once the supreme epiphany of Satan and the most promising hope that the Hurons would one day worship God as fervently as they were now following the whims of their tribal *okis*. "Certainly," said Brébeuf, who had spoken warmly of the "fervent simplicity" with which his Hurons had prayed during the drought, "if, should they some day be Christians, these superstitions help them in proportion to what they do for them now in vain, it will be necessary that we yield to them, or that we imitate them."[59]

This is, of course, but a lyric note in a cacophony of censure; it might well die unheard unless we staff it with Sagard's and Champlain's notations on tribal harmony [60] or with comments from the later volumes of the *Jesuit Relations* through which the Indians' "charity and union exceeding all power of conception" runs like a theme.[61] In this context Brébeuf's impressions suggest a feeling that here was a society more powerful to evoke the whole spirit of its members than anything he had known in civilized Europe. And this, perhaps, is the sharpest of those contrasts which the Jesuits, as well as the Indians, magnified into absolutes. For they were on the way to a central truth—that the real significance of the Indian lore they had seen revealed in drought, epidemic, and feast was not in such conflicts as between the seventeenth-century treatment of smallpox in Europe or New England [62] and the incantations of the Indians, or even in presumed affinities between tribal spirits and the continental Satan, for from our standpoint, at least, there would be little choice. The real meaning of Indian lore, they were beginning to see, lay rather in its expression of basic tribal patterns of life and belief. This was their own discovery,[63] though modern anthropology has made it familiar enough to us, and, with an enthusiasm like that of early sociologists who "discovered" the family, they invested it with the aura of myth. It was the myth that tribal society somehow held secrets for emotional expression and for living which they and other civilized men had hardly suspected. If the *Ononhwaroia* was to Lalemant pretty much Satan's show, its vivid revelation of communal feeling and action nevertheless became in the minds of the Fathers a compelling symbol of social unity and, eventually, of peace. Embossed in ceremonies like the Feast of the Dead, the symbol, as we shall see, was raised like a standard over class-torn France or set high to beckon men across the ocean to a haven of concord in Jouskeha's * beautiful country.

* A benevolent spirit, creator and governor of the universe, bringer of good crops and good hunting.

5 · CEMETERIES PREACH POWERFULLY

$\mathscr{T}$he gleam that illuminates the dark shape of yesterday's superstition is itself a shadow of superstition tomorrow. Perhaps because they affect us most closely, those stubborn repositories of superstition—the notions that grew up around spiritual and physical well-being—are most readily susceptible to change. On the discarded stones of superstition is largely built the history of religion and medicine. One has only to go back (to save himself the embarrassment of more recent illustrations) to the curiosities of the Crusades or of the Black Plague. And yet it is not far from the fires that "purified" the plague-saturated air supposedly drifting west in the middle of the fourteenth century from China over Paris to the sulphuric fumigations of influenza during the First World War.

The *Ononhwaroia*, the panacea of spiritual and physical ills, the most thorough and significant ceremony (except for the burial of the dead) in the savage repertoire of feasts, had already— before the coming of the Jesuits—been subject to the doubts of the more intelligent Hurons. Along with persons whom, as Father Ragueneau wrote, ambition, vanity, or avarice prompted to pretend illness [1] were others like the masters of the ceremony who begged Sagard "to pray to God in their behalf and to teach them some efficient remedy for their diseases, candidly admitting that all their ceremonies, dances, songs, feasts, and other tricks were

43

good for nothing whatever."[2] Faith in the medicine man had once been much stronger, Brébeuf learned.[3] The truth was that cracks had begun to appear in the solid front of Huron folk belief, and it was not easy for the Jesuits, astute psychologists though they often were, to assess the Indians' motives as they shifted between tribal superstition and expediency or skepticism. A story from Sagard illustrates the dictum that the most predictable thing about the Indians was their unpredictability.

I must relate how the commander of the [French] trading fleet, assisted by the other ships' captains, had with some formalities thrown a sword into the river St. Lawrence at the time of the trading in the presence of all the savages, in order to give assurance in the Canadian [Indian] murders of two Frenchmen that their fault was fully pardoned and buried at the bottom of the water. Our Hurons, who are adepts at dissimulation and kept an unmoved countenance while this was going on, turned the whole ceremony into ridicule and made a mock of it when in their own country again, saying that all the Frenchmen's anger had been drowned with this sword, and that henceforth for killing a Frenchman one would get off at the cost of a dozen beaverskins.[4]

The Jesuits, like the Indians, were in an era of uncertain credulity. Theirs was an age of mysticism as well as reason, an age in which visions led them along a well-grooved path to God, and the supernatural walked hand in hand with the scientific. The same Jesuit might hear the physicist Mersenne lecture on the laws of vibration and listen approvingly to tales like that of Noël de Merode on the life of Saint Brigide. She had been caught in a storm after keeping her sheep in the open country and had hurried to her dwelling. "Hastily unfastening her dripping garments, her eyes dazzled by a sudden burst of sunshine, she took a sunbeam striking through a crevice in the wall for a cord on which she cast her robe and mantle to dry." At that moment "a holy man and his following" appeared and conversed with the lady until midnight. Finally some of the group, who had for some time been watching the clothing on the sunbeam, said: "Good virgin, take again thy garments and dismiss yon sunray

er changes into a Turtledove, or, according to the most
on belief, it goes away at once to the village of souls. The
is, as it were, bound to the body, and informs, so to speak,
rpse; it remains in the ditch of the dead after the feast, and
leaves it, unless some one bears it again as a child." [14] In
arrow of the bone, thought the Hurons, was the germ of
ife.

en the last of the villagers had arrived in Ossossané, families
ry cabin unfastened their bundles of "souls" from the cross-
nd wept their last farewells over them. One young woman
rticular, the daughter of a chief, touched the heart of
euf. Opening the bundle of her father's and children's bones,
ombed her father's hair and handled his skeleton "with as
affection as if she would have desired to restore life to
On the arms of her children she slipped bracelets of porce-
nd glass beads, "and bathed their bones with her tears." [15]
s a scene repeated many times over the years; it must have
something like it that moved Sagard to say: "Christians, let
flect a little and see if our fervors for the souls of our rela-
confined in the prisons of God are as great as those of the
Indians toward the souls of their fellow deceased, and we
find that they have more love for one another in this life and
death than we, who say we are wiser and are less so in
speaking only of fidelity and kindness." [16]

out one o'clock of the day of the burial, all the Hurons
ut 2,000 people) went out of the village to the great central
-the common grave for all the dead of the nation—with their
lles, laying them on the ground "almost as they do earthen
at the Village Fairs." [17] A huge scaffolding straddled the ex-
tion with ladders leading up to its cross-poles. On signal from
captain the Indians scaled the ladders, "as if to the assault
town," to hang their bundles from the poles. This done, the
was lined with robes extending over the edges—forty-eight
large new robes, each of ten Beaver skins." [18]
seven o'clock those bodies still entire were lowered to

which has supported them since noon." [5] The story is typical of
what Pierre Coton, for instance, the Jesuit confessor of King
Louis XIV, may have found credible.

At this distance of more than three hundred years, the Jesuit's
belief in the miraculous seems hardly less palpable than the Indian's. But there was a difference; and the difference appears
with remarkable clarity in a curious tale related by Father Le
Jeune. A few hours after a young Algonquin convert had died,
"a great light appeared at the windows of our house, rising and
falling three distinct times." The dead man's relatives, seeing a
similar light playing about their wigwam, took it as a sign that
death was near. Le Jeune, who was "forty leagues from Quebec
in the cabin of the dead man's brother," saw the same phenomenon "at the same hour and on the same day, as I found afterwards
by comparing notes with Father Brébeuf." The frightened Indians could not be calmed with the assurance that it was a mere
flash of lightning; lightning, they insisted, did not occur in such
cold winter weather as this. "It is death. The Manitou is feeding
in those flames." [6]

It was easy for the missionaries to recognize as a bit of medi-
cal folklore the story of a French woman who, falling ill in New
France, was told "that she would recover if she would hang a
bunch of keys around her neck." [7] But sometimes it was a little
harder for them to distinguish superstitious elements in their own
thinking even when they appeared, *mutatis mutandis*, in Indian
lore. "A great invention of the devil . . . is this," wrote Sagard;
"just as with us one addresses a devout prayer to the man or
woman who sneezes, so contrariwise with them, under the
prompting of Satan and in the spirit of revenge, when they hear
anyone sneeze their usual salutation is nothing but imprecations,
abuse and even death invoked and called down upon the
Iroquois and all their enemies." [8]

The Jesuits, trained by philosophy and science to look askance
upon superstition, were still part of an age that had not yet
emerged from a too ready acceptance of the miraculous. Yet they

were now setting out to interpret the beliefs of a people that held stubbornly to its tribal customs but was showing signs of readiness to believe something better. And in all this there was much confusion—many false starts toward conversion, much misinterpretation of the Indian mind and motives. But there was one repository of tribal folk belief on which no shadow of Indian skepticism fell and which invariably left a single and lasting impression on the minds of those Europeans who were privileged to see it—the Feast of the Dead. "If there is anything in the world that is Sacred among the Hurons," Lalemant asserted, "it is their law of Burial." [9]

The Feast of the Dead

From almost every village in Huronia in the year 1635 long lines of Indians—two or three hundred men, women, and children in each cortège—wound slowly through the dark forest lanes toward Ossossané, or La Rochelle, the capital of the Huron confederacy. Now and then the silence was broken with eerie imitations of the cries of souls—*ha-e'-e', ha-e'*—as the Indians shifted the bundles of human bones on their backs or set down for a moment the litters bearing the bodies of the more recent dead. A "beautiful hanging robe" of beaver fur enshrouded each precious parcel; some of the parcels, arranged in effigies of men, were ornamented with porcelain collars and bands of long red fur. For seven or eight days these caravans with their cargo of bones and bodies converged upon the capital. As each procession arrived, the whole village came out to welcome it, exchanging many gifts and escorting each family to a cabin to hang up its bundles of bones on crossbars and with their hosts go over the poignant scenes of disinterment the week before.

It was now twelve years since the last accumulation of bodies had been removed from the temporary resting places in each

village and brought to the capital for fi[
ing the ceremony now, as Sagard and [
fore him, was deeply moved when h[
their dead "with a care and affection [
if they have dead relatives in any part [
no trouble to go for them." [10] As the [
relatives "renew their tears and feel afr[
the day of the funeral." [11] The sight o[
decomposition stirred the sensitive Fat[
the vanity of human existence.

I was present at the spectacle [he said]
all our servants; for I do not think one cou[
vivid picture or more perfect representation[
that in France our cemeteries preach pow[
bones piled up one upon another without [
the poor with those of the rich, those of th[
great,—are so many voices continually proc[
of death, the vanity of the things of this w[
present life; but it seems to me that what o[
casion touches us still more, and makes us [
prehend more sensibly our wretched state. [
the graves, they display before you all the[
and they leave them thus exposed long eno[
learn at their leisure, and once for all, [
day . . . ." [12]

The brittle splendor of the French cour[
of the camaraderie of farm folk—even the[
—veiled the face of death or made his visi[
death was close, recurrent, abiding, as the[

Yet to the Indian they testified more. Fo[
bones to him; they were literally souls. T[
esken, for souls *at-isken*, or that which is [
intelligent" captain of the Hurons told Br[
two souls; "the one separates itself from t[
remains in the Cemetery until the feast of t[

it eit[
comm[
other [
the c[
never[
the n[
new [

W[
in ev[
bars [
in p[
Bréb[
she [
much[
him.'[
lain [
It wa[
been[
us re[
tives[
poor[
shall[
after[
fact,[

A[
(ab[
pit—[
bun[
pots[
cav[
each[
of a[
pit [
"fin[
A[

The dread abyss, that joins a thundrous sound
Of plaints innumerable . . . from grief
Felt by those multitudes, many and vast,
Of men, women, and infants."

But not even the tumult of Dante's "city of woe" matched for Brébeuf the pandemonium of this pit. "Nothing has ever better pictured for me the confusion there is among the damned. On all sides you could have seen them letting down half-decayed bodies . . . . Ten or twelve [persons] were in the pit and were arranging the bodies all around it, one after another . . . . All the people passed the night on the spot; they lighted many fires, and slung their kettles." [19]

"As we drew near (next morning), we saw nothing less than a picture of Hell—fire and flames . . . confused voices . . . voices so sorrowful and lugubrious that it represented to us the horrible sadness and the abyss of despair into which these unhappy souls are forever plunged." [20]

But was it sadness and despair? The pit had a very different meaning for the Hurons. "By means of these ceremonies and assemblies, they contract new friendships and unions among themselves, saying that, as all the bones of their deceased relatives and friends are assembled and united in the same place, so also they themselves should during their lives, all live together in the same unity and concord, as good relatives and friends, without it being possible to separate or divert them from it for any misdeed or misfortune; and so in fact they do live."

It is a pretty sentiment that Sagard is here repeating almost word for word from Champlain.[21] But it is also sober history, if we may believe the almost unanimous testimony of the Jesuits who lived among the Indians in Canada. Let us give some of them a hearing.

Le Jeune: "They treat each other as brothers; they harbor no spite against those of their own nation." [22] "If so many families were together in our France, there would be nothing but disputes, quarrels, and revilings." [23]

Joseph Jouvency: "They thought the Fathers were madmen, because among peaceful hearers and friends they displayed such vehemence." [24]

Brébeuf: "If laws are like the governing wheel regulating Communities,—or to be more exact, are the soul of Commonwealths,—it seems to me that, in view of the perfect understanding that reigns among them, I am right in maintaining that they are not without laws." [25]

The pit is finally filled, the souls have taken up their harmonious residence in the necropolis, the robes bordering the crater are folded back over the bodies, and the whole is levelled off with mats and bark and heaped over with sand, poles, and stakes.

As on the afternoon of the day before, so now during the whole morning gifts were distributed by the dead, through the hands of the captains, to their living friends—a public execution of wills and testaments. An astonishing proportion of personal property, in view of the resources of the country, either changed hands or covered the dead. The French fur traders, had they been present, would have been appalled by the wealth that had been poured into the pit. "You might say that all their exertions, their labors, and their trading, concern almost entirely the amassing of something with which to honor the Dead. They have nothing sufficiently precious for this purpose; they lavish robes, axes, and Porcelain in such quantities that, to see them on such occasions, you would judge that they place no value upon them; and yet these are the whole riches of the Country. You will see them often, in the depth of winter, almost entirely naked, while they have handsome and valuable robes in store, that they keep in reserve for the Dead, for this is their point of honor." [26]

Having renounced the material things of this world the better to serve God, Brébeuf and Sagard were profoundly impressed that here, in a people not vowed to poverty and God, such selflessness regarding property could be found. Characteristically, Sagard was quick to draw the moral. The Indians "take few pains to acquire the goods of this life, for which we Christians torment ourselves so much, and for our excessive insatiable greed in acquiring them we are justly and with reason reproved by their quiet life and tranquil dispositions." [27] Twenty years before, a similar ceremony in Acadia had quickened in Father Biard a caustic comparison: "Judge from this whether these good people are not far removed from this cursed avarice which we see among us; who, to become possessed of the riches of the dead, desire and seek eagerly for the loss and departure of the living." [28]

As the unity supposed to prevail among the souls inextricably mingled in the pit echoed the social harmony of the living (a prime factor, as Sagard sagely observed, in their good health), so the gifts lavished alike upon the dead and the survivors were but a reflection of tribal hospitality and mutual assistance. Le Jeune, constantly under the necessity of prying funds from wealthy Frenchmen and corporate organizations—and not unmindful of the propaganda values implicit in this tribal philanthropy—was not slow to improve the occasion. "They are very generous among themselves . . . . One of the greatest insults that can be offered to them is to say, 'That man likes everything, he is stingy . . . .' They do not open the hand halfway when they give . . . . You will see them take care of their kindred, the children of their friends, widows, orphans, and old men, never reproaching them in the least, giving them abundantly, sometimes whole Moose. This is truly the sign of a good heart and of a generous soul . . . ." [29]

With the distribution of the gifts the ceremony was finished. The Hurons turned homeward to their villages, and Brébeuf retired to his cabin to write of what he had seen to his superior Le Jeune and to dream of building among the Indians a spiritual society on the foundation of this temporal community which Le Jeune had found so free from "the two tyrants who provide hell and torture for many of our Europeans, (and who) do not reign in their great forests,—I mean ambition and avarice." [30] For the moment the devil and all his works—the cruelty, bar-

barism, licentiousness, filth, and stench of the Indians—were forgotten, or rather reduced to their appropriate level in the scale of values. For in the eyes of the Fathers the apparent evil seemed exterior and accidental, the good natural and innate. The longer the Jesuits lived among the Hurons, the more genuinely they were convinced of their inborn capacity for virtue. Their feeling is reflected in a comment of Lalemant on the little tribe of the Attimagoueks. "Their nature," he wrote in 1647, "has something, I know not what, of the goodness of the Terrestrial Paradise before sin had entered in." [31]

The Jesuits, paradoxically, had crossed three thousand miles of ocean and a thousand miles of rapids and forests to find a society whose folkways and folk beliefs were not essentially different—beneath the encrustations of tribal sorcery and squalor —from the practices and tenets of their own Society of Jesus. The Hurons' austere acceptance of death, the tranquillity of spirit that stemmed from disinterestedness in property, the primacy of human values over material resources, the charity and self-sacrifice for the common good, the social harmony and native virtue —only the avowed recognition of God was lacking. Despite the differences of race and culture, the Jesuits felt a kinship with the Indians which perhaps no other European group could have realized. But it was not simply the similarity of Indian society to their own brotherhood that excited the interests of the Jesuits. It was the fact that these basically Christian patterns were not actualized in an esoteric institution organized in protest against, and for the reform of, a worldly, grasping civilization. They were the normal way of life for a whole people. We need not wonder, then, that the Jesuits conceived of their crude and lonely missions in the wilderness as the nerve centers of a new and fundamentally spiritual community combining psychological freedom with virtues invariably reminding them of the ancient Romans and with the fervor and social-mindedness characteristic of the early Christians clustered in the villages of Palestine.[32] If only, that is, the king's agents and the fur traders did not succeed in their attempts to corrupt the Indians with "civilization." Within little more than a decade, the nation of the Hurons would be only a tribal memory. In 1648 the Iroquois swept over Lake Ontario from the present state of New York and fell upon Huronia. Armed with Dutch guns and native fury, they wiped out the Huron warriors, killed or enslaved the captives, fired the villages, and murdered the Fathers. A handful of survivors fled north to the islands that led them like stepping-stones to Chequamegon Bay on the south shore of Lake Superior, followed by those missionaries who had escaped the holocaust. The rest—Brébeuf, Chabanel, Daniel, Garnier, and Lalemant—perished before the guns or at the torture posts of the Iroquois, and with them died the dream of a spiritual empire in Huronia.

Whether any shards of the broken dream could be excavated from remains of the early missions among the Hurons now mingled with other tribes at Chequamegon Bay or Sault Ste. Marie, it would be hard to say. There is a different emphasis in the writings of Allouez, Dablon, and Marquette, who established missions in northern Wisconsin and upper Michigan after the great dispersion, although elsewhere *la belle fable* persists in Lahontan, Lafitau, and Charlevoix. It would not have been easy for the idea of a society in which property and material goods were subordinated to human values to flourish in a land where men were soon to dip fortunes from the seemingly inexhaustible reservoirs of timber, iron, copper, furs, and fish. And yet the vision of wealth and opportunity that drew settlers from Europe by tens of thousands is not the proudest heritage of the Midwest; a more balanced judgment may in time see in the missions of the Great Lakes the gleam of a deeper insight.

But however tenuous may have been the impact of the Jesuits' interpretation of their experience in Huronia upon the life of the Great Lakes, there is no question of the effect which their *Relations,* read with intense interest as soon as they appeared, had in France. They were a stirring challenge, not only to the novitiates who yearned for everlasting blessedness in martyrdom, but to the laymen as well—the nobles, philanthropists, prospective colonists, philosophers, in short, all those who were interested in the renown of the French, the glory of God, the redemption of their own souls, or the dream of a new society.

The immediate effect of the *Relations* was not far from what Le Jeune, as a contemporary historian of the Jesuits says, had labored to produce: "to inspire a whole people with new ideals; to arouse them to contribute, not their money only, but their very souls . . . to look beyond geographical horizons, to rise above a false patriotism." For Le Jeune regarded the Mission as an enterprise "not merely for the spiritual benefit of every man, woman and child in France. It was a means destined by God to create a new spirit of faith and of fervor." [33] Not until the renaissance of religious feeling had spent itself and the missions in New France had dwindled away; not until the glory of empire had faded and disillusioned Frenchmen turned a critical eye upon their own country, did the social and political implications of the *Relations* begin their slow fermentation in the leaven of French thought.

Before many years the French citizen and peasant would begin to chafe under the absolutism of monarchy and the caste of privilege. Riding the groundswell of popular agitation, *les philosophes* were soon to feel, as the Jesuits had felt before them, that the utopian sentiments voiced in the American wilderness were the prelude, not to some fabled Atlantis, but to a social pattern imminently capable of realization. It was easy for them, thousands of miles from the smell and touch of tribal life, to transmute the Jesuits' realistic appraisal of Indian society into generalized abstractions on the golden age, a thought already present in Montaigne. The poet-lawyer Lescarbot, who accompanied Champlain to the New World, had endowed the Indians with the four cardinal virtues of the early Roman—courage, temperance, wisdom, and justice; when Le Jeune added to this the innocence of terrestrial paradise that he had found in the forests, the Indian became the symbol of the original, unspoiled goodness of human nature, surviving only in the "noble savage." Accounts in the *Relations* of Indian public ceremonies like the *Ononhwaroia* and the Feast of the Dead implied—simply by their descriptions of a tranquil and harmonious life and of a democratic council deliberating without laws and for the common good—a searching criticism of autocratic kings and a superficial culture. The disinterestedness in property which seemed to Sagard and Brébeuf the most impressive manifestation of the folkways epitomized in the burial rites was crystallized by Lahontan, in the heat of his personal resentment against his enemies, into a critique of European civilization. "It seems to me," he wrote in the memoirs of his voyages to North America, "that one must be blind not to see that the possession of goods . . . is the sole source of all the disorders that vex European society." [34] It is a short step to the social reformers of eighteenth-century France; they elaborated and deepened the pattern sketched by the Jesuits until the lines showed bold and broad in the writings of Voltaire, Montesquieu, and Rousseau. "If," says Gilbert Chinard, "instead of searching for the foreign origins of the *Spirit of Laws* or of the *Social Contract*, we should study their origins both in France and afar off, it is very probable that we should be able to find them in the *Jesuit Relations*." [35]

Long before the endless forests of New England had stirred the imaginations of the settlers preoccupied with maintaining their foothold on the Atlantic coast, the French missionaries had woven from the strands of Indian life and lore the fabric of a new society. Left unfinished in the Canadian wilderness, the fabric grew under a multitude of hands with frequent change of materials but no appreciable change of design until it caught the eyes of the French revolutionists. And it is not unlikely that it will be regarded with renewed interest wherever existence is sufficiently hard and human values sufficiently strong to stir fresh thoughts of the good, if not the abundant, life.

*T*hree centuries deep the Hurons lie; if their bones are not of coral made, at least there does emerge from the skeletal fragments of Huron folklore and folkways a tribal cosmos like the island-world built upon the turtle's back from the mud the muskrat brought up in his claws from the floor of the sea. We catch at this distance only momentary glimpses of it as it was crystallized in the writings of the French explorers and missionaries before it sank beneath the inundations of Iroquois invasion or the weight of the Hurons' own uncertainties. Yet the Huron synthesis of the complex elements of their environment and their identification with it was a rare achievement, exceptional in the culture of civilized nations though not uncommon among tribal peoples nor unique in eastern North America. Quite possibly the great Algonquin creator and culture god Manabozho had much the same meaning for his worshippers as the Hurons' Jouskeha; and the stream of Iroquois folklore, especially where it winds through the celebrated federal constitution of the Five Nations, mirrored a social harmony more clearly defined than that of the Hurons. Nevertheless, the Hurons afford a more fruitful approach to the historical backgrounds of the Great Lakes.

Through them, a segment of the highly developed lore of their Iroquois relatives was thrust northwestward toward the heart of the Great Lakes region, where it mingled with the beliefs of the Ottawa and Algonquins to the north and east and of the Tobacco and Neutral nations in Ontario's southwest "arrowhead." After they had been driven out of Huronia and had moved gradually north and west along the island arc of Lake Huron as far as Chequamegon Bay in Lake Superior, they naturalized their lore in new homes. Their folklore is, then, representative of the Great Lakes Indians.

The Hurons' impact upon the French was greater, perhaps, than that of any other tribe, especially during the critical "contact period," when French and Indians gained vivid and lasting impressions of each other. Lying midway between the mouth of the St. Lawrence, which Champlain entered in 1603, and the upper Mississippi region explored by Radisson and Grosseilliers and by Duluth from the middle of the century on, the Hurons formed the limits of the initial impulse of discovery and conversion and provided explorer and missionary with a proving ground for the next big push to the West. With seven Hurons Nicolet reached Green Bay, and it was the dispersion of the Hurons that brought the Jesuit Fathers to Lakes Michigan and Superior. Traders and missionaries alike found it convenient to deal with this numerous people: * they acted as middlemen between the tribes of eastern Canada and those on the upper lakes, and from their missions in Huronia the Fathers ventured out in all directions to plant the cross among the Indians of Georgian Bay and Lake Nipissing and among the Tobacco and Neutral nations.

Inevitably the Hurons were the most intensively studied of the Great Lakes Indians. Champlain's most intimate and interesting chapters deal with their folkways and his conversations with their chiefs, and Sagard wrote of them with a fountain-quill. Of the seventy-one volumes of the *Jesuit Relations*,† eight are devoted to the Huron missions; this remarkable compendium of folklore, history, ethnology, linguistics, religion, sociology, and personal

---

* Variously estimated between 16,000 and 30,000.
† R. G. Thwaites edition.

impressions gives us the clearest and most comprehensive picture we have of any tribe in the Great Lakes. The Fathers may not always have sympathized with tribal "superstition," and they were often severely critical of Huron folkways. But in the pages of the *Relations*—as candidly realistic and unconsciously mystical as the men who wrote them—dreams and demons materialize convincingly in a faithfully detailed setting of feasts and dances. And when these amateur ethnologists describe ceremonies like the Feast of the Dead, it is usually with the poet's feeling for human values. But in their interpretations of Huron society and the critique of European civilization which they derived from it, they rise above the plane of sensitive observation; they are adding the third dimension of cultural history. And—quite incidentally—they discovered and probed the deep sediment of Huron influence in the Great Lakes basin before the silt of European immigration washed over it.

We set out in these days to study a modern primitive people by measuring their craniums with our micrometers and their folklore with a Freudian yardstick. No such clinical gleam flashed in the eyes of the Frenchmen who lived with the Hurons. Their feeling was closer to ours when we first looked into the caves of Altamira, Spain and southern France, now opened after two hundred centuries of darkness. We gaze with unbelieving amazement on the lifelike sketches of reindeer and hunters that palaeolithic artists scratched on cavern walls at Lascaux, for instance, and on the sculptured bison starting from the rock. We speculate on cryptic symbols hinting at awed reverence for the gods of Stone Age tundras and feel ourselves something of the same wonder, something of the spiritual affinity men once had with their environment. But what must the French have felt when they dropped into the valley of the St. Lawrence and found a Stone Age world anachronistically alive and flourishing! The abstract perspective of the thousands of years that lay between their own culture and the Indians' was telescoped into a day; the sense of history was strongly upon them, prompting them daily to reckon up what they may have gained or lost by being "civilized." And in time they concluded that life came cleaner in the raw, where the environment was itself a personal dynamic and each emotion was elevated to the plane of communal expression, where everything unusual had its roots in spirit lore, and one felt at home in an organically complete little world.

This is the interpretation which the seventeenth-century French put on the folklore and folkways of the Hurons. It will satisfy us, for the significance of the Hurons in the story of the Great Lakes lies chiefly in their influence upon the French. The superstitious regard for the unusual which is natural to tribal belief became a useful tool for exploration in the hands of Champlain and Nicolet and a great aid to the cross in the hands of the Jesuits. There was, in fact, very little in their environment (including at times themselves) that the Indians did not regard as unusual—alive with spirits and the intimate presence of Jouskeha. And this quickening intimacy with the forest, this spirit of the *pays sauvage,* worked in the veins of the voyageurs, *coureurs de bois,* and of Champlain himself until it became an ideal of personal freedom and happiness.

But the demons ranged, too, in all that "savored a little of the uncommon." [1] The Fathers saw them shaking bark huts, heard them speaking through the medicine men, felt their presence in the arbitrary caprice of the Huron mind. Like the Saracens in Jerusalem, their hosts were encamped in this wilderness citadel of innocence; nothing less than a crusade would drive them out —a God-inspired crusade that would lift French Catholics to new summits of evangelistic fervor. In a land where dreams were sent by *okis,* were projections of the soul itself into a higher reality, the Jesuits dreamed of setting up by God's command a theocratic fellowship like their own. For they felt that once the devil was beaten and banished, they had only to prune Jouskeha's vineyard in which strong vines of instinctive religious impulse grew wild; and rich clusters of the same tranquillity of spirit, the same charity and disdain for riches, the same harmonious fellow-ship that ripened in the Society of Jesus, hung in embarrassing contrast with the fruits of French culture.

The dream was not to be—not in Huronia. But like the soul of a sleeping Huron it walked abroad in the night that preceded the French Revolution and took shape in the lives of parish priests and *habitants* in sunny settlements along the St. Lawrence.

The Great Interior

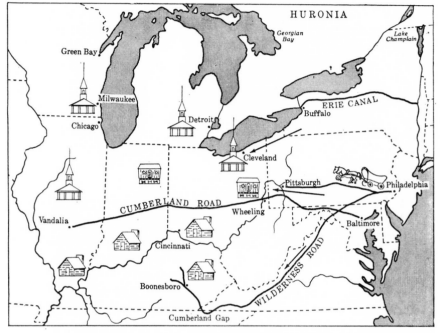

The Great Interior: Migration Routes and Settlement

 Yankees

 Pennsylvania Germans

 Southern Appalachian Scotch-Irish

olk beliefs and their impact upon his-
torical behavior in the Middle West derive their special interest
from the magnitude and rapidity of folk migrations into the
area—migrations that brought face to face fundamental assumptions about reality. The Yankee notions of settlers on the prairies
and along the Great Lakes clashed with the traditional "knowledge" of Pennsylvania Germans coming westward and of immigrants from Germany; they clashed, too, with the folk thinking
of homesteaders from the Southern Appalachians, many of whom
settled near the valleys of the Ohio and Mississippi rivers and
lent their lore and their values to the making of the myth of the
valley, the southern component of the folk image of the great
interior of America. The history and culture of the Middle West
reflect almost every aspect of this conflict, but it is the symbol of
the homestead that brings it most sharply into focus.

To the Pennsylvania German farmer, the homestead was an
organic little world—an intimate circle of family, stock, and nature that flourished through the knowledge of nature's ancient
lore. The homestead of the Lower Midwesterner was no less
rooted in folk knowledge, no less a hearth of tradition, than that
of the German, but he came to believe that he was a new man
cultivating the virgin soil of his lonely farm in a great new experiment in democracy. The Yankee, too, had caught the vision

of an agricultural Eden in which the homesteads of the great interior heralded the coming of the true America. To him, however, the homestead was not a folk heritage of land and lore (as it was to the Pennsylvania German) but a speculative commodity in the wagon of a roving entrepreneur—a rational symbol to be manipulated by other rational symbols like maps and mortgages. And it was not so much the Southern Appalachian settler's image of the center of a society of which all else was peripheral as it was the vignette of a progressive agricultural plant, the harbinger of railroads, industry, and cities.

The clash of these images of reality, intensified by farm journals and county fairs, neared a climax in the protest of the Patrons of Husbandry against the rising power of railroads and "combinations" that seemed to threaten the very sanctuary of Ceres. The protest flared again in the struggle of the Knights of Labor to counter the abstract, impersonal symbols of industry with a myth of the workingman's world fashioned from the farmer's assumption that the producer was the core of society, from the ethnic solidarity of Old World communities, and from the national tradition of human dignity and equality.

Industry had indeed moved from the homestead image of farmer and laborer to a world in which machines replaced men and patterns of production governed machines; and on the way it had refined the myth of a society engineered by reason and economic law. But the magic of the homestead image was all-pervasive: as industry developed into the characteristic economy of the interior, it drew increasingly upon that image, until—in the hands of men like Ford—it became Homestead, Incorporated.

But it is not alone the contrast between realities that is illuminated in the homestead symbol; it serves as well to illustrate the essential similarity of techniques of folk thinking by which different groups of settlers in the Middle West arrived at these realities—and at the myths that emerge from them. For each group had the same basic impulse to reduce its environment to a simple, understandable whole, to extend that formula to every facet of life, and to see in this private world an ideal pattern resting on an automatic equilibrium, applicable to all men in every age.

As the Indians in Canada had attempted to interpret their universe by classifying its multiple phenomena according to analogy and contrast, so settlers of the Middle West simplified their environment by arranging it into patterns of identities or opposites. They had brought with them, so to speak, their grandfathers' handbook of lore—of likes and contraries—to consult for any eventuality from birth to death; from these processes of folk thought the image of the homestead took shape. The Yankee—whether peddler, philosopher, farmer, or industrialist—found in his individual self the elemental reality—reason; his homestead, like himself, was a thing of rational symbols, and his world was polarized into the useful and the useless, emotional impulse and principle, custom and the engineer's design for the new society. Homesteads of Pennsylvania German and Southern Appalachian farmers were also patterns of subconscious equations: for the Germans the social world was one with the physical—subject to the same lore that codified the workings of nature; for the Southerners, the emotional values enshrined in ballad and hymn became metaphors of the social millennium envisioned in camp revival meetings, and the farmer was the virgin soil of a new society—natural man enjoying natural rights. He saw himself as the only real producer; by contrast, all the rest of society was derivative. This bifurcation of society tugged powerfully at men's minds: it went into the making of the homestead image of the laborer and again into that of the industrialist.

The realities that emerged from this folk logic were soon extended by each group to the whole of its private environment and then to society everywhere. In the myths that "canonized" them, they became absolutes—the Pennsylvania German's assumption of the everlasting validity of his corporate family life, the farmer's conviction that the valley and the prairie were the heart of the nation—a new Eden for natural man to dwell in, the workingman's transformation of the symbol of the eight-hour day into the timeless absolute of human values, and the industrialist's creed of an American way that rested upon economic postulates as immutable as the laws of nature.

Whether it was the individual, the social bond, or the pattern of production that was ultimately real, it was these images of reality that gave rise to the power manifest in the vigorous growth of the agrarian and industrial Middle West and in the drive toward equity in agriculture and equality in labor. As reality found its bible, so power found its theology, in the myths.

$\mathcal{B}$eneath the rich complex of Middle Western culture lie two salient factors—the physical unity of the vast heartland of America and the movement into this region of what is perhaps the largest folk migration in modern times.[1] There was an age when this unity was even more apparent than it is now, a glacial age when the rivers that intersect the heartland drained into the Great Lakes; only three centuries ago it was possible for the French to draw the boundaries of empire along the canoe lines from Newfoundland to New Orleans. But the lakes found their outlet to the East, and the rivers ran southward to join the Mississippi trunk: there were two distinct areas in the great interior.[2]

The contours of folk migration, following the river trails into the great valley or moving along the shorelines and over the prairies to the region of the lakes, paralleled in broad outline the dual profile of the Middle West. Folkways of Virginia and the Carolinas found a new matrix in Kentucky and again in southern Ohio, Indiana, Illinois, and Missouri; until almost the middle of the nineteenth century individual families of English or Scotch-Irish ancestry made their frontier mores, their ballads, and the lore of latter-day animism the norm of the Middle West.[3] By the 1840's, however, New Englanders and New Yorkers were beginning to implant a distinctively Yankee culture across the northern

panel of the interior [4]—an outlook no less individualistic or socially atomistic than that of the Southern uplands but which developed rather in an atmosphere of the rational and "realistic"
than in one of unconventional freedom and conventional folk
belief. And intermingled with the Southern migrants from the
Piedmont or again with the Yankees to the north were the
Pennsylvania Dutch,[5] whose colloidal folk culture stood in deep
contrast with their neighbors'. Inevitably there were local reactions: to the Yankee the Southerner was backward, often "superstitious"; to the Southerner and the German, the Yankee was
blue-nosed, uncompromising, at worst hypocritical; to most native Americans the German seemed old-fashioned, Old-World-
ish. But beyond these immediate, transitory attitudes were folk
beliefs oriented along the southerly axis of the valley settlements
and along the East-West line of Yankee migration.

The early Middle West was the valley West, a land of homesteads and Hoosiers along the riverbanks and the fringes of
timber. Hoof prints and wheel ruts in the mud and the axe cuts
on white stumps spelled out the word *homestead*. But here,
where the lines of the real and the romantic converged, the
farmer was "at home" in a larger sense; here were clustered
values of traditional and frontier life—the lore of medieval England and Germany and the democracy of Jackson, flourishing
the more in semi-isolation, for there were few to challenge their
validity. The new settlers from abroad—the Germans and Scandi-
navians who moved in by steamboat over the Ohio and Mississippi and the Great Lakes—served rather to enhance the ideal of
the homestead, to give it depth and vitality. And homesteads
were rising even beyond the line of wood and water, where daring farmers from the East pushed out into the long reaches of
grass and wind.

Few men were more cannily aware of the power of the word
homestead than Austin of the Illinois Central Railroad. On April
21, 1856, he dropped a suggestion to President William H. Osborn: why not have a sketch made of an "ideal prairie farm"—a

view of "the much dreaded rolling prairie with waving grain, some good-looking stock in the foreground, a living stream of water, handsome Maclura hedges, etc." In next year's publicity the cut was complete: a house with a half upper story, fences and fields of wheat and corn, sleek cattle, stream and timber grove, in the distance the train that was to carry the fat of the homestead to markets near and far.[6] We can only surmise what must have been in the minds of each of those who saw these widely scattered circulars—feelings from bitter laughter to long hard scrutiny or a quick gleam of hope; but the reactions of the major groups who peopled the interior—the Lower Middle Westerners, the Northern Yankees, and the German and Scandinavian immigrants—are explicit in their folk beliefs. These reactions, throwing into sharp relief the characteristic differences in attitude, reveal psychological substrata underlying historical developments in the two decades before the Civil War, and, more significantly, disclose something of the social power of myth.

The farmer on the Wabash or in the American Bottom may have looked upon this "ideal homestead" with the same suspicion he felt when he saw items in the agricultural papers on the arable, fertile prairie sod. But on second look the picture made good sense: it was simply an enhancement of what he already had, an idealization of the still-life image of the valley. The railroad was another stream of transportation—a stronger, faster current to carry pork and wheat eastward without spoiling on New Orleans docks. When he looked at the railroad, he thought of larger holdings, larger harvests: it was but the latest and best assurance of the inevitable prosperity of the interior. As it opened the prairies to more homesteads, to more free farmers, it was merely rounding out the interior which in the last decade had already grown with phenomenal speed.[7] The railroad intensified the idea of the valley as the land of homesteads and hastened the day of its destiny.

All this is familiar, and so it seems natural. But there are assumptions here—that the farmer and his way of life would continue to be at the center of things, for instance, and that the inevitable expansion of the interior simply reflected that fact—which appear surprisingly naive until we consider the power and persistence of homestead culture, until we turn from farms and railroads to folk belief. For these assumptions reflect the color-values of the farmer's social and supernatural landscape.

Like a psychological pharmacy, the minds of the people of the valley were filled with vials of folk formulae—specifics for every occasion. Many were gathering dust on the shelves or were used with half-amused, half-credulous excuses (it don't do any harm to make a wish the first time you enter a new cabin; it's supposed to come true). There were others, old stand-bys, that a man would do well not to forget in a horse-trade: sometimes critters with four white feet went begging like two-dollar bills. At births and weddings the cabin was drugged with folk wisdom (don't carry your baby downhill before you take it uphill, if you don't want it to go downhill in life; rain on the wedding day means just as many tears for the bride). And there were some uncorked in desperation for cholera and fever. But all alike—from the pink vials that made life pleasant and prosperous to the dark green drugs that warded off pain and disaster—contained the same ingredients. The force of analogy, distilled through centuries when folk put like with like, was basic still in the lore of Lower Middle Westerners, even in dim memories of a universe infused, like human beings, with will and feeling and in the quick jump from cause to effect. There was a strange significance, too, in "firsts" and their power to determine the course of what came after.[8]

In the little family worlds that spun round the axis of the homestead there were harnesses and roofs to be mended as well as futures to be forecast, and even of those who indulged a bent for proverbial wisdom there were many who did so merely because the occasion called for comment. Yet it is safe to say that although the Lower Middle Westerner was absorbed in the practical routine of farming and at times looked lightly on the lore of his ancestors his mind was none the less the product of age-old processes of popular reasoning continually reinforced by survivals of folk wisdom that were still untouched by formal education. Like the Pennsylvania Dutch he naturalized these processes in the new land, but there the resemblance ceases: for the Dutch cultivated their "Pennsylvania knowledge" in compact social oases, but the lore of the Southern uplanders was projected upon a region of individual homesteads that might be multiplied indefinitely where soil and freedom were lavishly bestowed.

The virgin soil was the Westerner's magic mill, grinding out not only porridge but wealth, schools and churches, political power and industrial might. If, that is, one were not too smitten with the ague to turn the handle. In this Western paradise, an Adam was no anomaly: like the land he lived in the farmer himself was a new creation, and the world of free, democratic, and independent farmers was a new society. There were recognizable details of fact in the foreground of this pictorial fantasy, and its far horizons and snowy peaks were daubed in by romanticism and spread-eagle rhetoric,[9] but the tones were built up from the primary colors of folk logic. The magic of a never-failing soil; the analogy of the individual with the land, and of society with the individual; the peculiar potency of first beginnings—of a new experiment in a new land—and the deterministic formula: as it has begun, so it shall continue to be; the absorption of social and industrial developments into the pattern of the homestead—these components of the myth of the valley parallel precisely the major processes of folk logic so richly exemplified in, for example, Scotch-Irish beliefs. It is no surprise that the myth should follow patterns of reaction stereotyped over the centuries; what is of primary interest is that these familiar folk processes had full opportunity to grow in the undeveloped Middle West (a situation unexampled, perhaps, in modern history)—not simply in local beds of "superstition" nor in romantic hothouses but over a broad area like prairie grass.[10]

The homestead culture of the valley was not alone the harvest of family chores and folk logic; every field was seeded with "the emotional component of projective thinking . . . made up of all those effects which accompany human relations." [11] In lonely cabins, at corn-huskings, quiltings, or village stores, fair Margarets died of "pure, pure love," and the twa sisters were parted over and again in fatal jealousy; young mothers left their homes to sail away with ship-carpenters while pale Penelopes poured out their woes unwittingly into the ears of late-returning lovers. The ballads sang, too, of woman's wit that snared a husband or foiled seduction, of backwoods murders and praise for the simple life, of hate and humor. There was little in frontier folk relations or emotional adventure which these songs from the Southern Appalachians did not express: here were plain folks [12] whose personal fates were hinged on passion; here were strong, clear motives, clashing at times in dramatic conflict. The "logic" of emotion lay in the moving appeal of these conflicts and in the fateful sequence of motive and action; and as folk wisdom reflected analogies of thought, so the popular ballads illustrated implicit emotional metaphors—judgments of value. In the larger affirmations of the homestead, the revivals and political gatherings, the motives and values which these lyrics sang of swelled in massed crescendo into the social ideologies of which the valley people made up the myth of the interior.

For half a century the settlers of Tennessee, Kentucky, Indiana, and Illinois set up great open-air tribunals in the piney woods and clearings, camp meetings where itinerant Isaiahs like Finis Ewing and Peter Cartwright convicted men and women of sin and brought them trembling to the bar of salvation. This was no quiet prologue in heaven in which God and Mephistopheles cast logic for the soul of man; Good and Evil mounted the witness stand in clashes of fearful intensity,[13] and only a fervent commitment to divine power could shake the grip of demonic fury, for in Methodist evangelism only passion could purge the soul of passion. This benign and universal Spirit, like the healing powers which some of the mountain people still invoked to exorcise the torments of disease, worked its mysteriously saving grace upon the mind and emotions of every individual, however insignificant he might be. It kindled a fellow-feeling, far transcending the secular brotherhood of house-raisings and log-rollings, and gave supreme sanction to value judgments in a society where dynamic human motives took the place of an impersonal law.

The Lower Middle Western farmer was at home, too, in the Fourth of July "camp meetings" and in political rallies. For these patriotic revivals, where local and itinerant speakers took up the task of exhortation, were—like their religious counterparts—periodic purges of pent-up desires and frustrations. In the heat of electioneering all the impurities of the day were absorbed into the person of an opponent, while the candidate one supported was refined to near-perfection.[14] And as the contestants personified the great issues that struggled in the arena or thundered from the "pulpit" on the Fourth—the national Sabbath— [15] so the ceremonies themselves were dramatic personifications of the power and destiny of the great interior.

To the farmer this was as it should be. The facts themselves gave pragmatic proof that the enduring core of the interior was the homestead. These warm, vibrant facts made an impressive anthem of notations in *Niles' Register* and the *United States Census*. Steamboats on the Ohio and the Mississippi converged like a Fourth of July pageant at Cairo, Illinois—floats that carried the products of two million Middle Westerners in an endless parade to Southern markets.[16] On the northbound boats there were families of the 750,000 German and nearly 73,000 Scandinavian settlers who would help to build a granary for America out of the Middle West in the decade of the fifties.[17] And beside these facts were others no less pragmatic—the mental and emotional images that shaped the homestead, or, to put it the other way, the images formed out of analogies common to all folk culture by the character of the new country. The farmer had, in a word, "humanized his natural environment and naturalized his human environment." [18] For the valley was not alone a world of plows and steamboats; it was also a world of latter-day animism ruled not by the impersonal laws of Nature but by a Creator whose extra-human will manifested itself continually from the simple subconscious sorcery of household beliefs to the unfolding of Providence in the great religious and political folk festivals. It was a world, too, where the man who pre-empted God's inexhaustible soil was sovereign; liberty, like the land, had no immediate boundaries, and the Ohio and Mississippi would sooner have stopped flowing than these two life-giving streams. Together they automatically guaranteed the security of the homestead; and in the narrow perspective of the nineteenth-century farmer it was easy to exalt this equilibrium to an absolute, in which the valley was the heart of an agricultural nation and the farmer the real, genuine American, the balance wheel of society. The interior was in truth a larger homestead.

The flood tide of German immigration had washed over the Middle West three years before the Illinois Central celebrated its completion with the homestead advertisement, but there were thousands still arriving who might see the "ideal prairie farm" posted on the walls of Chicago stations.[19] These German home-steaders were preferred stock for the new farmlands opening up along the right of way, but what did the immigrant himself think as he scanned the railroad's pastoral idyll? "A homestead! What a beloved word . . . !" He had left "a homestead such as has few equals in the world, cut through by brooks and streams, covered with hills and gently rising elevations, planted with everything necessary for man's needs and pleasures . . . ." [20] Would he find these things *in der neuen Heimat?* Where in this illustration were the undulating fields, the oak groves, the barn for stock and grain? Perhaps this was another "Last Chance! A homestead for a few dollars!" [21] Illinois was booming in these years, flushed with land-office promotion.[22] When one expected to stay, to set himself to understanding the behavior of the soil,[23] to build up an inheritance, perhaps in time to bring over his brother and his family, he chose carefully. For a homestead was not simply a *Haus* or *Heim* but a *Heimat*, a word pregnant with social and spiritual connotations.

> O kennt ihr den schönsten, den seligsten Laut?
> Die Heimath, sie ist es, so lieb und so traut.[24]

It suggested wistful memories of native foothills, "where silvery springs of the stream are murmuring"; it meant *Familienkreise* and Sunday picnics; and it might be interchanged with *Vaterland* or *Ruhe*—even the final repose of heaven.[25] As nearly as one word could, it embodied personal and social fulfilment; it brought the past into the present, and it touched the present at every point. The *Heimat* was the pivot of the immigrant's reactions in the new country: whatever preserved its integrity was good, whatever threatened it was bad. And so he was a Democrat when Democrats made it easier than the Whigs for him to recreate the essentials of the *Heimat* in an environment freed from the obstacles and the encrustations of the Old World, and he became a Republican when a Democratic administration blocked the passage of the Homestead Act and appeared to favor the extension of slavery. So, too, he opposed greenbacks and other "speculative" devices, but he was ready to try prairie farming and the newfangled reaping machines.[26] He was prepared to give up the German idea of statehood or change his dress and language and even his German name (nativists and Know-Nothings notwithstanding, these were but the historical accompaniments of his culture, and he had no impelling desire to perpetuate them in the New World),[27] but change his concept of *Heimat* he could not without cutting off his life at the root. And beneath the cultural incidentals of race and national temperament that distinguished other immigrant groups in the Middle West from one another—the Swedes and Norwegians (whose abilities the Illinois Central solicited with its "Swedish-Norwegian Land Agencies"),[28] the Czechs—any of those farming peoples, in fact, for whom the homestead was not merely a residence or an occupation but a genuine folk institution—lay the same fundamental attitudes. The personal records of these reactions have yet to be gathered,[29] threshed and graded, but the character of the yield is clear enough: it is the product of the kind of seed— the bank-barn thoroughness, the instinctive understanding of human agronomy and soil behavior, and the social integration and balance—that flourished in the homesteads of the Pennsylvania Dutch.[30] At a time when the homestead ideal of the valley had become a nostalgic lyric in Stephen Foster's repertoire and a symbol in the files of politicians and promoters, these immigrant folk attitudes gave it a vitality and a perennial endurance that lay at the heart of the farmers' strength and influence in the Middle West.

The immigrant farmer put himself at the center of the railroad's homestead sketch: the image it called up framed the whole of him, and through it his life ran vertically. But what blue horizons of "progress" must have opened when Yankees like that versatile entrepreneur John S. Wright looked over the cut! Perhaps it reminded him of those bright days in the early forties when, as founder of the *Prairie Farmer*, he had so frequently painted this idyllic scene in editorial pages or in addresses at the county fairs. Agriculture—"the interest of the magnificent empire . . . laved by the waters of the Mississippi," "the boon of Heaven to our race . . . the sole parent of value . . . the cohesive power by which our Union is preserved, and our liberties continued"; "the whole world know we hold God's farming country . . . and they look to us for great and worthy examples"; "the Genius of the Age has indeed set foot upon the prairies." [31] So did the Yankees in the North articulate the myth of the valley.

And yet the construction which the Yankees put upon the myth was significantly different from that of the Lower Middle Westerners. If agriculture was "of all other branches [of business] . . . the parent and precursor," if when you "improve the country . . . the town will grow," still "the same period which gave birth to [mechanical inventions] gave birth to a new state of thought and feeling and action, to a new order of society." [32] In land, the Yankee saw city lots as well as homesteads (Wright, for instance, had staked a claim in the new order with large holdings in Chicago real estate); [33] when he talked of inexhaustible resources, he meant ore and timber as well as soil; [34] when he planned for railroads, visions of advancing industry crowded upon those of expanding agriculture. To be free was to be "God's free man, treading upon the land which Heaven had bestowed upon him" [35]—as the homestead cut implied; and Wright's own *Prairie Farmer*, the forum of old notions and new methods, was hopeful of becoming the oracle of this land of homesteads. But it was also the liberty to apply those rational symbols that gave clear promise of developing the new interior—the contracts and surveyor's lines; the figures, notes, and bonds; the formulae of the new sciences; and the patterns of new corporations. Nothing could be more remote from the animistic folk thought still flowing quietly through valley settlements. And yet Wright— and his fellow Yankees who would soon be transforming logs and iron ore into the cities and corporate structures of a newer Middle West—rationalized their enterprise on the framework of premises revealing patterns of thought remarkably similar to those of the Lower Middle Westerners, though they had long since abandoned the images in which these premises had been expressed. At a time when supernatural law was giving way to natural, they had simply reversed the field. Peter Cartwright saw his environment in terms of human beings; it was human motive and God's will that determined the course of events; the world was simplified into a cosmic conflict of good and evil; and on the grace of God and the goodness in men's hearts rested the equilibrium of society. But Wright would have regarded society on the analogy of the environment; the sciences were disclosing a new determinism; the world was polarized into the useful and the useless, the exact and the inexact; and the equilibrium of society was assured by the inexorable operations of natural law. "Every rational creature," Emerson had said,[36] "has all nature for his dowry and estate," and when reality is reduced to reason, everything yields to formula: the landscape is changed by invention and society by law. If Wright was not yet ready to measure love with a thermometer and God with a telescope, he must nevertheless, as he glanced at the advertisement of the Illinois Central Railroad, have seen the homestead as a rational symbol, a formula for progress.

In Chicago offices, Yankees listened to the pleasant crescendo of railroad sounds—from the thin whistles of the Michigan Central and Michigan Southern engines when they entered the city in 1852 to the roar of the fifteen lines that made Chicago eight years later the railroad center of the nation.[37] These sounds spoke of many things. They spoke of laying open the vast prairie lands which valley settlers had had neither roads nor desire to enter. They spoke of the corn and wheat these lands were producing—harvests of wheat no one dreamed possible before McCormick began manufacturing reapers ot the rate of four thousand a year,[38] harvests that fed Lowell and Liverpool. The sounds reminded Chicagoans that their city was now the leading grain depot and would soon dethrone the Queen City of the West as the new Porkopolis.[39] But above all they trumpeted the vision of Stephen A. Douglas, whose epochal request of Congress in 1850 for free railway land grants (2,500,000 acres for the Illinois Central alone) would realize the destiny of squatter sovereigns and his own in "the great West—the Valley of the Mississippi, one and indivisible from the Gulf to the Great Lakes . . . the heart and soul of the nation and continent." [40] Within a few years after mid-century the valley was no longer *the* West: in fact and in symbol the North was taking its place with the valley in a new and greater interior.[41]

No one, it seemed, could symbolize the union of the upper and lower Middle West more powerfully than this Vermont Yankee who had become the champion of squatter sovereigns. Under his leadership the valley West—the land of homesteads—

had come into its own. When Douglas spoke of the unique and basic role that farmers played,[42] they remembered Jefferson; when he called them sovereigns, they thought of Jackson. He was a man who had the vision of the interior, and who would build ties and rails under that vision that would lead eastward to Atlantic markets and westward through the prairies. In this eloquent Yankee the West found its voice, a voice that harmonized with the baritones of the Democratic South and with the tenor of the young and strident North. With Douglas the homestead fell into place in the larger promise of the interior and the interior in the larger national myths.[43] In the middle fifties the West seemed indeed the heart of the nation and Douglas the genuine Westerner.

Only a Jeremiah could have felt any cracks in the foundation of this "wondrous temple . . . a soil exuberant beyond all measure . . . resources for material wealth utterly incalculable, a freedom almost ideal . . . one vast homogeneous race . . . ."[44] And yet the equilibrium of the interior was upset before it had become fairly established. Yeoman and Yankee alike had assumed that society would be in perpetual balance; but to the farmer the tremendous expansion of the fifties—the inevitable realization of Jefferson's dream—was like ever-widening circles on the unbroken surface of a lake; to the Yankee it was a springboard—fixed at one end, flexible at the other—for fresh plunges into promotion and experiment, as once the frontiersman had plunged from the settled areas to the West. In the minds of Lower Middle Westerners the homestead was the norm, and all else was defined by it: the factories that turned out plows and reapers, the railroads and lake routes, the elevators and meatpacking houses—these were but a fresh brood of Father Mississippi's children. But in the eyes of the men who built and operated these industries the Father of Waters and Mother Ceres were simply the physical postulates of a sound economic family. It was the same idea—looked at from different sides, but the difference was all-important: it was the distinction between sources of power, between a faith and a formula—that is, between the subjective emotional symbol of a homestead rooted in folk culture and the objective use of the symbol as the tool of rational control. In one sense the Yankee attitude was merely a coming of age, a recognition of myth as a symbol rather than as historical fact. In another it is an emancipation charged with the imminence of social imbalance: what is an *end* in itself—as the railroad's homestead symbol was for tens of thousands of native and immigrant farmers [45]—becomes the *means* for other ends beckoning far off on the horizon—the glint of ore, the gleam of manufactured things.

In the same year (1857) in which the Illinois Central published its homestead advertisement, when the myth of the interior was all but complete, the serene expansion of the Middle West was shaken by depression. There were some who felt that the farmer was a greenhorn in the speculative saddle [46] or that the dash for wealth had been made over muddy roads of forgery in wagons whose banking wheels were loose or broken.[47] But in the pall of those ominous months most people saw the consequences of personal sin, the retributive justice of an avenging God, and they turned to the warmth and light of religious revival.[48] Where else could one turn whose life was hinged on motive—as the ballads and the good book preached? Yet many felt that the sin was not wholly theirs: as they had done in their camp meetings and political rallies, and as folk have done everywhere, they channelled their ills into a being endowed with malevolent intent, into a devil in three persons—the railroads, combinations, and banks.[49] Farmers in central Illinois, though they may not have been aware of the abstract and empirical concomitants of social and industrial growth, massed in protest against rising freight rates and falling prices. And when the "Farmer's Congress" convened at the state fair grounds in Centralia the same year, its spokesmen knew that homestead culture and the myth of the valley had been struck at the heart: "the *producing* class," they said,[50] "should assert, not only their independence, but their supremacy." Thirteen years before the Knights of Husbandry raised their crusading banners farmers marked the infidel in the holy of holies.

The infidel was, of course, the Northern Yankee, and few farmers would have classed with him their great leader, Stephen A. Douglas. He had promoted homestead interests by law and by rail; he was the champion of the Jeffersonian West against the Whiggish East; he had articulated for them the formula by which they might share in the trade with the South and the progress of the North. But if the platform was unity and equilibrium, the planks were those of social disruption; if Douglas epitomized what the farmers of the Middle West thought they wanted, the cost of its realization nevertheless left them economically—and in a sense morally—bankrupt. There was even now the disquieting feeling that land and liberty no longer guaranteed the equilibrium of the interior, that the farmer was no longer the balance wheel of society. Fingering bills of popular sovereignty, new homesteaders from Europe and old settlers in the doubtful counties of Indiana and Illinois [51] were beginning to see that they could not be taken at face value—that these were but "shin plasters" issued only when it became expedient to repeal the Missouri Compromise, greenbacks of individual freedom to pay for the support of the slavery men. In their own minds, popular sovereignty was an end in itself; as a national issue it was only a symbol, a "temporary scaffolding" as Lincoln called it, for personal and party ends. To channel these disruptive developments into the person of Douglas would be to follow the folk technique of the farmers at Centralia; it would be hard to find, however, a more remarkable exemplar of what happened when the objective, individualistic Yankee applied the patterns of rational promotion to the homestead symbols of the valley. For the same role which the homestead enacted in the Illinois Central's advertisement the culture of the valley played on the larger stage of Douglas' platform for Western democracy and national unity.

Here and there in the valley West was a man crossing the rivers and the country on horseback through Kentucky hills, the steamboat stops on the Ohio and the mud-flat farms along the Wabash, Illinois, and Mississippi whose "keenest perceptions and . . . truest instincts enabled him to read human nature as men read a book." He knew, as the Northern abolitionists and Southern plantation-owners could not, that the common man lived much of his life within the pale of inherited belief and instinctive emotion, that God worked dramatically upon this emotion to change a man's—or a community's—life, and that it was *people*, more than ideas or property, that counted. Such things were in the Bible some folks read and in the ballads most of them sang—the pathos of unprovoked wrong and Jehovah's angry justice, the irony of a capricious fate and the irresistible push of Necessity. Given "sagacity . . . powerful fancy, and . . . vivid sympathy . . . together with the dedication of his whole soul to his work, and a studious and prayerful acquaintance with holy Scripture," one could transform personal feeling into social fact. Such a man the people understood as he understood them: "the earnest force and homely directness of his speech, and his power over the passions of the human heart, made him an orator to win and command the suffrages and sympathies of a western audience." Whether he spoke in a cabin, a crossroads tavern or a camp meeting, his hearers looked for the things that touched them in their folksongs and sayings—"a humor that was resistless," a pathos "softening the heart until tears stood in the eyes of all." Above all they listened to a man who "spoke much in metaphors . . . borrowed from the magnificent realm in which he lived," for that was the way they spoke and thought themselves whenever they churned their ideas to bring the cream.

These are William Milburn's words—about his fellow itinerant Peter Cartwright.[52] It is not surprising if some of us have been thinking the while of Lincoln, so closely do these two circuit riders resemble one another. On their long circuits they drank cups of folk laughter at puncheon tables and slept on straw pallets where pain lay sleepless the night before. They learned how to sweep aside frustration and doubt with words that were similes in themselves, to parry a blow with fist or anecdote, and to set abstract ideas in common metaphor so apt, so pregnant with meaning and emotion, that crowds laughed, cried, and shouted. These were the patterns of talk and the images that the farmer, the tavern keeper and the groceryman used every day; put side by side in vivid contrast and comparison, they seemed suddenly transformed into picture-epigrams, and people remembered them. On their trips through the country Cartwright and Lincoln learned to use the folk processes implicit in homestead culture— the factual and emotional analogies called metaphors and value judgments; and they learned to apply folk analogy's persistent reduction of everything to the human equation to the great issues of the interior.

In the middle fifties issues of every color—the politician's purple, the merchant's gold, the preacher's sulphur—had begun to fade into the blue and gray of slavery. People in border states were far from ready to clothe themselves in these uncompromising shades, but there were sensitive, persistent men in the valley who had seen chain gangs in New Orleans or who exhorted Baptist and Methodist farmers on themes of brotherhood. In characteristic fashion Cartwright and Lincoln set themselves to find and restore the point of balance in human equality, the interior, and the nation which black-and-white thinking threatened to upset.

There is a story which brings these two together in a religious meeting when they were rival candidates for Congress from Illinois. The story is as innocent of profundity as it is of abolition, yet it throws long fingers of light on the fundamentally different paths over which Cartwright and Lincoln would lead the assembly to a slave-free salvation. Cartwright had asked those of the congregation who wished to go to heaven to stand, and again those who did not wish to go to hell, and when he had observed that Lincoln did not rise on either occasion, Lincoln stood and replied: "I am going to Congress." [53] Abolition, like most issues, was to Cartwright a matter of religious conversion, in which the *good* comes before the *right* (". . . if the religion of Jesus Christ will not finally bring about emancipation of the slaves, nothing else will"); [54] to Lincoln the "definitions and axioms of free society" were the principles of Jefferson,[55] and he took his text—the *right* comes before the *good*—from the Declaration of Independence.[56] If Cartwright was "ashamed of nothing but sin," [57] Lincoln was ashamed of nothing but wrong.

This is the difference which runs through their addresses to the larger congregation of the valley. The young Kentuckian who mingled with Yankees in New Salem and Springfield had been profoundly stirred by the power of the rational: "all conquering *mind* . . . reverence for the constitution and laws . . . Reign of Reason" [58]—these phrases added statutory principle to the equity of personal feeling. Principle alone could wipe out the differences that stood in the way of a common humanity: embodied in the Declaration, it became the bond of freedom—"the only bond which immigrants have in the United States"—and the ultimate basis for emancipation.[59]

But it was principle tempered with long memories of flatboating and circuit-riding. His was no "one-eyed, one-idead, runmad procedure," as Cartwright branded abolitionism. He stood, like other people in the border states, on the middle ground between extremes,[60] the channel where he hoped "to hold the ship level and steady"—to preserve the equilibrium of the interior and the integrity of the Union.[61] "Much as I hate slavery," he had said,[62] "I would consent to the extension of it rather than see the Union dissolved." Echoes of valley sentiment—the feeling that there was not so much sin as sinners, not so much wrong as people wronged—are repeated in his "proposition that the thing which determines whether a man is free or a slave, is rather *concrete* than *abstract*." [63] With the logic of a county court he reduced the doctrine of squatter sovereignty to the simplest human terms: ". . . if any *one* man, choose to enslave another, no third man shall be allowed to object." And he falls naturally into the folk habit of identifying principle with motive: "Slavery is founded in the selfishness of man's nature—opposition to it, [in] his love of justice. These principles are an eternal antagonism . . . you cannot repeal human nature." [64] The house of justice that Lincoln erected upon principle he furnished with folk heirlooms from the valley.

Thunder and lightning fill the records of the Middle West from the storms that broke when folkways from the Mississippi Valley clashed with those of the Great Lakes; but in Lincoln the winds merged and—for a time—swept over the nation. At New Salem and Vandalia the young homesteader whose career fed on graphically pictorial analogies of folk logic and anecdote [65] sharpened his own tough legal wit against word-reasoning Yankees. Here and again at Springfield he may have wondered how the personal conscience of valley folk could be translated into the institutionalized patterns of social ethic. "We find ourselves," he told the Young Men's Lyceum of Springfield in 1838,[66] "in the peaceful possession, of the fairest portion of the earth, as regards extent of territory, fertility of soil, and salubrity of climate," but neither this nor Jacksonian freedom was enough to guarantee the unity and equilibrium of the interior or the nation against "disruption . . . from within—from mobocratic lawlessness . . . . Let reverence for the laws become the *political religion* of the nation." Nor again could unity be imposed from above by the sovereign power of principle unless it had "just application." [67] The point of balance in human relations was neither in the contagious conscience of revivals and rallies nor in the "ram's horn" [68] of Yankee dogma but where they converged in the declaration of "my ancient faith." [69] Valley and prairie were fused in Lincoln's thought—so far as homestead values could be fixed in political theory and law interpreted by the logic of feeling.

Douglas, too, had moved toward a synthesis of the interior: as

Edgar Lee Masters said, "the West of Douglas won in the Lincoln convention." [70] Yet this is but a half-truth: though it may have been difficult at times for their audiences to distinguish the platforms of the two Westerners,[71] they were acutely aware of the basic cultural differences underlying their approach to national issues. For the little giant from Vermont cultivated his Yankee doctrines in valley soil; but the Sangamon County lawyer transplanted seeds of Lower Middle Western folkways to the airy environment of Northern idealism. It was Lincoln's synthesis of these contrasting cultures—a "political religion" in which a "genius in the decisions of human accommodation" revolved about a center of principle—that prevailed in the election of 1860; for a brief period the democracy of the interior as Lincoln conceived it moved in the national orbit.

8 · YANKEE NOTIONS AND
PENNSYLVANIA KNOWLEDGE

$\mathcal{A}$nyone but a Yankee peddler would have dropped the reins to revel in the deep banks of maple red mingled with the yellows and browns of elm and oak that flowered the Pennsylvania countryside in Indian summer. Perhaps even the driver of the travelling department store along the road from Easton to Reading on an afternoon in the 1840's could forget the rattle and tinkle of his wares as they swung from the upper rack of his wagon. It was no country to hurry through: fat cattle, framed in sturdy fences, grazed between cornfields where timothy had grown the year before; patches of burnt lime spotted the dark earth; over against the side hill a loaded wagon pulled up the ramp and disappeared into the square darkness in the side of a big barn. York, Berks, Lehigh, Lancaster —these counties, he must have thought, are like nothing in New England. Here peace seemed planted like seed and bred like cattle.

The Yankee may well have remembered other visits out Lancaster way, some not so peaceful—when huge Conestoga wagons, thundering past with perhaps eight or ten tons of flaxseed, flour and salt, or as often of pig iron and whiskey, bullied him from the road. There were fewer now: the canals and railways were rapidly forcing them off the turnpikes. His own trade had suffered, too; he would have to move still farther into the back country or follow the market west, where towns and cities were budding along the branches of railways and rivers and lining the lake shores. Everywhere was movement, change—everywhere except among these Pennsylvania Germans.

The clatter of tinware drew the housewife to the door of the little stone house; from flower garden and orchard came some of the numerous *Kinner.* They seemed to have been expecting him: it was the time of year for his visit; perhaps the *alder Hawna* had crowed before the door that very morning. Intriguing outlays of spoons and scissors, perfume, combs and lace, even machine-made pins caught their eyes. And (as usual) something new—this time electroplated brass jewelry, very recently manufactured, the Yankee explained, in Attleborough, Massachusetts. But the farmer coming in from the field was unimpressed: these *Pokmon* were always selling such *Klanichkada,* with plating as thin as a Yankee's honesty. Where could his *liewe Dochder* wear it—to church, to apple-butter cooking? Better to leave the little muslin bag around her neck: its red-lettered INRI and the inscription inside had some useful purpose, at least, though it might not do to mention its efficacy to the Yankee.[1]

Well, if the wind blew that way, it was time to inquire about the crops, to admire the barn and the stock. Nothing, apparently, put the Pennsylvania German farmer in better humor. The fine solid grain, he learned again, had been planted in the waxing of the moon and in the sign of the Twins for a double-sized yield; it had not been harvested before the full moon. The corn was in full ear, as corn should be that is planted when the sign of the moon is in the head. There were places in Massachusetts, the Yankee allowed, where the farmers killed their pigs in the waxing of the moon, to swell the pork while cooking; as for him, he didn't set much store by it, though he'd read about such things in the *Farmer's Almanack.*[2] The potatoes had done well, too, the farmer added: they had been planted when the sign of the moon was in the feet so that they would strike root. And if the shingles had not been nailed on the barn roof by the same sign they would have curled up.

These nuggets of Pennsylvania knowledge were no new discoveries to the peddler: up and down the valley German farmers seeded and harvested their crops, roofed their barns, and built their fences by lunar law. They guided themselves with ritual exactness by the direction of the moon's horns and religiously followed the fullness thereof. But there were instances aplenty among his own New Englanders of the moon's mysterious influence, and of the seductive power of analogy in folk belief.[3] If Pennsylvania children born in the sign of Leo grew up strong and muscular,[4] goodmen of New England had the authority of the almanac for the belief that "animal food has a tendency . . . to make men ferocious like dogs . . . whereas vegetables incline them to docility and kindness."[5]

The sun was sketching caricatures of the Yankee's hanging stock in silhouette on the grass, and the cattle were moving toward the barn; it was time to leave for the tavern at Reading before it was crowded to the roaring rafters with peg-shoed wagoners. In Massachusetts or Connecticut he would have put up for the night with the family, perhaps, like Sam Slick,* leaving a brass clock on the mantle (warranted if well used) before setting out in the morning. Here he was a "foreigner"—with a reputation not quite so savory as the loaves of bread and the cherry pies now riding out of the door of the huge outdoor oven on long wooden paddles. But low banks of thunderheads were building in the south, and the old women had aired their nightcaps on the grass; [6] perhaps an agreement could be struck to lodge the Yankee "for and in consideration of a bran new tin milk-pan."[7]

Around the *Snits un Knep*, the *schwarts Brod*, and the many marmalades and catsups, the farmer grouped his numerous family. Good food, no care, he began—*Saurkraut un Shpek draibt alla Sar'ya 'wek.* In other words, proposed the peddler, "A fat Kitchen makes a lean Will."[8] To the Pennsylvania German farmer

---

* The pseudonym of Thomas Chandler Haliburton, Sam Slick typifies the shrewd Yankee clock-peddler quick to take advantage of a prospective customer.

that notion ran counter to the *Hoch-Deutsch Americanische Calender*, the Bible, and the *Geist der Zeit*,[9] but the Yankee had his reasons. Manasseh Cutler and General Putnam had been willing to forego Boston beans in the Bunch of Grapes Tavern [10] for the rights to a million and a half acres of land in southeastern Ohio; with double that amount Moses Cleaveland and his Connecticut Land Company were carving a new utopia of steady habits in the northern part of the state. And what a paradise awaited the right person in the valley of the upper Wabash! [11]

For the Yankee always somewhere else is paradise, muttered the farmer. He who remains in the mill grinds, not he who goes and comes. The garden spot of America, Pennsylvania, *do is wu der Hâs im Peffer sitst.* That was all very well, the peddler retorted, but the hare wouldn't have found much pepper in New England in spots where stone had a heavy mortgage on the land or in times like "eighteen hundred and freeze to death," when people moved West by thousands. They were wise, like the Yankee speculators who had staked claims—before the land office had opened its doors—on choice sections from Milwaukee to the Manitowoc River.[12] (The foxes, thought the farmer, got into the coop even before the chickens began to roost.) Thirty-six million dollars had been invested in unimproved lands in the western territory just prior to the panic of 1837.[13]

Grosswadder tilted his beard at the figure: that was Pennsylvania's public debt after the panic. Any connection between that comment and the peddler's was broken when the cherry pies slid onto the table and the cider rose in the cups. But the farmer was still troubled by the Yankee heresy. You would buy and sell land the way you do your *Klanichkada.* Each to his taste—*jeder Voggel gleicht sei eeje Nescht 's bescht*—but to buy land only to sell it, never really to own it! The peddler was amused. Land was a commodity, it was true—a commodity peddled on paper instead of in wagons and exchanged for money instead of "country pay" or those bright-colored parrots on the mantel. Our Amish neighbors would think it a sin, said the farmer, to peddle land that

God had placed in their hands to take care of; they must answer in church even for neglecting the soil. Well, the Yankee reckoned, speculating in land was hardly the same thing as farming. It was just as Tim Twilight * said to a customer of his who surmised that the almanac-maker had a long beard to make so many calculations: "The firmament to him is a sort of checkerboard, and the earth a bowling-green. Come, who buys my ware? Here's the Sun, Moon and Stars all for sale!" [14] When, ever since Moses sent scouts to spy out the land of Canaan, [15] could one find a checkerboard like the West or set up his own rules for playing the game? Maps were the almanacs of the West—at least to men like Cleaveland and Cutler.

The farmer shook his head. You Yankees think you can change the seasons, make the birds fly north when the snow falls, and shift the signs of the zodiac the way you set the hands of a clock. The almanac is *das Wort*—the Word of Nature; that you can't change. Maybe not, said the Yankee, but he had it from an old copy of the *Almanack* "that the Divisions of the Zodiac into Twelve Signs . . . is not the Work of Nature, but of Art, contrived by Astronomers for Convenience." Perhaps if he planted his fortunes under the new western moon, they'd come true— like those of the New-Mooners.

The farmer climbed back on his almanac as upon a rock in the middle of an eddy. John Bear says speculation "is a business with which farmers have little to do." [16] But the cows have to be fed yet. *Wer gut füttert, gut buttert* [17]—good fodder, good butter. He and the elder son left, the women folk cleared away the dishes, grandfather and the peddler lighted their pipes from the iron stove.

For fifty years or more, the old man mused, people have been moving West, many through Easton, Allentown, or Reading, a great many of them bag and baggage in the big Conestoga

---

* A fictional name given to a character representing a type of itinerant bookseller and peddler of almanacs in the early nineteenth-century *Farmer's Almanack.*

wagons. When Pennsylvanians—Scotch-Irish—left, the Germans bought up their farms and settled themselves or their sons on them. His sons and grandsons were all about him—*der Apb'il falt net wait fum Schtam.*[18] Where the peddler had crossed the bridge over the creek—that was the boundary of his second son's farm. You stretch your farm, observed the Yankee, the way a New England father used to stretch his sweater, cutting off enough each year to make a sweater for his son.[19] The grandfather seemed not to hear.

Sows over-littered eat their own pigs, the Yankee continued.[20] He was one of such a brood who had gone out on the highroad to do business with the wolves. It was a business in which you learned how to handle the devil himself. He liked the story (he'd heard it in a tavern) about the farmer who promised his soul to the devil in return for his putting up the farmer's barn before the first rooster crowed in the morning. Just before dawn, the farmer made a crowing sound, the rooster answered, the devil vanished. When we put up a barn, said the grandfather, all the *Freindschaft* come; in a day it is up. He had helped his sons get started—given them cattle, equipment, land, and had lent them money without interest if they needed it.[21] My rule is to let every one skin his own foxes, rejoined the Yankee; "a friend is more valuable than a relative," as they say. Besides, business is business: you couldn't let family considerations stand in the way. New London people liked to tell of a certain Joe Swain, who shipped to Barbados on the *Charming Nancy* with the family fortune in fowls. When the boat was anchoring on its return, the father shouted out to the pilot: "Is there one Joe Swain aboard there?" "No, he's drowned!" "Drowned?" "Yes, drowned, I tell you." "Fowls drowned too?"

Only the sound of the *Hausfrau's* steady churning followed the peddler's story, so steady the rhythm seemed frozen in time. Might stick a hot poker into the cream, joked the peddler; drive the witch out, you know, the way they used to do in New England. "Butter, that's a thing that's very much meddled with."

they say. A lady in Wentworth, New Hampshire, where he'd once run his route, heard a loud scream when she plunged the poker into the churn. The butter came, but a certain Mrs. Kimball had a bad burn on her leg. And in York State— A bit of saleratus sprinkled in the cream, the *Hausfrau* interrupted, brings the butter; though pokers were heated, she knew, in many homes in the county. The farmer came in with his son, and the grandfather retired to the little house at the edge of the lawn. He didn't hear so much now as he did once, the Yankee allowed, about witches in the kitchen, ghosts at cockcrowing or looking-glasses covered up when someone died. The devil haunts our theology, not our houses.[22]

The hour was growing late in German Pennsylvania, but the comment was suggestive, and the Yankee obliged. The devil doesn't bother them he's sure of, people say. But the preachers —they were always getting folks stirred up against one of Satan's causes. If it wasn't the notion of God as First Cause, it was intemperance, or the kind of people who moved West. But he didn't mind—so long as they didn't identify Old Scratch with speculating. Speculating could transform a man overnight: land agent one day, banker or statesman the next.[23] Why Moses Strong * in Wisconsin. . . .

At cockcrow the peddler was up and away, the greeting of the family still in his ears: "May your house be warm, your friends be many, and your sausages long."

The Yankee notions cart could hardly have differed more from the Conestoga wagon than the peddler from his Pennsylvania German host. Yet their folk heritage was remarkably similar, for they drank from a common cask of European lore that had aged for centuries. Witches rode down Connecticut lanes and Conestoga turnpikes; silver bullets traced unerring paths to the hearts of Yankee villains and Pennsylvania German ruf-

---

* An agent commissioned by Senator Hubbard of New Hampshire and others to invest in the Wisconsin Territory.

fians. If the powwow doctor had a flourishing practice in Pennsylvania, "root-'n-yarb l'arnin'" grew like a rank weed in New England. The moon was not less mysterious in Vermont than in Berks County, and clocks manufactured in East Windsor echoed as ominously when they struck thirteen as those made in Lancaster.

But the lore of the Pennsylvania Germans rumbled on almost into the twentieth century; by the end of the eighteenth the Yankee shay had begun to disintegrate, and the relics seemed like museum pieces to New Englanders themselves. Why had they, a people not less inherently credulous than the Germans, no less attached to their Old World culture, emancipated themselves from folk tradition a century earlier? They found less and less use for it, it is true—in buying and selling, in relations with family, neighbors, and parishioners, in sowing and harvesting, and in moving from one section of the country to another. But if this earlier folk belief atrophied in their daily life, it was because it no longer fitted the view of reality prevailing in New England—a pattern of myth fundamentally different from that of the Pennsylvania Germans.

A coil of concentric fences encircled the rich valley of southeastern Pennsylvania, enclosing family, *Freindschaft*, and neighbors. In frequent season the gates were flung open—for snitzing bees or apple-cookings, or for barter. Sons helped dig postholes; when they married, their fathers supplied the posts for the sons' adjoining fences. If a neighbor's fence was broken, a neighbor helped repair it. *Wie einer den Zaun haelt, haelt er auch das Gut;* as one tends the fence he also tends the farm—and the farm community.

But the coil of interlocking social relationships in this compact agricultural community was no less a spiral, reaching down to medieval Rhineland. "A man who walks in the footsteps of his forefathers . . . ," wrote Fredric Klees of the Pennsylvania Germans, "at least subconsciously . . . is aware of a sense of continuity, of belonging to the past as well as to the present and the future." [24] In Pennsylvania, as in the Palatinate, this corporate life, in which everything was intimately and minutely related, was a world in itself—a world moving upon the axis of harvest and husbandry according to the word of nature as it was transmitted through folklore from generation to generation. In its wholeness and completeness it was an organic microcosm in which the social nexus was the ultimate reality. And in the sense of oneness, the assurance of security and power, the elevation of a way of life to an absolute, and finally the faith in its enduring rightness, [25] lay the essence of social myth.

The organic little universe of the Pennsylvania Germans is only a modern reprint of the negative developed during the neolithic revolution, when an agricultural society emerged from a primitive world of nomads and hunters. The story of the climatic and economic factors in that change is an absorbing one, but the psychological is no less so—the principle by which the social group assimilated and adapted the mental modes of the life it had abandoned. Had they not fulfilled fundamental human needs and desires—the need to identify oneself with the environment as a whole and to control it, the desire for power and for security—these patterns of thought would not have been transferred. The neolithic farmer had all but lost the oneness of an environment in which, as in the world of the American Indian, plants and animals, birds and fish had souls like his own; he was by now on the threshold of the momentous discovery that there was a human nature apart from physical nature. But a sense of oneness he had to have, and he found it again in his human environment, whose harmonious relations he came to know as once he knew implicitly the laws of nature. Though sympathetic magic no longer brought the mammoth to his knees or increase to one's family, the seasonal ceremonies connected with sowing and harvesting wrought a like miracle. His myths no longer told only of the creation of the world, but of a society that was a world of its own.

This power of myth (we might better say *necessity* of myth) to perpetuate the basic habits of thought of a previous era and to assimilate them to the prevailing pattern has seldom been better illustrated than among the Pennsylvania Germans. The stellar "lords of life and death" shone above the Germans as they had above primitive men, but their witchery was codified in the almanac and applied to a well-developed agriculture. If animals no longer had souls, the stock was nonetheless an integral part of the corporate life: the farmer understood the needs of the cattle sheltered in the bank barn as intimately as when they shared his family cottage in the Rhineland, and he provided for their care even in his will.[26] The big horse seemed, as Benjamin Rush said, to feel with his lord the "pleasure and the pride" of his condition. The birds were

nature's clock, calendar and almanac. The day began with the first crowing of the cock and the song of the "early bird"; it came to a close with the vesper songs of birdland, the chickens going to roost, and the night voices from the orchard and the woods. The migration of the birds, that arrival and departure which was as reliable as it was mysterious, marked the change of the seasons . . . . The barnyard fowls . . . the driving winds . . . the falling mists and rains and the snow and sleet which swirled over the landscape,—all these were the visible parts of an invisible power, and it was believed that the birds could share some of the secrets with mortal men. They were one with the elements and, like nature itself, they spoke a strange and varied language. To them who had eyes to see and ears to hear was it given to know the mysteries of the weather, of life and love and destiny, of health and fortune and death.[27]

There were few in this organic Pennsylvania German society to whom such knowledge was not given, who did not grow up with eyes to see the magic it wrought in soil and stock, or with ears to hear the daily decalogue of Nature. For her commandments were revealed not to an educated elite through reason but to each through his senses; they were understood intuitively and maintained with an elemental faith.[28] The wonder is not that a lore brought down through so many centuries and assimilated so intimately into the corporate life of an agricultural community should have persisted almost into the present, but that it should have begun to fade so soon. That it did so is the result of two apparently paradoxical factors—that the culture of the Pennsylvania Germans was neither so isolated as to maintain its distinctive character nor so dominant in early American life as to stamp its pattern upon any considerable segment of the nation. For side by side with Pennsylvania knowledge there were growing up other myths, not least the notions of the Yankees.

Invisible passengers had crossed on the *Mayflower* as on the *Concord*, which brought the pioneering Pennsylvania Germans, and, as James Russell Lowell understood, Jonathan was conscious still that he lived in the world of the Unseen as well as of the Seen, but by the beginning of the nineteenth century the typical Yankee was increasingly embarrassed by their presence in his notions wagon. When he protested against travelling farther with them, he had his choice of two roads (for the way of protest against the traditional order is forked) leading from the unpleasant here and now to the promised land—the rational and the romantic.[29] Had Jonathan lived in Jean's older and more intricate culture, where myths of reform had less hope of realization in the immediate present, he might have fashioned a utopia that looked romantically to the past—to a simple village community that may never have existed, as Rousseau would have it, or to an ideal republic that synthesized the social virtues of the past, like Plato's.[30] But in the New World no such culture blocks lay in his path: the way of reason was open, and it led straight through the present to a limitless future.

The man who takes the way of reason through the land of opportunity travels light and fast. In the Yankee's cart the trappings of the invisible world, like the weight of Puritan orthodoxy, were so much ballast; so too, and not infrequently, was the family. His was no Conestoga wagon, carrying family and furniture across the country. There might, in fact, have been little furniture to carry—if one may regard the wills of some irascible Yankees as typical. There was the old New England lady, for instance, who rose from her deathbed and refused to die when she learned that her stepson would inherit the farm, and who for spite outlived him by eleven years. Few testaments could match the old 'Sconseter's, when on May 30, 1841, he dipped his quill in poisonous resentment against the members of his household; but after the virus of such instances has been drawn there still remains a chill of the impersonal in family relations. "Like the sun on a tombstone" shines the humor of the lady whose dying husband asked for ham and was refused because she was saving it for his funeral. The Yankee chuckled often over the doleful ballad of Johnny Sands, who, bent on self-destruction, had asked his bride to bind his hands before he flung himself into the water:

> All down the hill his loving bride
> Now ran with all her force
> To push him in—he stepped aside,
> And she fell in, of course.
> Now splashing, dashing, like a fish,
> "Oh, save me, Johnny Sands."
> "I can't, my dear, tho' much I wish,
> For you have tied my hands."

The young New Englander carried with him his father's admonition "let every feller grind his own axe" and his mother's copy of Watts on the *Improvement of the Mind*. For in New England, when the rational myth was taking shape, a son might discharge his filial obligations by learning to stand alone and by sharpening the edge of his mind on the moral law. Thus equipped he felt no nostalgic longings for the family circle; if he did, he failed to record them in his folk expressions, where "a friend is more valuable than a relative" is a more characteristic note. But it is not likely: he was in a sense his own family.

The Yankee whose way led through southeastern Pennsylvania must have been struck by the difference between the formal, individual pattern of his family and the close bond of traditional feeling among the Pennsylvania Germans. Individual families anywhere in New England grew hardy perennials of tradition, but there were no such gardens—constantly reseeding themselves—as in the Pennsylvania valleys. Having loosened the bonds of custom, the Yankees strengthened those of principle, enshrined in the spoken and written word, "in print a-life."

"Sayin' is doin'," [31] said Sam Slick, equating word with deed. It was a most useful equation: it made a man as good as his word, even when it was turned upside down, as many a Yankee peddler or lawyer knew. A blind horse might be traded with the casual remark that it didn't *look* very well today; the devil himself might be caught "fair and squar" by substituting sole for soul. It was the letter, not the spirit, that mattered, as in a contractual agreement. In a land whose very destiny was rapid expansion and development, the contract was a page from the Sibyl's books—the word invested with the authority of law and Scripture, and—through the equation of word and deed—with the prophetic inevitability of accomplishment. On the map of the land speculator settlements sprang up half-built; the Yankee who at some crossroads tavern met with other entrepreneurs and drew up a compact like that of the Ohio Company of Associates selected or fashioned a design, as at a neighborhood quilting bee, laid it out, and set to work on it.

"Life has a chart," says Sam, "as well as a coast," and you could "set your own compass and steer your own course." [32] Perhaps Thomas Chandler Haliburton was not implying that Sam Slick meant to carve the coastline to suit himself (though it would hardly be out of keeping, as we shall see, with a Yankee's faith in reason to control his environment), but that he drew up his own life-chart stood "to reason, to natur' and to logic." [33] And as the Yankee thought of himself, so he thought of society—a rational entity, whose relationships were largely impersonal, contractual ("when a critter is paid for his sarvices, there is no obligation"),[34] for whom "sayin' is doin'"—whether in colonial town meeting, where the town Mind presided, or in companies of land speculators, who mapped and blueprinted the West for profit and posterity. So completely did society reflect the personality of the Yankee (who was always improving the edge of his mind and of his axe) that William Ellery Channing could say: "the country, like an individual, has dignity and power only in proportion as it is self-formed." [35] And New Englanders found much beside humor in the White Mountain tales of the one-man town who sent himself as a representative to the state legislature and of the man in a neighboring town who, as the only private left after the military officers were chosen, admitted that he could form a column, even though it "racked him shockingly to display." [36] If the Yankee may be said to carry within himself the rational aspects of his family, he was no less his own society ("he's a whole team and the dog under the wagon"), his own culture hero [37]—in very truth, as Emerson said, "a counterpoise to a city."

On the New England stage and elsewhere, the Yankee character emerging from the expressions of the folk had become stereocast in a series of fragmented roles. In town histories, jokelore, and almanacs, these marionettes went through their familiar antics as the disingenuous rustic, the tough and testy sea captain, the American Gothic schoolmaster, or the wily peddler. But even as they played stock roles before provincial audiences, their prototype was moving—whole team and dog—toward a larger part in the expanding West.

The West into which he moved was not the land of the sunset —like so many Hesperias in the rest haven of romantic myth— but of the dawn, when reason scattered into flight the stars before him from the field of night. Like Adam before the Fall, he was "miraculously free of family and race, emancipated from history . . ." [38] and with eternity before him. But it was not the eternity of infinitude (an anathema to the Yankee as to the rational Greek) but days "marching single in an endless file," which a Connecticut clock-maker could lay out into hours, as his colleague the almanac-maker laid out his checkerboard. "Hours was made for man, and not man for hours," said the clock salesman. In the rational myth of the migrating New Englander, space, like time, was controllable, manipulable [39]—a commodity to be sold or speculated with,[40] or molded by his inventions. For the West was a projection of his own outlook, a creation—like himself and the society he moved in—of his reason. Reason was the granite in the Yankee character ("he wasn't born no how any way, but the thunder shook him out of a rock"), "the elemental reality" [41] from which the topsoils of regional and occupational types were formed. It was the man-in-man,[42] from the word-twisting trickster and the Yankee peddler to the itinerant vendor of intellectual wares at the lyceum.[43] It was the power behind the popular equation of word and deed as behind the faith in the efficacy of education or law—whether civil, moral, or natural—to shape the structure of society.[44] Struck with the wand of mysticism, it gave forth sparks of the divine reason.

Roughly paralleling the folkways which the Yankee followed after he had abandoned his companions of the invisible world was the path of reason travelled by the philosophers. While the common man's wagon jogged its individual way through the objective, contractual relations of work and trade to the assumption of a free and manipulable environment in the West, a stagecoach of intellectual whittlers was taking the ridge road to a rarified cosmos of their own. They had left behind the Puritans whose "speaking voice of God" spoke only too often for the clergy and whose world—"like a book wherein Gods wisdom is written"—was read and interpreted by the clergy. But they travelled by the book nonetheless—with frequent change of coaches as they rode over bridges of natural law and past temples of reason designed by the Supreme Architect, through heavenly cities governed by the social contract, to the all-embracing realm of the universal One, "where man carries the world in his head," and "no history, or church, or state, is interpolated on the divine sky and the immortal year." [45]

What the West was to the Yankee, the universal Being was to the Transcendentalists.[46] Profound differences lay between the Jonathan of folklore and the philosopher of Concord, but in so far as they start from the same premise of the pragmatic reality of reason and arrive at the symbol of a cosmos with which the individual identifies himself, they are both following the pattern of the rational myth. The salesman who believed that saying is doing and that "swapping facts is better than swapping horses" is no distant kin of him who reasoned that "the power to see is not separated from the will to do," that "thought must take the stupendous step of passing into realization," and that "the most abstract truth is the most practical." [47] Like an echo of folk expressions on the family comes Emerson's "O father, O mother, O wife, O friend . . . henceforward I am the truth's . . . . I will have no covenants but proximities . . . . I must be myself." [48] In the New England student of the western territories Emerson might well have seen his parallel: "genius is the naturalist or geographer of the supersensible regions, and draws their map . . . ." [49] And he could profitably have enlivened his thoughts on trusting in oneself because God is within one with folk tales of the Yankee's encounters with the devil. Old Scratch had become a rational, if perverted, being; and in denying him his due the Yankee had in part cut him down to his own size and in part elevated himself to the role of deity. It was this confidence in his own powers to control his environment that made intelligible the idea that one could "stand erect, go alone, and possess the universe"; and it was his identification of himself with that environment—fashioned after his own image—which put him on the same path with those who saw in themselves the image of the Over-Soul.

For the Yankee—whether peddler or philosopher, who, like philosophers everywhere, drank at the public fountain—was on the quest of the oneness he had rejected in the animistic world of unseen spirits still flourishing among the early Puritans and in the organic social cosmos "anachronistically" alive among the Pennsylvania Germans. Through the pragmatic promise of a free and bountiful environment, the Yankee looked ahead to the imminent realization of a rational order rather than backward to a remote and idealized society. In rejecting tradition, he put his faith in reason; in rejecting authority, in his own word. This was, in effect, his very soul—not the primitive soul of all created things, which was superstition, nor the soul of society, which was tradition. For man alone had a soul—reason—and it was this which linked him with divinity. It was the logical One in the illogical many—the core of the rational myth. Into it went all the needs and desires—for power, security, and identification—which had found fulfilment in spirit magic and Pennsylvania knowledge. For the Yankee absorbed into himself the values of worlds he had rejected. It was as true of Emerson as of the less speculative: "the new position of the advancing man has all the powers of the old, yet has them new. It carries in its bosom all the energies of the past, yet is itself an exhalation of the morning." [50] Whatever there may be in Transcendentalism of the romantic or the mystical (and the overtones are clear enough), the communion with universal Being was an absorption of the universe and of society into the rational, creative self. "Every rational creature," wrote Emerson, "has all nature for his dowry and estate . . . he is entitled to the world by his constitution. In proportion to the energy of his thought and will, he takes up the world into himself." [51] The symbol of Transcendentalism was not the Hindu wave, momently one with the ocean void, but the railroad, with power "to evoke the sleeping energies of land and water." [52]

Wherever the Yankee reached for the western stars, whether along the path of land speculation in the Midwest, or colleges in Ohio, town government in Michigan, economic organization and invention in Illinois, agricultural education in Iowa, utopias in Wisconsin, industry in Minnesota, or newspapers and righteous causes everywhere, faith in the absolute validity of principle led the way. With few limitations of time and space, it could be shaped into patterns at once capable of realization in a free environment and of acceptance by other national groups, as in the formation of the Farm Grange or the worship of the Constitution.[53] Freed from a custom-made tradition and tooled by reason, it provided an interchangeability of social parts; for the interchangeability of parts was a social before it was a technological fact. Yet if the warmth of Pennsylvania life appeared to the Yankee altogether too snugly centered in the hearth of habit and tradition to kindle the new society,[54] the glitter of Yankee stars seemed frosty and remote to the great mass of immigrants pouring into the Middle West after 1848. The conflict between the social myth of these peoples and the rational myth of the New Englanders (a conflict by-passed, except for occasional skirmishes, by the Yankees and the Pennsylvania Germans) was joined in the Middle West wherever traditional human know-how and intuitive relationships challenged the claims of a rationally articulated way of life—in the clash, for example, between the Continental Sunday and the Puritan Sabbath, between the force of a corporate personality and that of political action, or between the attitude that underlay centuries of barter and the increasingly abstract power of money and credit. Yet from the interpenetration of these myths there emerged a pattern audaciously forecast in Walt Whitman, who hymned the individual without the rational framework and the intimacy of human fellowship without the bond of tradition—a pattern that became distinctive for the Middle West and eventually for American culture as a whole.

9 · "GOD REIGNS, LET US GO ONWARD"[1]

*T*he cabin where Peter Cartwright expected to spend the night was still an afternoon's ride away: there was plenty of time to declaim to his horse,[2] while she picked her way over the sycamore roots along the trail, what he would say to his hosts or at the camp meeting he planned for this Scioto Circuit.[3] That was a brave name for a wild region of scattered cabins; it was only ten years since settlers had begun to cross the river into the Ohio country in goodly numbers—only five years, people said, since the buffalo had left.[4] But visit each family he must, even if it meant three or four exhortings a day.

He took his Bible from the saddlebag to read aloud a bit of the New Testament, but his mind was not in it: he was thinking of the family he had just left. There had been a supper last night of hog and hominy, corn bread and saleratus biscuit,[5] a long talk by the fireplace, and then prayer down on the knees on the dirt floor. It was the prayer that broke the surly husband, lightning-words to throw an awful glare on the tortured, swaying trees in the stormy blackness of his heart. And then ruddy, confident words, like the break of dawn.

He had stored them up unconsciously—words that had feelings and pictures in them—at corn shuckings, quiltings, and wood choppings; now he became aware that they had a special, driving force. And so he remembered apt phrases and images as he

rode the circuit—insects buzzing over a slough, a vine hanging from a tree, a dog shaking a rat.[6] "If God takes hold of your
father," he had told a worried young woman, "and shakes him
over hell a little while, and he smells brimstone right strong, if
there was a shipload of these sickly devils in him, they would
be driven out just as easy as a tornado would drive the regi-
ments of musquitoes from around and about those stagnant ponds
in the country."[7]

A man had to aim quick and sure to get his bobcat in one
shot, but it was a sight easier if you knew how the bobcat was
going to jump; and Cartwright was learning to throw "it red-hot
into [the] minds and hearts"[8] of his quarry. He would call "leading members of the flock . . . butting rams, or jumping ewes, or
sullen oxen, or kicking mules,"[9] and nobody could mistake him:
people of his circuit hewed their talk like their cabins from the
materials around them. They compared one thing with another as
they measured growing sons against their fathers: they stood
them back to back to size up facts and values; matters were
explained, proved, or settled by the logic of comparison.

There were people who knew men mean enough to steal
money off a dead man's eyes; there were farmers who boasted
that their whiskey was strong enough to draw a blister on a raw-
hide boot, that their fields were dry as a buffalo chip.[10] There
was a simple, uniform architecture in their logic as in their log
cabins, and it ran through the routine of life "from bornings to
buryings." When Cartwright had mastered that pattern, he had a
grip on his people: "you might hear in a single discourse, the thunder tread of a frightened herd of buffaloes as they rushed wildly
across the prairie, the crash of the windrow as it fell smitten by
the breath of the tempest, the piercing scream of the wild cat as
it scared the midnight forest . . . . Thunder and lightning, fire
and flood, seemed to be old acquaintances . . . ." And when
women "took their pipes from the chimney-corner at the close
of the exercises, saying to one another, 'Our young preacher is
a powerful piert,' "[11] he was well on the way to becoming "a

prophet clothed in garments of supernatural power," leading "his audience, willing captives, whithersoever he lists." [12]

There was hardly a family in the circuit, as he well knew, who did not think in analogies as naturally as they talked in metaphor: these stock pieces were almost the only furniture they had brought with them over the Alleghenies. The girls hoped that by shaking hands with young men across the communion table they'd soon be joined in wedlock with them, and that it would snow on their wedding day, for snow brings money. Young mothers watched to see whether a green veil—sure omen of the gift of prophecy—shrouded the faces of their newborn babies, they took care that their children's strength should not go into long and heavy hair, and they warned them not to pass in front of a casket.[13] Their husbands, like the Pennsylvania Germans, sowed, reaped, cut timber, and killed hogs by the light or dark of the moon and read the weather from the habits of squirrels and ducks. To the people of Cartwright's circuit, the world was a huge kaleidoscope, whose bewildering pieces fell by the twist of analogy or contrast into beautifully logical patterns of form, direction, texture, quality, process—patterns to cover everything that might happen from evening to evening and from spring to spring.

He might, Cartwright thought, let his horse choose which fork of the road to take, as Lorenzo Dow * used to do.[14] One road might be as good as another in this country where preachers "often swam [streams] on horseback, or crossed on trees [and] drove [the] horses over." [15] But he meant to keep a tight grip on the reins when he got to meeting: circuit meetings could be stubborn and restless; and sometimes haggling over a horse trade worried attention.[16] You had to talk hard and to the point, to use "methods of homiletic arrangement which learned writers on Sacred Rhetoric have never dreamed of." [17]

Often contrasts were more effective than metaphors: among these people things went "by contraries" as well as by analogies.

* An eccentric Methodist revivalist preacher (1777–1834).

To dream of the dead, it was often said, is to hear from the living. Clear eyes might reveal a clear conscience, but cold hands meant a warm heart.[18] It was an old folk formula, that things went by opposites—as old, perhaps, as paleolithic man's first pondering the succession of day and night, of summer and winter, or of life and death. Its hoary age was frozen in the lore of the seasons: a cold winter promised a hot summer; in March the lamb followed the lion, and mists in March meant frost in May.[19] Here where wild revels might be followed by wild revivals, where one could be whisked suddenly from sin to salvation, it was well to know that things went by contraries as much as by analogies.

Many of these formulas—like the one comforting the winter-weary with the thought that the days which were cold in February would be warm in March—had a kind of mathematical certainty about them (though not the kind that Yankee astronomers would recognize). Nature was reassuringly precise: you could tell from the number of times it thundered in February how often it would frost in May.[20] And what Nature started, she kept on with: if it rained on Monday, it would rain all the week; if it rained on the first day of dog days, it would rain for forty days thereafter.[21] What one did on the first day of the year was particularly important: it forecast his actions throughout the year. In this country people laid great store by "firsts" in getting a hold on the future.

But the young exhorter who had been fording many a stream of popular reasoning soon found himself, as he neared Marietta (the Plymouth of the West, its settlers proudly called it), swimming desperately in the open seas of Yankee logic. A thin-faced Yankee woman, "glib on the tongue," [22] entertained him with a bit of what he could expect from people who were proof against folk oratory, who thought him wicked because he pretended to preach the gospel without knowing so much as a point of Hebrew or a Greek accent,[23] and who held that man was a free agent, experiencing all his torments and bliss in this life. This might have been merely a Yankee's preference for education over "ignorance," science over "superstition," or law over custom. But Cartwright recognized instinctively that the conflict went deeper, that the grasp of an animistic universe by an understanding tutored in folk wisdom ("I learned this happy lesson not to fight against Providence")[24] was threatened by the belief in a cosmos apprehended by man's own reason. Against these tides he lashed out with lusty strokes: "If I were . . . to form a plan to contravene the laws of God . . . and crowd hell with the lost . . . , the Universalist plan should be . . . the very plan that I would adopt."[25]

He was more at home in his assignment to the Kentucky and Tennessee counties, where the devil had ridden circuit long before him. Any casual meeting (like the corn shucking, with its whiskey-bond of fellowship) might be one of the devil's "classes"; at every hoedown on a threshing floor he held a revival to rousing tunes like "The Frog With a Fiddle"; and rowdies and regulators alike paid him homage in their own way. These were mere liturgical performers at frontier shrines; the real devotees, the lasting converts, were those who sang the devil's "hymns," incantations that rose in thin Ionian or Mixolydian melodies along the "October-colored" valleys.[26] On an evening after chores the hearth or the porch became a folk stage where any member of the family might entertain the others with a repertoire of these ballads that sometimes lasted all night.

The ballads crackled with a humor as broad as a boatman's laugh—the elemental joke of things unexpectedly reversed, as when the old man thought he could do more work in a day than his wife in three but found

> As he gazed at the stars in the heaven,
> That his wife could do more work in one day
> Than he could do in seven.

Some ballads put the same turnabout into a quiet smile—like the song about the girl whose father had made her promise

> Always to answer the young man no . . . ,

and so when he asked

> Is there any real objection
> If a kiss I should bestow?

she answered archly

> No, no, no sir, no . . . .

Along with these were older songs sprung from the courtly sophistication that graced the romance of *The Green Knight*—ballads that moved subtly between irony and suspense. A feudal lord surprises his wife with her paramour and asks him:

> Oh, how do you like my bed, sir,
> Oh, how do you like my sheep,
> And how do you like my fairy queen
> That lies in your arms asleep?

And in nearly identical verses, the lover sings his affirmative reply.[27]

At one horizon of log-cabin philosophy were songs of a life with Common Bill and simple lyrics—

> I wish, I wish, and I wish in vain,
> I wish I was a child again;
> My wish, my wish shall never be
> Till green grass grows over me [28]

—as poignant and intense as the despairing cry of Goethe's Margaret at the spinning wheel. At the other were wistful yearnings for finery and adventure and folk forays into a predetermined unknown. If there was any feeling or situation that the "devil's ditties" [29] left untouched, it is probably the collectors' rather than Satan's oversight; and Cartwright knew that he must travel the devil's own circuit if he would draw the traditional patterns of folk experience into the orbit of Methodist evangelism.

But the devil had done much of God's spadework for him, had made a rich culture mold of the soil of Kentucky and Tennessee for the propagation of a personal faith. The ballads put the world in basic human terms, in motives that stirred unforgettable characters to highly dramatic action. Scolding wives, dishonest millers, faithful and fortune-wary sweethearts, cruel brothers, over-anxious parents—as clearly drawn a cast as ever Chaucer took from Canterbury Road—moved in piquant episodes through family storms, evening trysts, or murders in bramble briars. And in each lyric the listener recognized a neighbor or a neighboring cove.

To feel one with these personalities was to follow or reject unconsciously their patterns of conduct. Tags there were in plenty to point the way:

> Young people, lest this be your case
> Return to God and seek his face;

or again:

> A thief can rob you, and take all you have,
> But an unconstant lover will send you to
> your grave.[30]

Yet it was not these that people remembered so much as the dramatic situations, the value judgments implicit in graphic emotional imagery. Don't wait for happiness, the songs insisted; don't try to mold your son's or daughter's career too rigidly; don't seek the keys of heaven in a paper of pins, but marry for true love. Commandments multiplied in the ballad bible.[31]

As "the ballad singer phrases an idea in terms of things, unconsciously metaphorical," [32] so he spins his story in terms of recurrent emotional comparisons ("value judgments are all comparisons") [33] of good and bad in personal and social behavior. And as folk belief built up the physical universe with factual analogies and opposites, so too folk balladry conceived the social realm as the fabric of moral parallels and contrasts. Folk logic asked: is this like or unlike that? Folk feeling asked: is this better or worse than that? It was the same fundamental outlook applied to human relations. In the Kentucky and Tennessee circuits Lucifer had created an animistic cosmology that embraced the social as well as the physical world.

By Thursday evening most of the cloth-topped wagons had arrived and had edged into the shadows of the sugar maples and beeches that fringed the huge parallelogram; [34] and tents were already springing up inside the line of wagons. As the moon rose, people in thousands "visited around" or lay down gratefully to sleep in wagon bottoms and on the straw flooring of the tents —some perhaps with their Bibles under their heads to improve the prospects of the meeting with dreams of marriage.[35] Come Friday—the fairest or the foulest day of the week, people said [36] —dawn would break with the blast of a horn.

At the second horn family prayer—"fervent-believing prayer" [37] —went up all over the encampment. Soon came snatches of lad's warmth:

> Jesus, the name high over all,
> In hell or earth or sky,
> Angels and man before him fall,
> And devils fear and fly.[38]

The cosmic drama of hymns like this matched the dark conflicts of the devil's "ballets"; [39] there were others that radiated the ballad's warmth—

> The sweet comfort and peace
> Of a soul in its earliest love;

or breathed a ballad's impassioned feeling in a lyric prayer:

> Show pity, Lord, O! Lord forgive;
> Let a repenting rebel live.

Mountain folk at home in the symbolism of their songs warmed to the symbols in

> O sun of righteousness, arise
> With healing in thy wing,

and

> In hope of that immortal crown
> I now the Cross sustain.[40]

In every hymn thunderheads of nameless fears and "ancient half-pagan beliefs"[41] lay upon the horizon ("O! drive these dark clouds from my sky!")[42] or broke in sudden splendor:

> Lighten my eyes with faith; my heart
> With holy hopes inflame.[43]

But at the sound of a horn the singing stopped; people poured out of their tents to fill the benches.

The preachers were already on the stand, their hair turned back from the crowns of their heads and falling to their shoulders.[44] At the ends of the stand were platforms piled with pine logs like the truncated spires of a forest cathedral. Loud whispers from the benches were picking out Peter Cartwright, a keen-eyed catamount of a man, with oak burrs and slippery elm in his make-up, quick and sparkling as the Roaring River itself. But the figure who now rose before the benches was not Cartwright but a tall preacher in a round-breasted coat, short breeches, and long stockings, his shadow slanting behind him.

The meeting, he said, had gathered in its net bad fish as well as good. That was as it should be: here, if anywhere, the stupendous grace of God would rescue captives from the devil. Here was a glorious chance, not to consummate "spontanaceous" deals in barter and in love, as some of them seemed to be doing, but to throw off Satan's chains. The gates of hell shall not prevail, he shouted. He meant to level upon them the artillery of truth—the awful power of the Scriptures.[45] Many of these people, he knew, used that power in their own way: they would hold the Bible over their children's heads to stop nosebleeding or would make wishes and were sure, when they could find the words "and it will come to pass," that the wishes would come true.[46] The Word was a fearful and wonderful thing: it could work magic in body and soul.

He moved down through the rows, and another preacher raised his arms to exhort the crowd. "The great day of His wrath has come," he cried, "and who shall be able to stand!" [47] A nameless fear stirred in the benches—fear of unremembered sins, fear of an angry Providence that would shake them over hell during the earthquakes of 1812 and 1813. Perhaps, like Preacher Cook, they would leap from their beds in panic from the wrath of God when the ground shook beneath them and shout "my Jesus is coming!" [48] The ominous threat was all too real: the same Providence created the laws of nature and of morals and made them reciprocal—a universe whose facts were interpreted through conscience and whose values were known through the concrete imagery of the senses. The fires on the platforms had been lighted; pine knots were crackling and shooting sparks into the dusk. Providence was a Power at once personal and cosmic, uniquely intimate as a dream, inscrutable as the winter sky.

Cartwright had been peering into the dark line of sugar maples, where the smouldering campfires near the wagons blinked like stars in a pond. Warnings had persisted that a gang of rowdies would be stealing in to break up the meeting; he and his deputies would be ready for them. It would be much harder to crack the hickory-nut heads of unbelievers in the audience itself. Now he took his place between the platform fires, ready to tote the thunder in his fist and fling the lightning from his fingers.[49]

He set out to wield the earthquaking power of metaphor and symbol to open an abyss beneath their feet, to dangle these Common Bills and Cindy Ellens "hair-hung and breeze-shaken" [50] over the emotional bifurcation of their own ballads, where "evil stands out stark and goodness is . . . unqualified." [51] He would split their universe vertically from hell to heaven and from cross to crown into psychological absolutes—homespun and silk, ecstasy and dread, gospel and law.

To those who had little enough of the world's goods he shouted: "What shall it profit a man if he gain the whole world . . . ?" In "the great deep of a sinner's heart," there was no solid ground: he was "lost! lost! lost! forever lost." It was as if Cartwright were casting into the fires on each side of him all that life was made of—the joy of fine tableware, clothes, or horses, the hope and the security of schoolbook, account book, and lawbook. It was as if the fires were hungering for their very souls. But what brought these "tall sons and daughters of Belial" to "praying in mighty agony" [52] was that the very fabric of thought that made this kind of world possible or desirable was going up in smoke. In the Judgment fires the linear symbols of progress were reduced to ashes, and there was nothing left—nothing real but Providence.

The moaning of penitents rose and fell in the pine log benches as Cartwright "swung clear." If Providence could loose earthquakes and epidemics upon the sinful, he was saying, it was as vitally concerned for those who writhed in "agony for salvation." [53] Providence could wreak vengeance upon the blasphemous or protect the righteous from destruction—as it would soon prove again when a young Bloomington heckler was suddenly drowned, and when a large limb fell "without wind or any other visible cause" at a Sangamon District camp meeting, "but as the Lord would direct it, there was not a woman or child there when the limb fell." [54]

In the crowd other preachers were moving swiftly among sinners fainting from the exhaustion of fear and remorse, urging them to "pray on, brother, pray on," trying to stem those grim paroxysms of excitement, the "jerks," spreading "the heavenly fire." [55] From the stand Cartwright saw his moment coming: it was time to unloose "the puckering strings" of their mouths and bring them to glory. "O sinner," he shouted, "stop and think before you further go! Turn, and turn now. Behold, the day cometh!" [56] The platform fires played a lurid drama of light and shadow over his face: to these devil-distraught people he must have seemed the incarnation of that day.

He saw in their eyes the dark fatalism "that overcasts ballad skies . . . constantly with the irrevocable," [57] the common feeling that it was wrong for man to change what God had wrought ("If a fellow is born to be hung, he will never be drowned" [58]), the power of first beginnings to determine what came after, the "mathematical" precision of nature's behavior. He knew their resignation in the face of the inflexible. But the world of the ballads was above all human, a world of emotional absolutes in which Providence intervened suddenly and miraculously to set things aright.

In the hypnotic spell of Cartwright's exhortation the fires went unheeded: pine logs settled on one another in fitful showers of sparks. But the moon had risen; it poured along the "streets" at the four corners and cut a golden highway down the center to the stand. The preachers were already bringing along the highway a crowd of "shining and shouting Christians," and Cartwright was welcoming these "dead souls made alive," these "new-born souls . . . into the liberty of the Gospel." [59] Gospel was better than law; [60] the real Bill of Rights was Scripture itself. To these piney-woods people the Lord would give "light, liberty, and power." [61] In the fiery exorcism of camp meetings, through the inner regenerative power of Scripture, they would become a community in which the laws of nature and of morals were one and the same and were reciprocal—a world bodied forth in concrete images of conscience. In the "Nation of the Valley," [62] behold the day cometh!

*A*s he entered the gate at the Tazewell County Fair that 1854 September day,[1] the young reporter paused while a big wagon creaked hesitantly across his path toward an open plot that even this early in the morning was filling rapidly. Before the wheels had stopped turning, the children were leaping over the sides; the horses, tied to the rear, were soon munching the grass, and the farmer and his wife were unloading pumpkins, quilts, crates of chickens, and baskets of apples. It was good to walk through the freshly cut field, thought the reporter, after the long ride on the Rock Island and Bureau Extension Railroad from Chicago to Henry, the steamboat to Peoria, and Frink's Stage to Tremont—good to catch the smell of grass and fruit and of cattle and horses driven to their stalls. And the air—five acres of it—was alive and throbbing with the staccato of hammers, the squealing of pigs and wagon wheels, and the shouts after escaping fowl and escaped children.

Down the grassy thoroughfare sounds and smells met, mingled and separated, blending again in new combinations—like the groups of men supervising last-minute preparations of stalls and booths or examining the displays of farm implements. There were Griffith, Kellogg, and the Hodgsons trying to look busy with their horses. There were Matthews, Wallace, and Scott figuring that if no more hogs were entered than the lot that was already on the

117

grounds they should walk away with the two-dollar first premiums. And there were Clark, Bascom, Brown, and Saltonstall trading vital statistics on their cattle and arguments on the advantages of care and breeding. "Well-wintered is half-summered" was something they could agree on; and they reckoned James Brown of Island Grove was right about crossing native stock with Durham.[2] There were scientific laws of cattle breeding, and if you knew the language of science you could grow better cows the way you grew better crops. They had no sympathy with the downstaters farming in Tazewell County who said Nature knew what she was about, and no good could come of tinkering with her.

Some of these Yankees had settled Tremont about twenty years ago,[3] and they had a story they liked to tell. An enterprising individual had bought land there and had arranged that his wife should see a lithographic map with streets, squares, buildings, and trees, but when she visited the place there were nothing but jackrabbits to block the prairie vista.[4] But—such was the power of lithographic maps—there was now a very pretty village with shade trees[5] and farms like Seth Talbot's or Lloyd Shaw's all around.

Along the fairway to the left men were wandering about among the new machines glinting in the open sun. They guessed that the knives on Haines' mower wouldn't clog, that T. H. Smith's and Toby and Anderson's plows would show about the same draught on the dynamometer. The stubborn Illinois sod made them stubborn judges, but they had a flexible vision: a good span of horses could cross the green prairie ocean with plows like these. Mowers, plows, threshers, separators, corn planters, rakes, and reapers—here was proof of the boost that prairie farming gave to manufacturing. They boasted—as if they were partners in the business—that within a year or so the McCormick reaper would be turned out at the rate of three thousand a year.[6] Ideas like these, thought the reporter, made up the saying: improve the country and the town will grow.

People bent mainly on improving the country were crowding the end of the thoroughfare, where a large canvas stretched over them like a brooder house. On both sides of the entrance was the Ladies Department, a Sunday show of weekday skills. Altogether they made up a mosaic of the prairie homestead—paintings, fresh and packed butter, lace and muslin work, wool carpets, knit stockings, pressed flowers . . . . Beyond these booths spread huge crazy quilts of vegetables and fruits—bold patterns of apples, pears, plums, peaches, corn, potatoes, Isabella grapes. There were items here for the reporter's notebook: forty-five different kinds of apples in one farmer's display; preserved quinces and grapes; the deep glow of Mrs. H. R. Browne's plums. It was back in '51, he remembered, that the *Prairie Farmer* had thought it was time to bridle the "antiquated and somewhat superstitious notion" of pounding plum trees to increase the yield.[7] He made a few notes: Ladies Department, miscellaneous, fruits very superior, thronged with admiring visitors. Tazewell Adams and Eves were certainly heeding the call of the *Peoria Weekly Republican* to bring the produce of central Illinois' virgin soil to the fairs, to confirm the fact that "this section is not only the heart of Illinois but the heart of the West . . . the garden-spot of the world."[8]

It was almost time for the plowing match. The reporter made his way through lanes of lively chatter and knots of solemn appraisal to the shaft of sunlight at the rear. He walked briskly past the poultry fence, where a couple of men were on the point of awarding to a pair of long-necked Shanghais the first class premium these fine fowl seemed to be claiming for themselves, past the hog pens, to the plowing field. The crowd was already edging the quarter-acre arena to watch the oxen, six yokes of them, line up at the starting point. In a moment long billows of black loam were rolling off the plows, and the drivers were nimbly footing the furrows.

Children scurried after them, but their parents, knowing they would have a half hour to wait, renewed old acquaintances. They re-enacted the drama on the Thompkins farm the day before, when Ketchum's, Manny's, and Haines' mowers were put to trial. They exchanged recipes for Indian loaf cake and hominy pudding and testimonials matching the story that a Tazewell County baby had been born with a green veil shrouding its face and so would have the gift of prophecy. They debated whether northern flint corn with its regular kernels was better than the crowded southern gourdseed. They claimed with a twinkle that they could tell whether chicks would be pullets or roosters by the sex of the first visitor on New Year's Day. And they asked whether anyone had seen the new Amish who had come from Pennsylvania to join the others along the river; some were venturing out of the timber into the prairie, and it was a good thing for Tazewell: [9] they were fine farmers. Now and then they looked out into the field and allowed that Franks, Wood, and Kellogg seemed to be ahead.

The reporter strolled through the crowd, tasting opinions as he had the samples of cake and cheese in the Ladies Department. It struck him that here—without benefit of booths, canvas, or committees—was the heart of the fair, the crowning exhibit. He could envisage pens with the placard "What Farm Machines and Blooded Stock Will Do For the Country," stalls with the sign "Folklore in Central Illinois," the tabernacle "God Reigns, Let Us Move Onward," an enormous tent with the banner "Politics."

At times that tent overshadowed all other displays. A farmer near Tremont reckoned that Douglas would cut a swath through his foes at the Springfield State Fair next week. He put slogans into Douglas' mouth that he had seen in the papers: when Kansas and Nebraska entered the Union, they would be free because a free people would control them; slavery was a local institution, and it was wrong to intervene; the motto of the Sucker state was "state sovereignty and national union." But "Douglas" was a fighting word: he was only, replied another farmer, a "northern man with southern principles"; Germans in Peoria knew,[10] if some native Americans didn't, that slavery was wrong and must not be allowed to spread into the new states. Bystanders rushed to back the Tremont farmer, and for a moment Tazewell was secured for Douglas. It was in these middle counties where "cow-milking Yankee Puritans" and "Egyptians" [11] met, thought the reporter, that disputes on squatter sovereignty plowed the deepest furrows. And yet it wasn't so simple as Whigs against Southerners. These men were farmers, too: what they assumed about their homesteads, what they took for granted about the future of their homesteads—this should make a difference. The talk grew hot; they didn't know the plowing match was over and had to ask who won. They were told it was Milt Franks, using a Toby and Anderson plow.

As the crowd left the field, the wind sprang up, whipping the dust into people's eyes. Men looked anxiously at the big canvas shelter and at the roof of the cattle shed; there was a scurrying after husbands, children, wives. The children whimpered that the storm would spoil Orton's Badger Circus; but the wind died, the circus went on, and they then and there made up their minds that when they grew up they'd play like those musicians, ride the gaily tasselled horses with the same graceful aplomb, or perform the feats the giant did. Everybody agreed that this was better than the horse racing, the tournamenting, or the baby shows that were lately beginning to debase the county fairs— the best thing, in fact, that had come to Tazewell.[12]

While the nodding crests of the circus horses moved out through the crowd, men were pulling and pushing a wagon toward the center of a grassy field. This was the stage for the annual address, the blue ribbon premium of the fair. There was a pattern for these rituals: by now the reporter could draw up his outline in advance, whether it was the minister, the editor of a farm magazine, or the president of the agricultural society who stood upon the platform. He would offer dirt-farm advice; he would urge farmers to improve their soil, stock, and science, their "land, labor, and learning"; [13] he would pay artful respects to the ladies; and he would paint sunrises over the homestead and rainbows over the future of the Mississippi Valley.

The speaker had mounted his platform and was looking out over the audience—several hundred, counting those who sat in wagons ringing the outer edge. Some, he knew, were simply drawn to the group, but many had been reading his *Prairie Farmer* editorials as regularly as they read the skies. "Farmers and Citizens of Tazewell," he began, "although agriculture may lack the elements of excitement possessed by other subjects, it yields to none: ministering to them all, it feeds them all." [14]

John A. Wight was no novice at these fairs, the reporter reflected—last year at Kane County, day before yesterday at McHenry: as surely as he stood in the center of the crowd, this doctrine put him at the core of their thinking. Ministering to them all—there was no need to say more. Everyone knew that the farmer did not merely talk about things, or put them together, or buy and sell them. He created them. He was the only genuine producer; the others—the lawyers and preachers, the working and business men—were nonproducers. He was the soil of society; factories like McCormick's, towns and cities— these were the crops.

In these days everything was changing, Wight went on. "Think of the steam press . . . the railroad . . . the electric telegraph . . . . All our moving, acting, and thinking are in some sense of a different sort from . . . those of our early days." Let no one think that agriculture, "like Dogberry's 'reading and writing, was a thing which come by nater.' The grand comprehensive want is *more knowledge. Knowledge is power* . . . over matter, over principles, over every thing. Agricultural knowledge is agricultural power."

Wight's gospel reached the ears of the downstate settlers of Tazewell, the genial "hog and hominy" people, like the echo of a bell high in the thin steeple of a Yankee church. They had heard it before, and they shook their heads over it. Maybe reading and writing didn't come by "nater," but did he mean that cows and pigs and corn came by the book? They'd spent a life-time learning the signs of nature; if they weren't real, what was? As for the Emersons, the Shaws, the Talbots—men who managed fairs, collected and classified insects, and wrote on fruit culture and hedging—to men like these Wight was beckoning his followers from Mt. Sinai out of the bondage of "Egypt" into the promised land. He was revealing to them a decalogue of agricultural lore, a new code of signs to be learned. It sounded as if he meant that the press, the railroad, and the telegraph had made all the difference, but if you listened closely you knew that it was the signs that really mattered—that changed your moving, acting, and thinking. When you had learned them, you had power over matter, over principles, over everything.

The speaker paused—for emphasis partly, and partly because of a spirited exhibit of wrestling between two future farmers that had not been duly entered in the program of the fair. Many of the male members of the audience abandoned their concern for the progress of knowledge to follow that of the wrestlers. Wight ignored them and plunged into his theme.

"While there are people who will feed half-boiled cabbage to a patient laboring under the cholera, or salt pork to one half-convalescent from the typhus fever, both of which I have myself known, none need think there is not a chance here for improvement. I will not promise [the farmer any new idea] from this address, but there is a continual address to him from all these grounds during these two days. Pumpkins and pigs and poultry talk to him; horned beasts give sermons on good beef; implements and products say *improvement*."

What would they say to the Amish in Tazewell County, wondered the reporter? Would they talk in lbs., %'s and $'s? Or would they speak in the ancient idiom of earth—the shaggy coats of cattle and horses, the signs of the zodiac, the elemental pantomime of growth? These were not dialects of the same tongue: they had no common roots and could not be translated into one another. They were opposite ways of expressing the same world

—if (as he doubted) it *was* the same world. The Amish, and many of the Southern upland settlers, knew their homesteads as a panorama of pictures, a pattern of sounds. They caught these images in the bright red, yellow, and blue designs upon their barns, in the autumnal melancholy of their ballads. But the "movers" from New York and New England shaped the images of their prairie homes into an alphabet—a set of symbols stripped of all externals. That was the heart of the difference. For if you went from image to image, as the Amish did, you were moving deeper and deeper into the rich warm world of intuitive revelation. But if you linked letter with letter, idea with idea, you were spelling out an ordered universe in a logical scheme of laws and principles. In one homestead you read the omens of heaven from the leaves of farm lore; in the other you floated reason's kite on a string of symbols and brought down the lightning from the skies.[15]

Knowledge "underlies all our hopes of progress," Wight was saying; "it embraces the whole agricultural gospel . . . . It is mind that governs the world." It was as if he had said: "In the beginning was the Word . . . ." This was the revealed Truth, the Reality behind the signs. Last year at the State Fair, the reporter remembered, he had heard another witness to the light intone to the multitude: mind is "the great motive power of the universe . . . the steam power of the eternities . . . that all-embracing, all-conquering power that has produced all else here and all else worth producing on the face of the earth." [16] With this gleaming new implement prairie farmers could plow the tough sod of ignorance, reap the harvests of progress, open the "great green ocean" of the West, as Jonathan B. Turner had said to the multitude, to "that iron commerce that is to mark [the] triumph" of Illinois. And now Wight was telling his audience: "Knowledge, like money, propagates itself in geometric ratio . . . . The road that runs by your house will, if you follow it, lead to the end of the world."

The way of knowledge was the highroad to Eden. You were

leaving behind homesteads "unpleasant . . . unhomelike" (how many the reporter had seen on his way to Tazewell—their front doors hidden from the road by hog yards, rail corn pens, woodpiles, old sleds!).[17] "Admit that [the love of Eden] is sometimes rude and untutored," he had said last year; "still it is here; culture will do the rest." You were riding through a smiling countryside that a "correct taste springing from a love of nature" had transformed from burdock, mustard, plaintain, and knot grass into a garden of shade trees and fruits and flowers—"the seminal reflections of the first paradise." You were drawing nearer to the homestead set at the top of Wight's own paper—the pastoral vignette whose "circle is magical and elastic and encloses 'the dear home' of every Prairie Farmer"—a home that had "a countenance and a language, too," where images of "domestic peace and rural happiness" assimilate its dwellers "to the order and neatness they continually see around them," filling "the mind [with] a beauty of character and conduct." [18]

Looking around at his passengers, some of whom were stirring restlessly as if they would have been quite content to get off anywhere on the road and enjoy nature's gifts uncultivated, Wight drew rein at the very gateway of Eden. "What may we not hope for when the full effulgence of knowledge shall have penetrated all our rural districts and infused itself through all our rural operations? The farmer everywhere delivered by it from that excess of toil which bows him to the earth . . . yet with labor enough for physical health and intellectual elasticity and moral soundness . . . able to do all that his calling and position require . . . as God meant him to be, the fairest type of manhood upon earth." [19]

Such was the vision of heaven. It was a homestead set gleaming upon the broad prairies of knowledge—the home of nature's own brand of man. In the "Genesis" of Wight's Bible there were only those who produced and those who did not. And he who fed them all did so less with his hands than with his head. So from the vast virgin prairie Wight had selected a handful of primeval soil—reason; and from it he created the farmer. Here stood the fairest type of manhood on earth—unfettered with toil and custom, stripped of superstition. Like Euclid, Wight looked on Beauty bare.

Having extracted the raw stuff of reality, Wight grew upon it the lush vegetation of Eden. From this primeval clay he saw farmers springing up everywhere through the Mississippi Valley; he saw farms as clean as a business ledger, industry growing like ears of corn on the stalks of agriculture, homesteads aglow with happiness,[20] virtue, beauty. He saw the prairies, once the fibrous roots of farm lore had been cut, grow vigorous and full upon the taproot of knowledge.

The millennium was at hand; there was "a good time coming." For a moment the reporter could see that apostle of knowledge, J. B. Turner, standing there in the wagon as he had stood before the multitude in Springfield. "When the millennium of labor shall come," he heard him say, the farmer will be "as much above all other professions . . . as farmer Adam was before the fall above that same fallen farmer now," with "a loftier character than any other living man—man fully restored from the fall." [21] The image faded, and he could see another evangelist upon the pulpit—the impassioned form of Peter Cartwright ushering in the kingdom of God. In the revival meetings of Springfield he had called upon God to shake sinners "hair-hung" over pits of hell and then had brought them screaming, moaning, and singing down the aisles of grace to the glory of conversion.

The Book of Revelation lay open to both, but how different the paths to the new heaven and the new earth! To Cartwright knowledge put up almost impassable bars; to Turner it was the ladder of salvation.[22] To the "Egyptians" in Tazewell, Yankee education took the color out of Paradise and the melody out of God's voice; to the cow-milking Puritans—however Turner might scoff at the "school-men and professors of our day" for giving children "no other idea than that God made the world out of the nine parts of speech" [23]—it was the grammar of agriculture that would restore them from the fall.

The wagons that ringed the crowd began to move away, pulling their shadows after them, and the people spilled out over the fairground. Children ran to stumble over the stakes and entangle themselves in the ropes as the big canvas came slowly down. Moments like these, the circus, the squealing and cackling, the green and orange smells of the fair, would stick in their minds all year. Their mothers were already busily wrapping things up to take home—preserves and quilts and pastries, images of the newfangled canned fruit and of garden plots and green hedges. And their fathers were loading the wagons with pumpkins and poultry and pigs—daily sermons on improvement.

Piled high with produce, stock, and ideas, the wagons were soon winding out of the gate and down the road. The reporter watched quick gusts of wind lift the dry dirt beneath the wheels and the horses' hooves. Were many of Tazewell's farmers, he wondered, travelling "from dusty bondage into luminous air?" There would be some who had lifted their eyes from the "oak openings" of occasional insight within timberlands of tradition to the vast open prairies in which only hardwood groves of custom studded the sweep of knowledge. But there would be few farmers rolling homeward through the red blaze of sunset who had caught Wight's revelation of reason, the vision of light anatomized. Their vistas were still wrapped—like the little farm houses dozing in the warm shadows of the setting sun—in symbols of things seen and felt, in metaphors of things loved and remembered.

And yet Wight was no prophet crying in the empty prairies. In the minds of homegoing farmers were bright flashes from the radiance of his gospel—the silver sheen of "money, that abstract and supple measure" [24] of value, the steel gleam of plows and railroad tracks, the golden fleece of improvement. If they still moved more naturally from reality to image than from reality to abstraction, they nonetheless understood the saying "God has ordained that knowledge is power." [25] Had it not been so, Wight could not have set the stern helmet of Athena on Ceres' rustic brow. He would never have tried to clear away the woodpiles and old sleds from the front yards of their minds—to persuade them that farming is a science, and that to be a farmer was to be a creature of reason, the only "true farmer when the millennium of labor shall come." [26] As they lumbered slowly into the night, it was not hard to believe that the only true democracy must be made up of such farmers, that there was a reciprocal relation between cultivating your fields and your mind, and that knowledge made the homesteads lying asleep in the prairie moon at the end of the road into vignettes of progress, happiness, and character.

"All our moving, acting, and thinking are in some sense of a different sort . . . ." He would get the full text of the speech, the reporter decided, when he returned to Chicago. He penned a final note: two thousand present "consisting of old men and young, matrons and maidens, together with the boys and girls— a very satisfactory audience." [27]

11 · THE QUEST OF CERES

*A*lmighty Father, Maker of Heaven and Earth, and Giver of all Good, we return our heartfelt thanks to Thee that we are permitted again to meet each other here for work in this glorious cause. Endow us with prudence . . . that our labors may be blessed with a liberal harvest; and when we are called to lay down our implements on earth, may we . . . receive that welcome plaudit, Well done, good and faithful servants.[1]

There was a low "Amen"; then heads and voices were raised in the still June air. In the unnatural sheen of the evening sun, the Patrons gleamed in stiff patterns as they stood singing beside their chairs; and the baskets on the tables, the oaks, and the house and the barn stretched out in deep green silhouettes upon the lawn.

The Master of Harvest Grange, his sash slung from his shoulder and his pouch from his belt, took his place before them. It was good to share the bounties of picnic baskets and comradeship. Some of the young couples at the tables, he noted, had not neglected either.[2] Perhaps those who were not fourth-degree members would be willing, while the business meeting was in session, to help arrange the parlor for the initiation.[3] A number of Patrons arose, and the youngest children took it as a signal to slip away to the barn and the willows along the creek.

The Master turned to the order of business. There was the re-

129

port of the Committee to Aid the Patrons of Northwest Iowa. The five hundred families ruined by the grasshoppers, said the chairman, were no longer threatened with starvation, but the clothing, seed, and money sent by Harvest Grange had been most welcome.[4] There was the report on the question of joining the Jasper County Mutual recommending purchase of stock in the company. The Patrons' elevator at Monroe and the Co-operative Association store at Newton were firmly established; with men behind this venture like J. W. Murphy, secretary of the company and a stockholder in the association, the risk should be well worth taking.[5] And it was so voted.

In the parlor of the house, men were moving tables to "altar" positions, and women were hanging frames on the wall behind the tables—Flora's bouquet of everlastings, Ceres' huge wreath of various grains, and the wax Siberian crab tree laden with fruits to symbolize Pomona.[6] There ought to be an emblem to hang over the doorway, a lady suggested—like those that Foster and McFarren made for Granges.[7] She had tried one, but the heavy materials wouldn't take the stitch. Her sewing machine, though, was as "nice as a new pin": she had bought it through the Patrons' state agent at a real saving. It was the same with the groceries, said another, that she had got through the Grange from Chicago retailers; after the depression last year, they couldn't have made do without Granger prices on foodstuffs and farm machinery.[8]

They still needed a couple of tables, one of the men reminded them—for the Chaplain and the Lecturer; the sewing machine, covered with a cloth, would do for one. These covered tables, he added, resembled a spiritualists' convention. The sun, slanting low through the long narrow window, kindled a red glare in the mica squares of the stove. The room settled into a cozy repose: the women sat about in the gathering dusk, and the men moved out on the little front porch. Now and then snatches of conversation about table tippings and spirit hands reached the men as they talked about feeding meadow or swale hay; and tales of locating water with "water witches" filtered into the parlor, where the talk had turned to custard cakes and mock lemon pies.[9]

From the porch it appeared that the business meeting had closed: the air was intense with argument. They could hear one Patron say, "If Any Party Stands Between Us, Let It Die," adding that the question of railroad rates had bankrupted both parties as thoroughly as they had the farmers here in Jasper County, and that it was time to overthrow the old parties and re-establish popular rights.[10] They called to the women inside and joined the group, now in the midst of choosing a slogan for its banner in the big Fourth of July celebration only a couple of weeks away.[11]

That slogan would have been better last year, another farmer replied, when the Anti-Monopoly party polled half the votes in the county; he'd prefer "Build Up and Foster Home Industry." [12] Fight fire with fire; [13] show the monopolies that the farmer was independent, that he did not have to submit to extortion and unjust discrimination.[14] And show the middleman, too—that smooth gentleman with his matched grays and fine carriage— that the farmer did not need a chain of agents to inspect, insure, weigh, ship, and store his produce. Too much money stuck to the fingers of the middleman; farmers had to fight an army of them as big as the standing army of the British Empire, and the census proved it.[15]

A trim lady rose abruptly. She had read a great deal and had a way with words, and she had been chosen Lecturer. If it's fight fire with fire, she said, wouldn't "In Union There Is Strength" be better? Monopolies thrive on combination—railroads combining with other railroads and with eastern brokers. The whole country is at their mercy. Farmers have begun to match their combinations with co-operation—the only way to restore the balance, to get justice, equal protection and advantages, and a fair share of wealth.[16] And Jasper County is an excellent example of co-operation—the largest number of Granges in the strongest Grange state in the Union.[17]

Here and there fireflies pricked the dusk; the sky drew closer, and the children were returning from the creek. But no one stirred from the lawn: all perspective of time was erased in the immediacy of feeling—in the anxiety to trace the heresy and restore the Faith.

"Strength" was a good word, one man agreed, but "union" was only a part of that strength. "Farmers, You Are The Strength Of The Nation" more nearly expressed it. It was as Grand Master Dudley Adams had said a few years ago: the farmer was the real producer; railroad men and manufacturers "do not produce a pound of meat, a bushel of wheat, a yard of cloth, or a pig of iron. They cannot subsist a month without us. We can without them. The farmers have got the lines, why don't they drive?" [18]

A voice came from the edge of the group. The farmer *feeds* them all, yes; but the farmer *pays* for all, too.[19] What good did it do to produce if it cost so much to get things to market? Rates were excessive and discriminatory; the way they were set up, Omaha was situated between Chicago and Iowa. As Governor Carpenter said, railroad rates were "the skeleton in every Western farmer's corn-crib." [20]

We're examining these slogans, came another voice, like a pen of prize steers: we're agreed that each is a blue-ribbon winner, but we don't know which to buy. We'll have to take one and get on: the initiation is still ahead of us. And then someone brightened like a lamp with a new wick: the Farmers' Declaration of Independence should be of some help. It was in the *Iowa Homestead* about a year ago. The hostess left and in a few moments returned with the paper and a lamp.

When in the course of human events [she read] it becomes necessary for a class of the people, suffering from long continued systems of oppression and abuse, to rouse themselves from an apathetic indifference to their own interests . . . .

She skipped along: they had heard it read so often they knew it almost by heart:

We, therefore, the producers of the state in our several counties assembled . . . do solemnly declare that we will use all lawful and peaceable means to free ourselves from the tyranny of monopoly, and that we will never cease our efforts for reform . . . .[21]

Reform the tyranny of monopoly—that was the general feeling. Someone called out "Corn Must Go Up, Monopolies Must Come Down," and suddenly they were all on their feet talking together in little knots.

Monopolies on patents, prices, rates, elevators—it was an infernal yoke.[22]

The people gave the railroads privileges—land grants and bonds —and they used them for oppressing the people.[23]

My corn goes up now—in smoke (there was grim laughter; some of them knew what it meant to burn their corn to avoid the freight).[24]

This was the slogan they would carry on the Fourth of July, Farmers' Independence Day. Yet it was not a slogan they had been searching for but a symbol—a symbol that would sum up the heresy undermining the natural order of things. And it was here in the sanctuary itself—the myth of the great interior—that they had discovered it, the image of the railroads (a sure extension, it had seemed, of the promise of the Middle West) demonically bent on the farmer's ruin.[25] A prairie poet had painted the promise and the ruin in two strokes:

> O prairies so vast, ye are vassals at last—
> To-day we rivet your chains.[26]

Grangers spoke of the "infernal yoke" and of the contrariness of things, and everyone knew what they meant—that the power which was to be a partner in progress was weighting the scales in its own favor,[27] that everything from prices to politics was out of balance. This was the oppression and unbalance that went into the word "monopoly"; this was the reason why it could mean not only discriminatory rates and monopolistic control of patents and elevators, but middlemen, unequal tax loads, hard money, and hard times. It was a personification of predatory inequity:

> When the engine's screams break his midnight
>   dreams,
> He will wake with the old affright,
> And murmur low, as in years ago,
> "Fierce howls the hungry wolf to-night." [28]

These Iowa Grangers brooded over the image of "Monopoly," visualized it in high-priced plows and low-priced corn, and drew moral conclusions about it. It was a strong symbol—personal, single, and concrete; it had power to stir emotion and action. But it was a synthesis of wrongs, not an analysis of causes.[29] It could not shape for them the shadowy werewolves that stalked their farms once they had removed the fences between subsistence and commercial farming—had exposed their independence to the makers of farm machinery and thrown their crops and stock open to the fluctuations of distant markets.[30]

The train was rumbling against the low hills to the east; through the open door of the house kerosene lamps laid a narrow corridor of light along which Patrons were bringing in their chairs. Beyond these hills were shadowy symbols that could not be internalized—symbols without color, body, or shape that lay outside the Grangers' way of materializing hopes and fears, right and wrong, in iconic molds.

These symbols had nothing to do with emotion or ethics; they were part of the remote world of abstractions—market quotations, investment speculations, patterns of corporate structure —that made up a different kind of reality. When the railroads came to Jasper County, it had seemed that this reality was one with the farmers'; it had seemed that they would carry the bountiful present into the more bountiful future. Here was none of the utopian feeling that compensated for an intolerable present; this was the other facet of myth—the projection of the agreeable "now" into tomorrow.[31]

But the Grangers who had watched the shadows lengthen over the lawn were beginning to feel that this "tomorrow" no longer belonged to them but to the new capitalism. It was no longer a future of making two blades of grass grow where one grew before but of luxuriating economic symbols. Like rails, these abstract units could be laid end to end across impersonal distances; like cars, they could be made up into endless new combinations. It was these that were replacing the old symbols of progress; these were the units in a new network of power upsetting the old equilibrium. If Patrons were unaware of the polar differences between their folk images and the abstractive symbolism of industry, they were nonetheless determined to restore the balance, to set things aright. They were writing to the *Iowa Homestead*—"a sort of general minutes of our order": [32] "out of darkness comes forth light"; and again: "out of evil is brought forth good." [33] And they awarded the prize to Mrs. Tucker because her poem said in simple absolutes what they had been thinking in hundreds of Grange meetings:

> We come to build a nation's hope,
> To slay the giant Wrong.[34]

Armed with angry votes, they were marshalling in the corridors of the state legislature to confront the giant with statutes of restraint; [35] in Grange halls and Grangers' homes they were building their hopes by relighting the lamps of the immemorial myth of agriculture.

The room lay hushed in the flicker of oil lamps. Like candles enshrined they cast a ceremonial light, illuminating solemn faces and homespun coats, bun-topped heads and white-dotted calico dresses. Before the altar of the Overseer stood the initiates. Crickets through the open window drummed incessant litany, and a voice was saying: "The position of Husbandman . . . binds you in a closer tie of brotherhood." [36]

Then the guide beckoned them on to the next altar, and the room stirred as if to acknowledge their presence. "Brothers," the Lecturer intoned, "to live in the country . . . we should love the country. To love the country is . . . to inhale the fresh air of the morning, as if it were the sweet breath of infancy . . . to perceive this glorious temple all instinct with the presence of the Divinity, and to feel a holy joy . . . . This is to love the country, and to make it not the home of the person, but of the soul."

As if the initiates had been ascending the steps and were entering the temple, the Patrons filled the room with singing; the Master greeted them: "Brothers, I say to you, 'Well done, good and faithful servants'"; and presently they were standing before the three altars at the end of their pilgrimage. "No man," spoke Ceres, priestess of faith, "comes closer to God in his daily labors than the Husbandman." "When you see the blossoms open in the spring," said Pomona, "hope is there for the luscious fruit." And Flora said: with flowers "God decorates His footstool . . . . Encourage their culture, and dispense your charities." The initiates turned to the Master. "Another season in the work of our Order has passed," he said. "Let us strive to make our lives as harmoniously beautiful as are the works of Nature."

Wearing their new sashes like the streaks of dawn on the shoulders of the hills, the initiates joined the circle of Patrons, and the Lecturer rose to speak. She held a sheaf of notes, and from time to time she would glance at them:

Ceres lives once more in the Grange (Ceres, Flora, Pomona —these were no mere offices but living symbols of woman's place as a Patroness of Husbandry) [37]

Making and keeping the beauty of the world (no other class could match the Patroness and her husband as natural landscape gardeners—as partners in a work of precious influence on society; children must be taught that labor does not live alone upon the land; it is bound in wedlock to beauty and to intelligence, walking not blind, but open-eyed among the works of God) [38]

Realizing in education the foundation of all other features of the Grange (on this rests all that is truly great and noble; along its path woman walks to equality with men in all her inherent rights).[39]

The group clapped briskly: she had neatly shocked the ripe grain of their thinking. In a moment the whole room was astir. The men figured they'd better look after the horses, but their glowing pipes were soon clustered together in the darkness of the lawn. The babies and little children asleep in bedrooms, kitchen, and pantry had to be visited on tiptoe. The young Patrons were looking about in anxious expectancy—as if what they had so long been waiting for was, and yet was not, going to happen now. There were dark hints that it was not—that he had lost his way or had been delayed too long at the Forest Grange meeting. Would the Adams sisters sing "The Farmer Girls" while they were waiting? The sisters obliged and were singing "Plow, Spade and Hoe" when the ballad man entered.[40] In a moment they had made a circle about him, and all was "calm and placid as a mud puddle."

> On a stormy night in winter
> When the wind blew cold and wet,
> I heard some strains of music
> That I never can forget.
>
> I was sleeping in the cabin
> Where lived Mary fair and young,
> When a light shone in the window,
> And a band of singers sung:
>
> "We are a-coming, sister Mary,
> We are a-coming by and by;
> Be ready, sister Mary,
> For the time is drawing nigh."

And then he sang "William Tailor" and "When This Cruel War is Over" and was going to sing "The Soldier's Dying Wife," but they called loudly for "Time Enough Yet":

> I at length told her her passions were wrong,
> And more, that I scorned to be fooled with so
> long.

> She burst out laughing at seeing me fret,
> And she hummed out a tune: there is time
>   enough yet.
>
> Early next morning her maid came in haste
> And begged me forget all that had passed.
> She said her lady did nothing but fret,
> And I told her think on "there is time
>   enough yet." [41]

There seemed to be no bottom to his saddlebags of song, whether of traditional ballads or popular broadsides. He could dim their eyes with the sentimental or the supernatural or wrinkle them with rollicking humor. He could draw out buried feelings and set them vibrating in strong rhythms. Like the picnics, the dances, and the rituals—but far more intimately—the ballads bound these Patrons together. They could have heard him to the end, but it was nearing midnight—time, as one Patron put it, "to break ground for home."

Ceres, as the Lecturer had said, lived again in the Grange. This night an Iowa farmhouse was her temple and the meeting a ceremony of homage, revitalizing in ritual, reaffirming in spirit, the myth of the great agricultural interior. This night—as on so many nights in 1874—she had been reassured that her daughter, the hope of progress in the Middle West, would be restored, that the ancient balance of economic life would right itself.[42] In a harassed quest from Grange to Grange she had traced her at last to Hades: Pluto had swooped down upon her in his iron chariot and was holding her enthralled in a monopolistic hell swarming with demonic middlemen, politicians, and elevator owners. Now Ceres was face to face with Pluto, and her devotees were rekindling the fires on her altar to refresh the purity and restore the might of her divine power.

That a pall hung over her power seemed to her worshippers inconceivable. But somehow it was no longer assured by their mere numbers; and the virgin soil of Iowa was now in fief to Plutonic powers of freight, storage, and market. They who had not been helpless before the prairie sod, the drought and grass-hoppers, the "lung fevers" and typhoid, were not even sure that they still held the reins of democracy.[43] Had God sent a plague upon them, they would have accepted it as punishment for their sins; this they had done nothing to deserve, and they felt a deep sense of wrong.[44]

It was not enough to be "good and faithful servants" if they were to be "slaves" [45] in the end; or to be "blessed with a liberal harvest" if they were to be cursed with "combinations." [46] They must fight like with like, monopoly with union. In union there was strength to gain redress from the outside—not from the political parties ("the one would not, the other could not grant it") [47] but through "granger laws." * And there was strength from within—the mutual enterprise of buying and selling, storing and shipping, "the magic word co-operation." [48]

It was co-operation that would restore the balance so cata-strophically upset when Pluto carried off Proserpina and brought the chill of fear upon the land. To most Patrons, alarmed by the threat to their inherent right, it would bring back "equal and exact justice to all men." [49] Last February they had written into the Declaration of Principles at St. Louis: "We desire a proper equality, equity and fairness, protection for the weak, restraint upon the strong; in short, justly distributed burdens and justly distributed power. These are . . . the very essence of American independence." [50] But there was one who drew from a deeper well—from the artesian flow of folk assumptions: "If we take two pails, each half full of water, and lade out of one into the other, one will become empty and the other full . . . . This principle holds good throughout all nature . . . . Of late this natural and free equilibrium has been encountering an adverse current." [51] In the imagery of Jasper County, corn must go up, monopolies must come down.

---

* Laws in Middle Western states seeking to regulate railroad rates and practices, called "granger laws" because they were drafted in good part in response to agitation by the Patrons of Husbandry.

In the wonder-working of co-operation there was indeed much of magic, but there was more of vision. After the age-old manner of tracing the prophetic fire to its ultimate source and then of linking origin with mission, they said: "The Goddess of Liberty will smile on her offspring, and the Providence that guided our fathers in the dark and stormy night of the Revolution will foster this movement." [52] They prayed God to bless "this glorious cause," "destined to mark an era in human progress." [53] They beheld in heaven an open door and heard a voice like a trumpet saying: Co-operation is "a great natural law . . . an emanation from the Great Giver." [54]

"Our institution," they had come to feel, "is a pretty good church in itself; its precepts . . . will lead to the enjoyments of the great 'harvest feast' above." [55] It was in very truth the house of Providence, a master symbol within whose vault the various lesser symbols played their part—the music and lectures, the solemn ritual, the stained glass panels of folk images, the holy book of Declarations of Principle and Independence. It was reality enshrined in myth.

The myth was rich and full: Patrons had brought all the fruits of mythmaking and laid them at Ceres' altar. They brought a highly cultivated variety of "natural man" ("our lives as harmoniously beautiful as are the works of nature") and set it beside the offering of "natural rights." [56] They rebuked non-producers with lavish displays of that hardy type "farmers are *the* producers." And having arranged a neat and simplified pattern of analogies and antitheses,[57] they crowned it all with the wreath of the absolute—plaited throughout without a break from Paine to Providence.[58]

In the garden of the great interior all facts leaned toward the sunlight of the myth. They were synthesized, too, in unity of image and of impulse—in synoptic slogans, ceremonies of initiation, the emotive symbolism of the ballads, the order of the Grange itself. The metaphors that came naturally to Patrons' lips brooked no middleman of abstract relationship: they reached reality with intuitive directness and depth—whether in homespun images of yokes and water pails, or in earth divinities of ancient lore.[59]

These symbols imaged a myth that enshrined not one but many realities. Clusters of natural man were cut from romantic vineyards imported long ago from France; from rational orchards came notions of equality, liberty, and natural law. There were ears from pragmatic cornfields (with a few kernels of determinism)—assumptions that what "had made this country great" would continue to be. And these—vineyards, orchards, and fields —were from the "Giver of all Good."

In the warmth and glow of the Grangers' meetings, the myth bloomed with bright fragrance. Its light reached out across the dark fields, assuring Patrons that their order was "one of the great powers of the land," [60] a power that could set the bit in the teeth of monopolies [61] and stir a "commercial and political revolution." [62] But the "Providence that guided our fathers" had fostered not revolution but restoration—the renewal of faith in the old realities. And as the men of business and industry packaged various realities all as pragmatic merchandise and shipped them over rational rails, so they were all initiated by the Grange into the same degrees of the concretely and intuitively human. This was the horizon that circled their outlook like a line of low, well-loved hills; this was the meeting place of Patrons, "the home of the soul."

As they gathered up their baskets and children and drove off across the prairie, the midnight train was already cutting through these hills. It would be bringing Proserpina back, but only for a season. From time to time the fruit would wither at Ceres' shrine and the wicks grow dry in the lamps. From this time on Ceres must share with Pluto the promise of the great interior.

$\mathscr{T}$he raw March wind whipped away the
light and warmth from the doorway of the Cleveland city armory
and shot fine spray into the faces of the men pouring out into
the street. It spun a trail of fiery ashes from James Brady's pipe
when he reached the intersection and snuffed them out on his
companion's shoulder.

May 1 is a long way off.

A good thing, too, Brady answered; there's a lot to do before
then.

You mean more thorough organizing—what the speakers were
talking about tonight?

Well, yes—organizing and giving people the right idea about
what we want. Take what Tuckerman said tonight about the
danger hanging over the country from "parasitic classes," from
their increasing in power. People will stop there; they won't
pick up what he said next—that if workingmen were better
organized there wouldn't be any outbreaks between capital and
labor; we could rely on arbitration. They'll read "parasitic classes"
in the papers and figure that the next step is to turn the parasites
out of their Euclid Avenue palaces.[1]

But the public is with us on the eight-hour day, at least: everybody at the meeting accepted the resolution favoring it.[2]

Feast of the Dead, from *Les Voyages de Champlain*

Yankee Peddler, by John W. Ehninger. Collection of the Newark Museum

County Fair. Courtesy of the Cleveland Public Library

Gift for the Grangers. Courtesy of the Library of Congress

The Standard Oil Company Works in the Cleveland Flats. Courtesy of the Western Reserve Historical Society

The Ford Plant at Highland Park, Michigan, in 1914. Courtesy of the Ford Motor Company

The gray stone buildings cut the wind, but they dripped with cold ooze. The dampness frosted the bleak shop windows and crimped the posters billing "Peck's Bad Boy" at the People's.[3]

Most people aren't against shorter working hours; they're afraid, though, that it's just an excuse for the men to toss everything into the eight-hour hopper. And they're nervous enough now.

They had reached the river and were following it southward toward Newburgh, past shipyards rising like skeletons on parade and piles of lumber looming up suddenly into the mist, past the eerie windows and the high whine of planing mills.[4] Their talk went back to the meeting: there would be no eight-hour day anywhere unless unions all over the country presented a solid front on May 1—that was the tone of the speakers.

Powderly thinks we're bringing the men into the Order too fast as it is, said the organizer. That's why the Executive Board called a halt on us until the middle of next month.[5]

You can't blame him, answered Brady. This fight with Jay Gould has got everybody looking our way; now they think the Knights are behind the eight-hour day, too. Powderly doesn't like the idea of using this as a drawing card: you know what he thinks about strikes.

Well, it's hard not to organize new assemblies when whole shops come and want to join.[6]

The lurid light of a foundry raced along the railway tracks, played fitfully over men unloading at a freight depot, and outlined the black contours of oil works. Here in the flats Welsh, Irish, and Scotch laborers ground out hours filled with sweat and smoke or caught a sullen sleep in houses lacquered with soot from the trains running through the streets. The Bohemians had their homes "on the hill"—little cottages with garden plots for sun and soil to meet; but they worked in the same mills and foundries.[7] It was a world of nights without days, years without seasons. Or rather there were two seasons: "layoff" was one, "back to work" was the other.

It was men like these that the locomotive engineers' P. M. Arthur meant when he said that if they had two hours less work they'd have two hours more to loaf at the saloon.[8] Brady's anger burned again at the thought; if Arthur Keitel had not protested that what the men really wanted was "nicht Bier sondern Brot," he would have said what was on his mind—that two hours less work would make workmen not less but more human.

That's even more important to them, he said to his companion, than better wages. They want their simple, decent, human rights. They want what the good Lord meant them to have.

They want what's coming to them, all right—including better wages. When they see what goes out of here—oil, hardware, stoves, sewing machines, meat, chemicals. . . .

And are told by you organizers that iron and steel alone are capitalized for over ten million dollars. . . .[9]

Well, maybe they don't know that, but they do know that the coal coming into Cleveland from one direction and the iron ore from the other add up to something big. These poor devils down here in the iron ward think they should be getting more out of this thing than they are.

And when they try to get it? They're locked out, like the men at McCormick's and on Gould's system—or like the Knights at Myers and Osborn's stove works here in Cleveland.[10]

They moved briskly through the maze of rails and factories and crossed Walworth Run, where the stench of slaughterhouses, mingled with smoke, hung low in the heavy mist. These flats— the choked, throbbing valley of the Cuyahoga River—were the heart of industrial Cleveland. In this volcanic pit John D. Rockefeller, Mark Hanna, and many lesser men were molding monarchies of steel and oil; to carry its lava flow of goods George Tomlinson and Alva Bradley were building fleets that fanned out over the lakes.[11]

From this pit, too, men had poured out less than a year ago—in July, 1885—to protest the latest of a series of wage cuts by the Cleveland Rolling Mills. They had gone to the city offices of the plant, and they had talked to Mayor Gardner; then with impatient desperation they had listened to fiery William Gorsuch and to men denouncing the "purse proud residents of Euclid Avenue." They had marched—a band three thousand strong packed with Poles and Bohemians—upon the Union Steel Screw Company, thinking that the Chisholms, who owned the rolling mills, were operating that, too. They had injured the president, Fayette Brown, and their leaders had been arrested. And when—some weeks later—another crew had been installed in the mill under police protection, they had besieged the gates with a thousand men and had fallen back after twelve had been wounded. Their needs had become so desperate that a relief committee had been organized to meet them. A minister, George Dowling, had mingled with the mob and had written a novel called *The Wreckers;* by that he meant the strikers, not the techniques that turned both iron and men into machines. For a few months the city lived in dread. Could the Poles and Bohemians—apparently the hard core of the strikers—be treated as Americans, be taught to respect American institutions? Would the whole labor situation get out of hand? Was all this a renewal of the trouble of 1877? Was it part of an ominous prelude to a national crisis? On September 27 wages had been restored, but smouldering unrest continually fed the cloud of suspense that hung over the city.[12]

When you get the chance to know these fellows—the Poles and Bohemians, I mean—they're no more ignorant, no more revolutionary than the others.

Well, answered Brady, you can't blame people for thinking so after the big strike.

Perhaps not. But you can't be around Bohemians as much as I have without knowing what goes on. The singing, the good times, the plays and gymnastics—the sort of thing they used to do in

Bohemia. They're back in Bohemia again—at least for a night. And before daylight they're back in the factory enjoying the fellowship of misery.

They stood for a moment on the corner where their paths parted. By now the wind had died, but the cold stung their ears. A half mile away the furnaces glowed with a blood-red fire.

At any rate, said the organizer, they've got power in numbers— more than they'd have in separate trades.

I don't know. Sometimes I think the Central Labor Union goes farther than we do; it sticks to what each trade wants and what it can get. Of course, it's dealing only with skilled men, and we take in everybody. They've got a short goal—wages and fighting power; we're trying for the long run—education, one big union, a partnership between labor and industry.

Well, we're getting stronger every day.

For a moment Brady was silent, staring at the lamp that made a frosty circle of light on the curtain of the window across the street.

I'm not sure, he said, that it's just numbers—or even organization. It's the numbers that are waking up.[13] The stir and pounding down there in the flats drowns out what they're saying, but it won't be long—maybe May 1—before they'll be talking loudly enough to make people listen. People hear the rumbling now— that's why they're afraid, but they don't know what the workingmen are saying. When they do, there'll be a new day.

If you mean tomorrow, it's not far away.

Brady laughed. Goodnight, he said.

Off Superior a narrow street twisted south into gray darkness; at intervals dim squares of diffused light crossed the road and climbed the buildings opposite. The organizer walked past and then wheeled abruptly upon his shadow and entered: a tall glass might shorten the distance home. He moved down the long room to a space at the bar beside a man reading a paper between preoccupied draughts of beer. Presently the man looked up and pointed to an item on Powderly: he was willing, it said, to lay open the secrets of the Knights of Labor if Jay Gould would bare the methods by which he had piled up his wealth and let the public judge. What did he think of that? Fair enough, the organizer replied, but he liked better what Powderly said—a little farther down the column—about the war "in which every business man, every commercial man, every professional man, every workingman will be invited to enlist."

That must be the kind of war this article was about, the man said sardonically, turning the pages to an item on the big mill strike last July. Here it was: the Cleveland Grays, the home companies of the fifth regiment, the Cleveland light artillery and the Gatling gun battery—all in the fight to keep order. And "now the whole country is exercised with fear arising from the conflict between capital and labor."

It might be, replied the organizer, but he didn't think so: Powderly said (he turned back to the first page) "no converts will be made by physical force."

Well, the man insisted, he wouldn't convert anybody by talking, by arbitration; he'd never beat Jay Gould. And he shook a finger over the story of the deputies held accountable for the shooting of the nine strikers (the ninth died last night) in East Saint Louis. You couldn't beat the system: it was too big; you couldn't get hold of it.

He drained his glass with an angry gulp and motioned for another. It says here that they fined John Panek ten dollars for violating the Sunday closing law, he said to the bartender.[14] Maybe that Sunday law was all right and maybe it wasn't; anyway, things used to be different. The bartender nodded. Relieved for a moment to be off the Gould crisis, the organizer chanted:

> In eighteen hundred and forty-eight,
> I learned to take my whisky straight . . . .

There was laughter behind him; then somebody picked up the ditty:

'Tis an illygant drink and can't be bate,
For working on the railway.[15]

A brakeman sitting at the table protested: you'd think nobody but railroaders drank whiskey. The retort shot back: no, but
they're the only ones who brag about it. The bubbles rising in
the conversation put a glint in the eyes of an old miner from
Pennsylvania: he knew something about big talk in the barroom:

In the barroom, in the barroom,
  Where big diggers congregate,
A-shovelin' coal and a-layin' track
And a-pilin' back the slate.

If you want a car of coal,
  You'll never have to wait,
If you call upon the digger
  In the barroom, in the barroom.[16]

The smoke curled toward the gas lights and then shot up
against the yellow, artificially patterned ceiling. This was the
last night in Cleveland for a couple of sailors—the last before
they shipped out for the straits of Mackinaw City on the first run
of the season. It would be a cold trip—on this fifteenth of April
there was still ice in the straits [17]—but no matter; they put down
their glasses and rapped out a rhythm on the table:

In the month of September, the seventeenth day,
Two dollars and a quarter is all they would pay,
And on Monday morning the *Bridgeport* did take
The *E. C. Roberts* out in the lake.

We went through North Passage—O Lord, how it blew!
And all round the Dummy a large fleet there came too.
The night being dark, Old Nick it would scare.
We hove up next morning and for Cleveland did steer.

Now the *Roberts* in Cleveland, made fast stem and stern,
And over the bottle we'll spin a big yarn.
But Captain Harvey Shannon had ought to stand treat,
For getting to Cleveland ahead of the fleet.[18]

In the absence of Captain Shannon, suggested an ex-lumberjack from Michigan, perhaps the sailors ought to stand treat. They were willing, provided the lumberjack would match them with a song.

> When navigation opens,
> And the waters run so free,
> We'll drive our logs to Saginaw,
> Then haste our girls to see.[19]

And then he turned to "The Jam on Gerry's Rock"—the brave, sad story of how the foreman, young Monroe, broke up the log jam and died in the avalanche.[20]

The organizer put on his hat: there were still two more days to the week. He made his way to the door through the smoke and the chatter and the thin quaver of a song:

> He's only a miner, been killed underground,
> He's only a miner and one more is gone,
> Killed by an accident, there's no one to tell,
> His mining's all over . . . .[21]

The wind whipped his hat, and he huddled his shoulders against the brim. It was surprising how these songs came out when the men were relaxed. He didn't envy the lake sailors starting their run to the straits tomorrow—Friday, of all days; as for the lumberjacks, there were more ex-shanty boys than shanty boys. But there were ways of coming to grips with the danger— even of getting the better of it. Miners, jacks, sailors, railroaders —they all had a way of breaking up their worlds into human components, into little emotional units. They met ice and log jams, storms and cave-ins, as if they were demons that they could fight with strength, skill, and daring.

He reached Prospect Street and turned left. Perhaps the man at the bar was right after all: this Gould trouble, this whole conflict between capital and labor was too hard to get hold of— too big to break up into emotional images, too vague to meet as a personal challenge. To many people Gould made a good devil, but there was more to it than that. Powderly certainly had the right idea—of meeting corporation with organization, arbitrary principle with the principle of arbitration. But could he pull the men with him? In the mine, in camp, or on ship, they cut down their troubles to their own human dimensions; in the vast domains of oil and steel, they were left without pick, cant-hook, or rudder: what then, when trouble came? "Now the whole country is exercised with fear," the paper said today. Nobody knew that better than he, but he was just as sure that the editor was afraid of the wrong thing.

Along the street other squares of light fell across the road; to the southeast the sky burned with angry, intermittent glow.

James Brady sat down in his office in Room 41, Weckerling Block, to sum up the work of District Assembly 47. It had not been easy to organize in Cleveland, he wrote: a year ago there were only eleven assemblies with memberships of from fifteen to forty. Now there were forty assemblies, each with one hundred to three hundred members. And there were plans to set up an employment agency and a co-operative. He went on:

Among the recent additions of local Assemblies . . . are four or five German Assemblies, the members of which take a great interest in the Order . . . . We have some five or six Bohemian Assemblies which also work well, the only drawback being that they are not able to have the A. K. and Constitution in Bohemian, they having to be interpreted to them by some competent member.[22]

His thoughts went back to the meeting last April when he and the organizer were setting up an assembly of Bohemians. Most of Cleveland's Bohemians were tailors, carpenters, saloonkeepers, masons, or coopers in Rockefeller's shops;[23] but these were the men who worked in the mills. Silent and resolute, they had listened closely while the interpreter spelled out what the Order meant. Some things he said were as natural to them as the smell of hot steel—that they along with other American workingmen were part of one big union, that their solidarity would bring them pride in themselves as laborers and power to win better hours and wages. But what of the talk about Powderly's legalistic structure of arbitration? There were moments when the room seemed empty—as if all this was as resplendently remote from their feeling as the palaces on Euclid Street.

Beneath the men's heavy jackets beat rhythms not very different from those Brady's Irish ancestors had fed into his blood. There were forlorn cadences of love forsaken that Bohemian women had sung in the hay fields:

> Weeding poppies gay,
> Alas! alack-a-day!
> That such joyous tender wooing
> Lasted not the poppies blowing.

There was the primitive beat of lyric hopelessness in the cry "All joy is gone":

> All joy is gone
> Now I am left alone!
> .   .   .   .   .   .
> How well does ploughing fare
> With no horse, no plowshare?
> .   .   .   .   .   .
> Like ploughing such as this
> Is loving when amiss.

From the peasant heart came the words "All joy is gone," as totalitarian masters of a later day—more relentless than the Austrian conqueror, the archbishop, or the landlord [24]—well knew when they forbade Bohemians to sing them.[25]

But not all was shadow on the slopes of the field. Women tossed hay into the sunlight to the saucy lilt of *Sly panenky silnici, silnici, silnici:*

> Tripping maidens on a day . . .
> Met two huntsmen on the way . . . .
> Where, fair maidens, do you go . . . ?
> Which will be mine, I would know, I would know . . . ?

Or they tossed their heads to "Little Dove" ("It was not a dove, it was a bird in air; since you will not tarry, dear, then naught I care") or to the proud peasant, the *sedlak* strutting like an old peacock:

> To his field he rides bestride,
> Two watches wears with pride,
> O see! O see! O see! how foolish he! [26]

Peacocks and proud peasants make a natural picture. So, too, do poppies, doves, and love. They are related images; like views in a stereoscope they merge to create a mood-picture in depth, an emotional image with a third dimension. But plowing and love—how can such things be put together? No logic equates them, no visual magic blends them together. Like folk groups everywhere, Bohemians fused images—even unrelated images— in the heat of emotional congruency.[27]

Bohemian workingmen had for generations been "thinking" in these metaphoric images. Now Brady and his Knights of Labor organizers were spelling out to these silent men what the Order could mean to them—note after note in a melody of the new day in labor. Were they following the narrative line of the melody; were they listening to the logic of its cadences? Or were they trying to fit each note into a chord—into a fuller harmonic context? They could hardly have done otherwise: the world of Bohemian folk was made up of contextual patterns—comprehensive symbols of reality created by the same metaphoric imagination that was at work in the folk songs. The image of home—one's own home, the center of the love and obedience, the devotion to parents and respect for elders embodied in the folk figure of Babicka, was itself a composite picture. Like love and poppies, it blended with another depth symbol [28]—the land of Bohemia. "Where is my home?" asked the national anthem. "Waters through its meads . . . streaming; mountains with rustling woods . . . ; vales . . . bright with flow'rlets . . . earthly Eden." [29]

Had these Bohemians fitted the principles of the Knights into their world of contextual symbols? They had said little, but they had joined, and their chapters were thriving.

April inched toward May through a series of squalls. There was trouble along the river among men loading vessels with coal. The viaduct molders were still on strike. "The labor cauldron continues to boil and bubble"; there is "no certainty when the next strike will be." [30] The Knights of Labor, concluding that it was war between themselves and Gould, decided to send two thousand dollars a week to aid the strikers.[31] There were moments when the sky seemed clear: people crowded into the Tabernacle to see the dogs and looked forward to welcoming Doris' Inter-Ocean Circus on May 1.[32] A special meeting of the general assembly of the Knights was scheduled in Cleveland for the last week in May: Cleveland Knights, guessed their leaders, were not planning strikes; the city would be quiet.[33] But observers anxiously scanned the skies toward Chicago and New York: manufacturers in New York, the *Plain Dealer* reported, were convinced that a general strike was being planned for May 1; there were "ominous indications that a bitter contest between labor and capital is near at hand . . . apprehension that we are upon the eve of serious labor troubles . . . men fear the coming storm." [34]

Storm warnings were unmistakable: "antagonistic forces," the *Plain Dealer* on April 28 noted darkly, "are drifting nearer and nearer the point of collision." Antagonistic forces? What force could workingmen bring to bear against industry's weld of material and scientific power? Could the threat of strikes and boycotts match the might of corporate investment? Tons of ore— almost five million by next year—were flowing through the Sault: would these and the tons of finished products (150,000 from the Cleveland Rolling Mills alone) be balanced by the sheer power of numbers—swelled daily by immigrants like the Germans and Bohemians alighting at Union Depot fresh from the fatherland to make their homes in Cleveland? [35] Machines and factories were multiplying; Samuel Wellman and the Otis plant were introducing the new technology of open-hearth steel.[36] Could these be countered by the skills that workingmen had developed during a half-century of ideological training in the rights of man, social reform, co-operative stores, Greenbackism, slogans like "Knowledge is Power," "Politics is Bread"? [37] Did the phenomenal growth of Powderly's Knights balance Rockefeller's technique of merging small units into an industrial colossus? Could the impact of impersonal, rational symbols in this nerve center of the Middle West—symbols for exploiting tremendous natural and human resources—be matched by the fact that now for the first time in America masses of unskilled workmen were joining the skilled in a vast folk uprising against the numbing weight of machines?

The late April sun beamed down on the Square, and the wind from the lake had lost its sting, but chill gusts of restlessness swept the streets. A new code of wind signals was to go into effect on May 1—"the cautionary," "the directions," and "on shore"; [38] but what was there to signal a plunging labor freighter into dock? Men gathered at mill entrances grimly named the factory whistle "the American devil"; [39] inside the vast, grimy darknesses they muttered that they were losing their very humanity, as they were gradually losing their skills before the new machines; [40] the long shadows at quitting time ate into the hours they would have for relaxation with friends and family. At home the *Journal of United Labor* reminded them that they—the real producers— were not getting a fair share of the wealth they produced, that their world had lost its equilibrium.[41] In meetings of the Knights, the talk glumly revealed that not even the most powerful workingman's organization in the world was proof that they could negotiate their differences with industry: sometimes Knights were fired because they were Knights.[42]

It might be that these were merely rumblings on the horizon— an exaggeration like the report of a general strike on May 1.[43] It might be. But dispatches kept pouring into the offices of the press: mob tempers were seething in Milwaukee and Pittsburgh; the gigantic demonstration planned for New York's Union Square on May 1 was taking shape; last Sunday in Chicago— Easter Sunday—"streaming crimson banners and hurrying groups of swarthy-faced foreigners" paraded and fired off "blood and thunder" speeches.[44] From scattered sources came reports that on Saturday, the first of May, socialists were planning to rise up and take over the country; here in Cleveland, said Friday's *Plain Dealer*, it was alleged that last February 20 they had purchased two thousand rifles; on May 1 a well-drilled army would parade the streets.[45]

Saturday afternoon, Brady remembered, he had shopped for Sunday's family picnic. The gulls were wheeling above an outbound freighter that traced a silver curve across the shiny surface of the lake. Around the Square horses twitched sleepily in the sun and shade beside empty buggies. There would still be time for Doris' Circus—a colorful coda to an entertaining week. Sunday night the German stock company had offered "Familie Hoerner," and "Passion's Slave" by John Stevens had been running all week at the Cleveland Theater; Thursday night people crowded into Music Hall to listen to "The Red, White and Blue" and other band favorites and to hear Governor Foraker speak.[46]

Friends had stopped Brady on the street and asked wasn't this an odd time for a circus to come to town—when the whole city was awaiting a huge eight-hour-day demonstration? And Brady had replied he knew of no demonstration—none planned by the Knights, at least; the "demonstration" was all in the papers. The papers were full of eight-hour arguments: editors, economists, labor leaders—there was a column for anyone who wanted to march in the parade of opinions. Powderly had stayed on the sidewalks, but that canny master Samuel Gompers had walked at the head of the procession, waving a richly brocaded banner on which he had woven a dinner pail and a home, the lamp of learning and the American eagle, the cross, and the scale.

The eight-hour day creates work for the unemployed, it more permanently employs those at work, makes wages more permanent and regular. (These were the dinner-pail arguments.)

The man that works eight hours a day places a higher estimate on his home, his family relations. . . . He is . . . a better husband, a more devoted father. . . .

He will require papers, he will require books. . . . It enlarges the sphere of his intelligence. . . .

He is a safer citizen. . . . [Reduction of hours] is to the best interests of our country. . . .

[The eight-hour day] is in line with the social and moral progress and advancement of man as laid down by the golden rule. (It was John J. Jarrett * who had added this.)

The reduction in the hours of labor controls to a great extent that oft quoted law of demand and supply . . . . (Or, as George Gunton † put it: it sets in motion "the natural and silent operation of economic forces.") [47]

Were the weaving of folk-honored symbols into the eight-hour banner and the intensive maneuvering over the last two years for this day all part of an elaborate staging? [48] Gompers had long since been an apprentice in labor stagecraft, yet for him this was no mere pageant but the dramatic expression of a fundamental myth. This was "the one great movement benefitting all, hurting none"; it was "more far-reaching in its beneficent influences than any other measure known to man"; it reached "the lowest stratum of society." [49] Step by step the myth had taken shape: the merging of workingmen's dreams and realities, the extension of these equations into every artery of their lives, the transformation of

* Ex-president of the Amalgamated Association of Iron and Steel Workers and Secretary of the American Tinned Plate Association.

† English-American author of books and treatises on economics, President of the Institute of Social Economics, publisher of *Gunton's Magazine*.

reduced working hours into the timeless absolute of social and natural law.

On May 1 it was clear—perhaps for the first time in America —that the labor freighter had become a genuine folk vessel, the image of reality for the skilled and the unskilled, native-born and immigrant. From its flagpole flew the stars and stripes of the myth—the dream of equality, dignity, the promise of the good life implicit in American prosperity, simple human values, an equilibrium that would ensure that these things might not soon pass away. The cargo they had produced had shifted to industry's side of the hold, and the ship was listing. Now—through the eight-hour day—the freight would be balanced; now the ship would sail its even, automatic course.[50]

Sunday morning the Reverend Sturtevant preached a sermon —"The Ideal Society." There was distrust now, he said, but "the coming age will be one of mutual faith."[51] Men solemnly agreed that the eight-hour day was "right and proper if kept within orderly limits,"[52] that there was probably enough mutual faith in the city to prevent violence. Then suddenly on Thursday morning, May 6, fanatical circulars appeared at critical points of the city: one had been posted, sometime the night before, on the Central Police Station itself; Officer Hildebrand had discovered another on a billboard on Broadway in the Bohemian section; they had been scattered freely around the mills in the old Eighteenth Ward.[53]

Brady had taken it for granted that there would be no demonstration last Saturday, but this was another matter. He, like everyone else, had been following the bloody Milwaukee riots and the mounting tension in Chicago. He had visualized the killing of one of the strikers at the McCormick Reaper Works, the mass meeting on Tuesday at Chicago's old Haymarket Square to hear Spies, Parsons, and Fielden, mounted on a wagon, call for revenge, the bomb thrown into the squadron of police, the search of the *Arbeiter Zeitung*, where copies of the "revenge" circular had been found. These—here in Cleveland—were the same: "Rache! Rache! Arbeiter, zu den Waffen!" [54] Agitators had been working, he well knew, among the Bohemians in the twenty-fourth, twenty-fifth, twenty-sixth, and twenty-seventh wards.[55] Would this shatter the fine beginning he and his organizers had made among the immigrants? People were only too ready to blame them for anything that might happen.[56]

Rumors, in fact, had been circulating that five socialist groups —all immigrants—were meeting weekly on Croton, Lorain, and Columbus Streets, on Payne Avenue, and in Newburgh.[57] And there were uglier rumors. If only people would—as he did—set them off against what his friend Karl Tuma, editor of *Volnost*, had said—that about half of the two hundred socialists in the city were Bohemians, a mere backwash of the twenty thousand living here.[58]

What would these thousands think when they read the circular "Workingmen, to arms!"? Now and then some of them would talk to Brady about Thomas Paine—about things like "Ye that dare oppose not only tyranny, but the tyrant, stand forth." [59] They would talk of Paine and Jan Hus in the same breath—crusaders not for anarchy but for human freedom. Paine said you could "produce Revolutions by reason and accommodation, rather than commit them to the issue of convulsions." [60] Well, that was about what Powderly thought, too; perhaps this was one reason why so many Bohemians had joined the Knights. But sometimes they seemed to be as far away from Powderly's court of arbitration as they were from the industrialists' machine-tooled calculations. They would stand on the shore and watch the logical symbols ebb and flow.

Industrial thinking was like Lake Erie itself. On its shores rose conceptual structures of finance, engineering, and corporate control; its vast, impersonal waters carried iron, coal, workingmen, and oil beyond all visible horizons. No extraneous tracery of hills or trees were reflected on its even surface. Its levels rose and fell with the winds of economic law.

In Bohemia, the "waters through its meads streaming" were springs, not inland seas. They welled up from the bedrock of metaphoric imagery in vales bright with poppies; they bubbled endlessly, falling endlessly back upon themselves. Villagers came one by one to drink from fountains of self-fulfilment in folk lyric and folk craft; they came together to fill communal buckets— in Sokols, in choral groups like the Lumir, and in the Tyl dramatic societies. For these were the ritual tableaux of metaphoric reality.[61]

Bohemians in Cleveland built their homes at these springs, far from the flash floods of labor rebellion and from industry's great lakes. Here, as in Bohemia, native lore and folk ritual flowed fresh and constant—a continual renewing of reality. Their lives were somehow—Brady hardly knew why—in balance. This was nothing like the immutable principles, the natural and economic law that industrialists claimed to live by. It was, rather, like the balance that the Knights had been searching for, a scale on which basic human aspirations might be kept in perpetual equilibrium. Brady's *Journal of United Labor* had been reminding him insistently these last few months of what that equilibrium should be. It was in equality, or in harmony.[62] It was in "the equilibrium between the powers of the individual and the collectivity," or in social evolution.[63] Again, it was in "the equity and solidarity of conditions," or in justice, "the sum total of liberty, equality, and solidarity." [64]

These dominating heights of the labor myth were dotted with Bohemian cottages. Were they not, after all, the foothills of the mountain where Krakonos lived? Krakonos, King of the Mountain, kept his eye on the village. He watched people like that old peacock, the *sedlak*, riding about with two watches, or the tailor who cut short Krakonos' fine coat material in order to keep some for himself. He disguised himself as a wealthy merchant and took sly vengeance on a greedy innkeeper and his wife who found only old vegetables in their chest in place of the finery they had expected. He might even do away with the incorrigibly greedy, as he did with the servant sent to his garden by a rich woman to gather herbs to heal her husband. Krakonos filled the servant's pockets with money and forgave him on condition that he never return, but he stole back for more and lost his life along with his money. Krakonos was sly and mischievous: he could play pranks on the villagers, but he could laugh when they were played on himself. He befriended the humble and healed the sick; he was a Robin Hood in the forest of human relations, taking away from pride, adding to self-respect. He was peasant Bohemia personified—the power of setting things right in the heart, of keeping the balance in village society.[65]

What was Brady to say about these Bohemians in his report to the *Journal of United Labor?* He picked up his pen and wrote: "I believe that properly instructed in the aims and principles of our Order they will make good members." Did he suspect how close they were to these principles, how far their own personal and social equilibrium, dramatically imaged in the folk culture hero, had predisposed them to accept the new order poised by the Knights on the pivot of the human spirit? He did not say, but of one thing he was sure: "When our Organizers first organized them I was fearful of their creating trouble on account of the movements of the anarchists at that time, but I am happy to state that if any known anarchist is proposed for admission he is promptly rejected." [66]

Lake winds unseasonably chilled the delegates of the Knights from all parts of the United States and Canada who met on Tuesday, May 25, in Forest City House,[67] but inside all was warmth and glow. They sang "Blest be the tie that binds our hearts in mutual love." They took pleased notice of Terence Powderly's magnificent portrait in pounded brass hanging near the office counter in the corridor of the hotel and of the leaders they had known so long by name—John Jarrett, Richard Trevallick, Henry George, Adolph Strasser, and Samuel Gompers.[68] They warmed to the reports of the thousands who were flocking to the Order.

The chill returned for a time when Strasser's cigar makers launched a stubborn fight; [69] but looking back, men remembered this as a great day for labor. And yet it was not in the corridors of Forest City House or in the lobbies of Glass Hall [70] that the high drama of labor was being played but in the lives of the men in the Iron Ward and of the tens of thousands whose dreams these delegates brought with them.

Now, in the dramatic months of 1886, these dreams had become articulate. Flames from the furnace of folk feeling shot into the night sky—the torch of a holocaust in the minds of many, a beacon of the new day to the men themselves. The realities lit by the flames—realities revealed in the metaphoric imagery of the Bohemians, in the emotional components into which laboring men (miners, railroaders, sailors, lumberjacks) resolved their work, and in the drive of the Knights toward social harmony and equality—released an enormous power. To Gompers' trade-unionists this power was economic—"control over the basic things of life," "the foundation of organized society." [71] For the followers of Terence Powderly "the new power dawning upon the world is that of the workingman to rule his own destinies." [72] But the vast folk movement to stage within or without the organization of the Knights an "elemental protest" [73] against the maneuvering of intangible economic symbols, against the impersonal symbols of machine technology—this mass awakening found a volcanic surge of power in the vitality of primal human motives. In meetings and demonstrations, in the long walks home from the yards and mills, men shaped the myth—that human values were a law in themselves. From the factories of folk thinking emerged the symbol that imaged the myth—the eight-hour day, a symbol that spoke of many things in many tongues. Its flame dyed every aspiration with its own color; it illuminated expanding horizons until it seemed to shine for every man alike; its unwavering beam was the pivotal focus of human law. Before the year had passed, workingmen would be turning from the Knights to Gompers' new

American Federation of Labor; in years to come the furnaces in the iron wards of the Middle West would now and again be banked. But once they had been fired, industry would have to form its ideological steel in the crucibles of folk belief.

$\mathcal{T}$he plant superintendent at Highland Park in 1914 stood watching an intricate maze of overhead trolleys, chain-driven assemblies, and moving platforms converging with measured pace. As he watched, a new automobile every twenty-four seconds [1] rolled off the terminal—the product of a synchronized magic the like of which had not been seen before. There were others, too, with an eye for mass technique—within this plant, in Chicago, Pittsburgh, in cities across the continent— who watched as invisible lines of assembly, carrying precisely interchangeable units, converged upon the production of a simplified, standardized myth.

The specifications for the myth had been drawn up by amateur and professional "engineers" scattered from farm to factory office. They ran as follows:

Motor:
> An individual free to act in accordance with his own view of his interests and so
> responsible for his own economic fate in a land of equal opportunity . . .
> self-reliant . . .
> working with initiative and reason (practical realism)
> to win (in wages or capital) the rewards of work . . . .

Chassis (of standard "natural law" steel):
> Free enterprise operating in accordance with the competitive instinct of all mankind . . .
> as inexorably as the law of gravity (provided that there was no interference from government)
> to achieve production regulated by supply and demand . . .

Body (from rolling-mill stock of logical argument):
> Industry the source of wealth (other institutions being derivative of industry) . . .
> prime indicator of national progress (its labors, like Hercules', performed in the service of mankind) . . .
> engaged in the pursuit of self-interest and at one with the goals of the human race (human rights are at bottom property rights) . . .
> its harmonious relations like those of the American family, its essential nature like that of the common man . . .
> born with democracy in the days of the Founding Fathers and growing side by side with freedom from that time to this . . .
> in corporate form, the key to order in society; in its consistent wholeness, the one reality in the modern world . . . valid for all societies . . .
> through its mission of raising standards of living, through its conviction that its self-interest serves the community interest, and through its identity with democratic goals the core of American society and the most representative American way of life . . . .[2]

As it rolled off the assembly line, the myth gleamed in the national sunlight. There was a fascination in the myth itself; but there was more in the factory that produced it—in the raw materials of reality, in the shapes of power forged from them, and in the folk techniques of ideological assembly.

Above the din of the lathes and the chomp of the presses rose the gritty hum of a remarkable machine, a drill that punctured a cylinder block simultaneously with forty-five holes in ninety seconds.[3] Machines like this, said the master of Highland Park, "multiply the power of the hand"; [4] and he had a passion for them born of the discovery of Truth. The machine was a catalyst of freedom: it could lift "farm drudgery off flesh and blood and lay it on steel and motors"; [5] it gave "refinements to colleges and homes; man's rise in intelligence [could] be charted by this machine civilization." [6]

The machines at Highland Park were stretched out as in a vast stable—powerful organisms with a long evolution, a gestation period, a dramatic birth.[7] If they were not "the only absolute truth in the possession of mankind," they were solid segments of material reality, with "an elemental force, blindly creative, like nature." [8]

In these Augean stables stacks of heavy castings, motor fittings, chassis frames, axles—parts for the 182,000 automobiles completed within the year [9]—stood in endless stalls. To set them moving, as King Expansion had ordered, was a labor beyond anything the brute efficiency of machines could accomplish. Now it happened that there were two rivers flowing near Highland Park. The River of Interchangeability actually coursed through the plant itself; nearby was the River of Automatic Sequence, a smoothly flowing stream that rose in the land of flour milling and meandered through harvests of wheat fields.[10] In a matter of months these rivers were channelled together and loosed upon the stables. They began slowly—a trickle of magneto assemblies; then a flood of steel strips and automobiles poured out.

Here, as it seemed to the men at Highland Park, and as some philosophers had always insisted,[11] was a different kind of reality. It was not the reality made up of things: raw materials, machines, and even men (since they were interchangeable now) were no longer real in themselves but only in so far as they were channelled into an automatic pattern. The new reality was Process, a technique with incredible power. "It [was] this pattern that [was] actually productive, not the individual." [12] The man who installed it in his plant called it the "New Messiah," [13] a power that would change the world.

It was the pattern that was productive. But to the plant superintendent charged with seeing that each belt and trolley ran at precisely the right speed, that the assembly line reached each station at precisely the right moment, the pattern itself rested on the exact, inexorable cycles of time. Six feet every sixty seconds: [14] that was the ultimate arbiter, and every operation in the plant was geared to it. Like a mammoth clock, Highland Park was the embodiment of the greatest of abstract symbols.

In the drafting room, in the pattern and experimental departments, men were busily manipulating other symbols. These symbols had no weight, shape, color, or extension, though they stood for things that did. They were self-contained essences having no necessary connection even with the things they stood for, things that might rot or rust. They were like letters of a word: the letters were everlastingly good though the word might change or die. There had to be symbols before there could be machines and assembly lines.

Highland Park was sailing, as once Hercules had sailed in quest of the fat cattle of Geryon, in Apollo's golden bowl. Now of all the symbols that made up the bowl, the cleverest was the stock certificate, a symbol of two other symbols—currency and certificates of ownership.[15] With a paper properly marked with these abstractions "a man who had never seen a locomotive could say that he had a railroad in his pocket." [16] Last year a man had died who had in his pocket not only railroads but steel mills, a legend whose international influence proved just how powerful these abstractions could be.[17] This year they were turning out an ominous flood of Chevrolets.

But enterprises like railroads, said the directors of Highland Park, were too often "factors in the stock market"; they were "run . . . from banking offices."[18] And having a railroad in one's pocket was of small value unless it hauled supplies to the plant. Stock symbols could tie a company up with banking corporations or with other companies, and that must never be. The directors had only to look around them to see the potentialities of concentrated power. They could see it in general motors combinations, in steel, lumber, meat packing, and flour milling[19]— combinations that were closing the frontiers of enterprise so rapidly that Congress had become alarmed and, in the last two years, had tried grimly to curb them.[20] But there were other ways of organizing them by weaving a horizontal network of interests. They had organized step by vertical step—making their own parts, treating the ore in their own furnaces, buying their own coal and iron mines—moving steadily through every stage of production in a vast spiral of integration.

Highland Park was an ascending ring of production, an inverted pyramid of departmental divisions. But it was immensely more: it was a coiled synthesis—machines, symbols, process—of realities and powers. Watching the growth of this automatic, autonomous structure with its own laws of being, men noted that it was a state within a state.[21]

Another plant on a somewhat larger scale is in building at Flat Rock . . . . We have dammed the river. The dam also serves as a bridge for the Detroit, Toledo & Ironton Railway, which was in need of a new bridge at that point, and a road for the public—all in one construction. We are going to make our glass at this point. The damming of the river gives sufficient water for the floating to us of most of our raw material. It also gives us our power through a hydroelectric plant . . . . The men will have plots of ground or farms as well as their jobs in the factory, and these can be scattered over fifteen or twenty miles surrounding—for of course nowadays the workingman can come to the shop in an automobile.[22]

On a stretch of farm land fifteen miles from Detroit an industrial homestead would soon be springing up—like many other factory communities except, perhaps, that the Engineer at Highland Park had carefully planned it.[23] He had selected the land ("everything," he said, "is produced from the earth");[24] then he had dammed the river and bridged it to bring in materials and generate power for manufacturing. "There we shall have the combination of agriculture and industrialism," he promised;[25] these two, along with transportation, "hold the world together."[26]

The homestead at Flat Rock would be a little world in itself, held together by growing things, making things, and carrying things.[27] The men would have farms as well as their jobs in the factory: farms, after all, were the greatest of factories—no mere rural occupation but the business of raising food.[28] On idyllic acres reaching out fifteen or twenty miles from the glass plant, the Engineer could see men "working with material which we did not and could not create, but which was presented to us by Nature," putting into their farms "the human element which makes the fruitful seasons of the earth useful to men."[29] He could see them unconsciously working out the economic and the moral fundamentals:

For the day's work is a great thing—a very great thing! It is at the very foundation of the world . . . . Work is our sanity, our self-respect, our salvation . . . .[30]

They would be driving in from their farms as the morning sun glinted off the bridge over the dam and taking their places at the machines. The machines would be spaced with ultimate precision —no space, no time wasted. "The most beautiful things in the world," said the Engineer, "are those from which all excess . . . has been eliminated"; "cut out useless parts and simplify necessary ones."[31] And this, too, was an economic and moral fundamental.[32]

The Engineer studied the blueprints of his industrial homestead. The plans were as steely bright as the rails of the Toledo and Ironton Railway; they had all the concentrated economy of the dam that was also a road and a bridge, that provided both draft for transportation and power for production; they were as translucent as the glass that would soon be moving in continuous sheets over semi-automatic rollers. Here as at Highland Park ("a department is a little factory in itself") [33] men and machines would be perfectly synchronized; in an organization in which "one part is so dependent upon another," the men would move in a tightly disciplined, coolly impersonal pattern.[34] No stubborn Dionysius stood in the way of realizing this industrial Republic. On the farmland at Flat Rock its logistical precision of work and technique would presently be emerging, clean and clear as a mathematician's dream, on the foundation of economic and moral certainties. It would be a world complete and self-contained, a rational homestead.

Cut out useless parts and simplify necessary ones. In the Engineer's homestead there was nothing that did not reduce to the great One of production, to making and transporting things. This was the dam that supplied the power, the machines that, like books, gave men ideas; [35] the awesome precision of symbols; the continuity of assembly—"a lever to move the world"; [36] the mainspring of integration. There were moments when the Engineer seemed to see human nature itself as a creative power. A man's "personality" had little to do with whether he had "been in Sing Sing or at Harvard," [37] whether he had come from Chicago or Czechoslovakia; its essence was his "rate of production." This was his guide in his work, his status in the shop, the ratio of his intrinsic value.[38] Symbols, too, whatever their original shade, took on the same productive coloration: "time is money," money is a "part of our transportation system," an "engine of production." [39] Even the necessary parts had been simplified in the industrial homestead at Flat Rock.

The elements of the Engineer's Republic now building here were meticulously tooled: they were interchangeable with Flat Rock or Highland Park plants anywhere—or even, the Engineer thought, with the structure of society itself. He could see the nation tooled on the pattern of Flat Rock: "We want those who can mould the political, social, industrial, and moral mass into

a sound and shapely whole . . . . We want men who can create the working design for all that is right and good and desirable
in our life," [40] men who can plan the nation's progress with the
logic of plant management ("each step has to be regulated"),[41]
whose dream of universal justice can be realized by perfect-
ing the wage system.[42]

In the Engineer's eyes, the good society was simply an extension of the carefully regulated power and process that hummed
so smoothly in the plant, the "working design" [43] of the truths he
had discovered there. For these revelations were not only for
Flat Rock; they were universally true.

There is something sacred about wages [the myth was moving in
absolutes]—they represent homes and families and domestic destinies . . . . Wages are bread boxes and coal bins, babies' cradles and
children's education—family comforts and contentment . . . . There
is something just as sacred about capital which is used to provide the
means by which work can be made productive . . . .[44]

This was no part of the blueprint, a design that stripped human
nature to the productive bone. But the Engineer (as makers of
rational myths have always done) was putting back the flesh—
cradles, education, contentment—on the skeleton he had constructed. The pulse of life was the reward of work—wages and
capital; they were the primal urge, and they were sacred.[45]

"Every spirit builds itself a house," another individualist had
said.[46] The rational homestead that the Engineer was building
seemed to him "the mainstay of all the finer things which the
home represents"; there was "something just as sacred about a
shop that employs thousands of men as there is about a home." [47]

When one looks about . . . at the young workingmen who, on the
strength of their jobs are marrying and setting up for themselves, at
the thousands of homes that are being paid for on installments . . .
when one looks at a great productive organization that is enabling all
these things to be done, then the continuance of that business becomes
a holy trust.[48]

The myth was complete—a sound and shapely whole.[49] The
Engineer's horological soul had discovered its chronometrical

truth,[50] and upon it he was building his industrial homestead. It was a homestead in which young men who were expressing their essential natures in productive work might live in exact social justice among the comforts that spilled out of the cornucopia of the shop, fired with the fervor of keeping as a holy trust the business that made these bounties possible. It was a world in which these young men might rest secure in the realization that "business is a reality" [51] with its own immutable laws ("the laws of business are like the laws of gravity") [52] or, rather, a synthesis of realities, each with its special form of power. These were the logical absolutes—the steel frame of a chassis that would support the body not alone of industry but of the nation itself.

The Engineer's ideas had been born on a Michigan farm; they had grown up in the myth of valley and prairie—the myth that machines were "hired hands" to lighten the work, that they were created to increase the yield and the market, that they were the natural fulfilment of the promise of the homestead. But the articles of the myth had been transferred one by one from the vignette of the farm to the panorama of the factory. The change was embodied in the workman at Flat Rock whose shoes carried the soil of his farm plot into the plant. It was not on his farm that he symbolized the genuine American. It was the synchronized pattern of his work at the plant that made him the prime producer of the wealth that built homes, schools, and churches. The homestead had been incorporated.

The process of incorporation was the classic one of rational mythmaking. The Engineer had Yankee notions; reason was at the root of things; the world was made up of rational units condensed in rational symbols. He had Emerson's horological soul, and the world was made in its image. He had the Platonic vision of society as a rational One like free enterprise, a "tightly integrated, consistent system" . . . "homogeneous in time and space." [53]

This was the rational myth, as remote from other myths as a Yankee peddler's cart from a Conestoga wagon, or as an anemoscope from an Indian's finger moistened to the wind. And yet all mythmaking—from the Hurons' forest lore to the creed of a Detroit industrialist—follows the same folk trails; and the same winds blow spring on all men's dreams. The Engineer, like a Mennonite farmer, made of his world a simple, understandable whole; [54] like a Southern Appalachian settler, he fitted together facts—and ideas—by analogy.

It would not be long before this folk "science" would reduce the life of every American—whether he was buying and selling, marking a ballot, enjoying his home and friends, or worshipping Providence—to the pattern and principles of free enterprise.[55] Business would soon become one with progress, with freedom and patriotism, with the family and "the people," and finally with the divine plan for a happier humanity. What was true of each of these would be true of business, and what belonged to the nature of business would belong to each of these. And soon this streamlined System would be extended, as once farmers had extended the ideal of the homestead to include the nation, to every crosspath of American life. The blood of business would seem to run through the body of the nation; its ideals would be those of society itself, its way "the American way."

The way of business would come to appear to the men of business as immutable as the path of the stars; it would appear to follow orbits of economics and of human nature, to gleam for all men in every century. It would seem to rest on a self-adjusting equilibrium,[56] to be, in a word, "natural." And the nature of business—a rationally ordered System homogeneous in space and time—would emerge as "reality," a System releasing the tremendous power of technology and technological integration. In the naves of banquet halls, in the pulpits of public forums and the choir lofts of the press, the liturgy of the myth would give homage to the glory of reality and to its all-embracing power.

History and the Myth

$\mathcal{T}$he accumulation over the last few years of materials illustrative of folk belief has provided historians with a broader base of interpretation than has until recently been possible; the evidence is now at hand for an approach to the understanding of the historical behavior of the whole people—of the mass substratum of society as well as of its more conspicuous or dominant elements. These materials have helped, too, to reveal the basic assumptions of folk groups about their mental environment—about what is ultimately real—and to disclose processes of folk thinking which have led each group to focus upon its own view of reality and to invest it with universal validity.

Settlers in the great interior, like other folk groups, concentrated their experience into a single organic nucleus of reality and portrayed it in a symbol that imaged the whole. However one nucleus may have differed from another—as, for instance, the living universe of the Hurons or the social nexus of the Pennsylvania Germans from the Yankee individual, each was a reduction of the environment to the human equation, to a little cosmos that could be understood and controlled. That folk groups should have arrived at these nuclear realities by such equations is not surprising: folk thought had from time immemorial been classifying, analyzing, and interpreting the environment—both physical and mental—by analogies. And it is not hard to see how folk thinking made this focal center of reality the more homogeneous, the more truly a community of essence, in proportion as the elements that were equated with one another were reciprocally related in a mutual interchange of qualities. If the spirit-invested forest was the human nature of the Huron writ large, then the Huron in turn could become an *oki,* a being that savored of the supernatural; once democracy and capitalism (to choose a contemporary example) have been equated, what is true of the one is assumed to be true of the other. Having simplified the environment to a nuclear center, folk thinking extended the formula to society as a whole and, as the myth clothed it with eternal verity, exalted it to an absolute. So it was, for instance, that the Middle Western farmer projected the equation of himself and nature as the norm for the whole interior of America and then magnified that norm to a universal pattern of life.

From these centers of reality folk groups derived the inner dynamic that helped to mold the history of the great interior. For power stemmed from a core of implicit assumptions about reality and varied with the nature of these assumptions. When that core was a community charged with the pervasive spirit of Providence, power was prophetic and evangelistic; when it was a world of rational abstractions, power was manipulative, combinatory, pyramidal.

The symbols that imaged reality and power—symbols like the Huron *Ononhwaroia,* the Pennsylvania *Familienkreis,* or the Highland Park Engineer's blueprint of the good society—were at the same time concrete epitomes of myth. They embodied the animistic oneness of the human and the physical world in Canadian forests. When the narrower community of men supplanted that of man and nature, they imaged a social cosmos in which nature took its place as part of the family circle. And when the individual sloughed off social bonds and emerged as the nucleus of reality, they pictured a world erected on the primacy of feeling or—if the man-in-man was a thing of mind rather than emotion—on the pivot of reason. For the individual, having reduced the world to himself, re-erected it in his own image: like the Yankee, he "sumtotalized" society; like Plato and the industrialists, he returned along the path of reason to a new One of man and nature.

It is in the larger sweep of history that the rational—and the romantic—myth should be regarded as a return to the oneness of the primitive cosmos. In the narrower context of the great interior, in which both the romantic and the rational were protests against a corrupting or constrictive present, the Jesuits in Canada turned to an idyllic past, but the Yankee looked ahead to a utopian future.

Whether it was in Canada or in the Middle West that utopia was to be realized, the myth validated the aspiration to achieve it. There were moments in Middle Western history, however, when something like the good society seemed to have been already achieved; in such moments, myth became a canon of orthodoxy. And when the orthodox pattern of the environment appeared to be threatened with disruption or perversion—as it seemed to the Hurons, the piney-woods people of the camp revivals, the Patrons of Husbandry, and the leaders of industry—myth restored the integrity of their being and reaffirmed in symbol and ritual the ultimate rightness of their world. To each folk group, the assurance of this ultimate Truth rested on formulae that guaranteed its automatic sway. The folk thought of settlers in the early Middle West fixed on the deterministic formula "as it was first, so shall it continue to be," and the myth forged the link between origin and mission. But for all folk groups the myth expressed some moral, economic, or natural "law" that kept their several worlds in constant, self-adjusting equilibrium.

14 · REALITY, POWER, AND MYTH

$\mathcal{A}$ ny fact that illuminates motivation and behavior which have shaped past events or have been shaped by them is grist for the historian's mill. No area of belief or activity falls outside his province, provided that it yields objective data susceptible to critical analysis and to verification by accepted criteria. The realm of reality discoverable in such data has until recently excluded the beliefs and behavior of the great mass of common folk because popular reactions appeared to be event-making factors only in relation to leaders or leading groups and because popular beliefs were felt to be inarticulate or shot through with the irrational. But a lively interest in the wealth of folk expression has lately revealed an articulate and meaningful area of common life, and "fact" has become an elastic concept, covering not only events, actions, documents and statistics, but the environment disclosed in signs and symbols from which, says Susanne Langer,[1] "we weave our tissue of 'reality.'"

The archaeology of folk belief has made it increasingly possible to discover and assess the motives and actions of the *whole* people, rather than to derive them by inference from the attitudes and achievements of their leaders or from the records of some currently pre-eminent group. Reality—the mental environment that underlies mass behavior—has been gradually extended at the base by a study of what people *believe* to be true and act upon,[2] a study of ideologies, for example, or of the role of myth in modern political propaganda. That base has been broadened further by the growing awareness that there is a substratum of popular psychology, a reality system which each individual "has in common with all other members of his society,"[3] an "implicit dominant ontology" which "all the material structures and functions of culture . . . even all the customs and habits" follow.[4] And beyond these psychological frontiers lies a "reigning cosmic philosophy . . . as fundamental to a particular climate of opinion as are its economic foundations to a selected social scene."[5]

Students of power have recognized that it is within these spacious frontiers of reality that power relations are to be explored. "The basic symbols," observed Lasswell and Kaplan, "formulate the most general perspectives concerning interpersonal relations in the society; specific power facts are responded to in these perspectives."[6] Power, says Quincy Wright, is "a psychological phenomenon which springs eventually from the attitude of individuals toward group symbols";[7] and Riesman would agree: "people interpret power configurations on the basis of their psychic needs."[8] As the patterns of reality change, the forms of power must change also, varying "from age to age, with the interests which move men, and the aspects of life to which they attach a preponderant importance."[9]

The basic assumptions that embody prevailing views of reality and power have been articulated in almost every form of written and spoken language: epic poetry, incantations, novels, advertisements, creeds and constitutions—in whatever form the current needs and idioms prescribe. These modes of expression epitomize history in legends and metaphysics in concrete images; they look backward into an immemorial past or forward to a utopian future; they reflect social ethic and national mores; and they merge the aims and the ends of action. For a concept so rich, diverse, and sweeping there is but one word—the generic term *myth,* "a form of poetry which transcends poetry in that it proclaims a truth; a form of reasoning which transcends reasoning in that it wants to bring about the truth it proclaims; a form of action, of ritual behavior, which does not find its fulfilment in the act but must proclaim and elaborate a poetic form of truth." [10]

In primitive animistic societies myths portray the "re-arising of a primordial reality": [11] they recreate the origin of the universe, the gods, or the race, convey a sense of oneness—a "co-ordination of cosmic and social events," [12] or enshrine race memories. In more highly organized communities, myth reflects social reality —the theocracies of Egypt and Babylonia, the Greek polis paralleling social with natural law, the clan structure of the Roman gens, and (in the Middle Ages) the social organism. Myth often expresses the individual's protest against society—whether it is the romantic quest for oneness with a primitive environment or the search for a rational cosmos. And again in the twentieth century the propaganda in the name of racial purity, the utopian manifestoes, and the ideological advertisements of the American way of life confirm the conclusion that myth discloses the mental environment (now an uneasy marriage of romanticism and technology) that is implicitly accepted.

As a revelation of reality, myth must also bear a vital relation to the power forms and symbols that reality makes feasible. If power is a "control over value practices and patterns," the symbols which crystallize these values will have "causes and consequences in power relationships," symbols that function "directly in the power process, serving to set up, alter, or maintain power practices." [13] The political symbols expressed in myth are usually in the form of constitutions, laws, and treaties, or again in ceremonials and mass demonstrations; [14] but power symbols may reflect any aspect of social reality—whatever provides a foundation for, or an explanation or justification of, the theory and use of power. Each myth "in its own time and place serves the necessary function of mitigating fears and validating hopes, of harmonizing implacable fact and indefeasible desire, of reconciling that which appears necessary with that which seems just." [15]

But our study gives us reason to believe that we may go further, that myths not only serve essentially the same functions but are also formulated in the same way—by the same fundamental processes of folk logic. Whatever "philosophy" of reality people in any age subscribe to, they will interpret their universe or their society according to observed (or learned) resemblances and contrasts; they will assume that the elements identified are reciprocal in form, quality, or power; they will reduce everything possible to the human equation—to whatever human thought and feeling can use for its own purposes; and having arrived at some magic formula or factor most congenial to their particular needs or status they will claim for it a universal validity.

We can assume, then, that characteristic "reality systems" may be identified for animistic, highly organized, and individualistic patterns of society; that these "realities" provide the symbols of power by which people seek to consummate what they believe to be real (or wish to become so); and that, by very similar processes of folk logic, they formulate in myth both the nature of the reality system and the justification of the power relations arising within it.

15 · COMMUNITY OF ESSENCE:

THE MYTH OF AN ANIMISTIC UNIVERSE

*S*cratch the epiderm of the civilized man," wrote Wallis,[1] "and the barbarian is found in the derm." However true this may be for other aspects of primitive culture, it is certainly true for the concept of reality: survivals even in highly civilized countries continue to conflict with or modify more "advanced" assumptions, in comparatively isolated areas during normal times but in a goodly segment of the population in times of crisis.[2] So far as it is possible to reconstruct primitive reality from inferences about early literate and preliterate cultures and from contemporary primitives, its essential features seem to be as follows. "The whole man confronts a living 'thou' in nature": [3] he and his physical environment are of one order, one society, apprehended by one mode of cognition—an undifferentiated universe in which man and nature are in a reciprocal relation, the qualities and properties of the one interchanging with those of the other. The reactions of nature are thus psychological—those of helping or hindering, productive of friendliness or anger, giving expression to pleasure and pain. When men and things are still not distinguished from one another and are reciprocally related, there is also no discrimination between facts, values, and sanctions—between what defines and designates, what constitutes good and bad, and what approves and disapproves. Primitive man analyses by classifying, notes the great contrasts of life and death, light and dark, sky and earth, land and water, and the great identities—the regularity of celestial phenomena, the recurrent cycle of seasons, the similarity of parent and child. And when he begins to distinguish between aspects of nature and between himself and nature, he enriches the all-inclusive symbols of contrast and identity with more specialized group symbols, crystallized in magic and ritual—the dramatic re-creation of the world as he knows it.

When the universe is presented in symbols channelling fact, emotion, value, and will; when it is in one social relationship—and that a reciprocal one—with man; when it is regarded as a living thing having mind and soul, then everything is invested with a "contagious or radiant potency." The source of power is that which may be derived by sentient beings from other sentient beings, whether they are vague supernatural powers like daimonia and numina or, as later, symbols of personification. To bring about what one desires or prevent what he does not, these powers must be cajoled, entreated, bent to compliance through prayer. The magic word and ritual drama, fixed symbols of a reality to be consummated, draw their potency from a two-fold identification: the word and the act are, in the first place, identical with the "reality" they represent; and the expression and pre-enactment "produce" effects identical with what is desired. Identity, like contrast, is close to cause. The conversation and negotiation with the supernatural Presence, the attempt to make it feel and act as one wishes it to do, makes primitive "science" a psychology rather than a rudimentary physics and primitive power a passive kind of control.

The manner in which animistic myth reveals an ordered concept of reality and the sources of power is vividly illustrated in recent American Indian lore, particularly in ceremonies of the Osage, Pueblo, and Huron. These rites suggest no cosmogonic contrast of light and darkness,[4] no broad differentiation of earth, sky, and sea from chaos or night, no great natural hegemonies or hierarchies of nature gods: for these fundamental phases of animistic myth we would do better to turn to the mythologies of Egypt, Persia, and Greece. But they do portray in an intense and consummate form the cosmic background, the identity of being and reciprocity of power between man and nature, and the pervasive indwelling spirit of an animistic universe.

"Gradually it became clear to me," La Flesche recalled of "a sacred dance-drama and a prayer" which he witnessed among the Osage Indians, "that the rite as a whole was of a cosmic character; that it was a dramatization of the movements of certain cosmic forces whose combined power brought forth material life upon the earth and set it in perpetual motion." [5] As John Collier concluded: "through its . . . intense enactment, not the individuals alone, but the tribe, commingled with the universe and contributed, not merely received, meaning and power." [6] Collier's own testimony of a Pueblo rite in 1926 illustrates even more graphically the role of myth in expressing reality and power in primitive belief.

The occasion as a whole was a summoning by the tribe of many spirits of the wild, elements or cosmic kin known from ages gone by . . . . As the hours moved on, a displacement of human and mystical factors seemed to take place . . . . Forces or beings normally invisible, only half-personal yet connecting with the hidden central springs of the empirical life, are a dominating fact in the Pueblo (in the tribal Indian) mind. The Indian's relationship to these forces . . . is a partnership in an eternal effort whereby, from some remote place of finding and communion, the human and the mechanical universes alike are sustained.[7]

This interpretation recalls the Jesuits' impressions of the Huron *Ononhwaroia* in seventeenth-century Canada—the celebration of a primitive "All Saints' Day" in a three-day festival of "the upsetting of the brain." Here the spirit-invested universe became a communal reality, the bond of men and nature was forged again, and from it the Hurons drew the power to purge themselves of whatever was destroying their lives and to restore the integrity of their being. It could be said of the Huron, as Collier said of

Stone Age man, that "his animistic and magical world-view led him to an assumption which became one of the molding forces of history. That assumption, which he worked over into his institutions, was this: That intensity of consciousness . . . was effectual in the magical control of nature through co-partnership with the gods." [8]

"It is not the 'act of God' but the shaman's spell that is coercive," observed Lasswell and Kaplan.[9] As masters of ceremony Indian medicine men and Egyptian priests formulated the symbols of a unified, living reality; as mediators of the supernatural they perfected the techniques of obtaining power. Under their leadership society focused basic animistic assumptions and channelled emotion, absorbing all forms of power—social, economic, or military—and all phases of life. If "to penetrate to the heart of a civilization we ought to begin with a knowledge of its gods," [10] the surest approach to the historical interpretation of millennia of tribal communities and theocratic imperialisms are the myths— the codes, rites, ceremonies, epics—embodying the reality and power of animism.

For two centuries American history, too, was affected in certain areas by a kind of "latter-day animism"—in concentrated force in early New England and among the Pennsylvania Germans and Southern Appalachian pioneers, and more generally diffused during the westward expansion among the common folk of the country. For these people, as for earlier and more primitive cultures, the invisible world of spirits was a reality; the Pennsylvania Germans worked in close co-partnership with an almost human universe and patterned their lives on its moods and rhythms; and common people everywhere looked upon the divine being as Providence, intervening alike in the processes of nature and the intimate lives of men and disposing His awful power to punish or reward. But the historical interest of latter-day animism rests not so much on these familiar aspects as upon the assumptions that underlie them. These assumptions reveal an implicit acceptance of a holistic environment, whose physical and psychic elements stood on the same plane of reality and were correlative. Whatever existed derived its significance in terms of what was good or bad for human beings. It was a predominantly moral environment, expressed not in scientific formulae but in valuative metaphors: [11] that which was good was correct, that which was bad was incorrect. There was no neutral ground of fact where one could stand to view the world objectively, no Dantean limbo of impersonal matter. The fundamental processes of folk logic—identity and reciprocity, contrast, and the deterministic quality of origins or "firsts" (processes as vividly illustrated in American folklore as in any primitive classification of the universe)[12]—shaped the environment into subjective, moralistic symbols.

The fenced-in farms of German settlers in southeastern Pennsylvania and the lonely homesteads of the Southern Appalachian migrants to the Lower Middle West were components of a cosmic reality providing a source of power daily for work as well as for social and spiritual fulfilment. The myth that sustained this subjective universe was a faith; its followers were devotees. Folk "knowledge"—the lore of strongly animistic symbols expressed in ancient adages, ballads, folktales, and hymns—furnished a design for living in which moral, customary law took precedence over civil ("Gospel is better than law," people said), in which bank barns and homesteads symbolized the basic values. Among the Pennsylvania Germans a common dialect and a common stake in the land gave the myth a quietly enduring strength; but the Southern Appalachian settlers, whose atomistic homesteads lacked the social nexus of the German communities, found periodic affirmations of the myth (in revivals, hoedowns, and barbecues) an emotional imperative.

To those who spread their sails before the winds of the new science and the new industry, the flotilla of latter-day animism seemed stalled in perpetual calm; to believers in linear progress, these groups appeared to revolve in an undeviating orbit. Even contemporary writers sometimes refer to achievement like that of the Pennsylvania Germans and the Southern Appalachian highlanders as "culture lag." It is true that their way of life was static—in the sense that a faith is static—and that they were suspicious of novelty and change: leaving their cultural parish meant adopting a new faith.[13] But their resistance to change, their apparent weakness, came not so much from their lack of one kind of strength (an objective, theoretical outlook) as from their possession of another—the strength of the immemorial myth of a single, subjective world.

The segment of America they knew was a "community of essence,"[14] a reciprocity of power between the farmer and nature that made him, "natural man," the balance wheel of society, the germinating, productive core of civilization. Mythical thinking concentrates and focuses the whole of what is experienced into a nuclear center, whose pregnant symbol images or "contains" the whole.[15] When pioneer reality was imaged in *Heimat* and homestead, "progress" could mean only intensification, enrichment, fulfilment of an accepted order of things. For the Pennsylvania Germans this implied a progressive enrichment of the land and of human resources; for the plain people of the Lower Middle West it implied the continual absorption of new technological developments—the railroads, steamships, mines, and factories—into the agricultural norm as its natural enlargement. This was one of the major projective components in the myth of the great interior—the myth of the Middle West as the real, natural center of agrarian democracy. No less significant was the projective turn given to the doctrine of "natural man" by the emphasis on the human equation and on the idea of God as a personal Providence. Democracy was to be achieved not so much through reason or by agitation for rights (they appeared to have been largely attained in the social equality of the Middle West) as by mass conversion to realize and restore what God had wrought. In religious revivals and political mass meetings the plain people of the Middle Western frontier reaffirmed the great emotional symbols of the creed and rededicated themselves to it.

*I*t is difficult to imagine a time when men did not think in social terms or were not involved in their social heritage,[1] or when they did not regard themselves as human beings as well as integral parts of a holistic environment. Social intercourse and sanctions shaped the individual; social ritual made past and future a coherent, unbroken verity; there was as real a co-existence, as complete a reciprocity, between individual and society as between man and nature. Tribal groups were no strangers to control over social values or to complex associations and interlocking blood relationships; but their patterns of organization were elaborated and institutionalized within the periphery of dominant animistic assumptions.

When the change came, it was a matter of emphasis and direction, an increasing preoccupation with social relations until they became the foci of reality. As the physical universe of nomadic hunters narrowed to an agricultural environment,[2] the grander, fiercer phenomena that beset tribal life grew relatively remote, and the natural forces affecting agriculture—seasonal changes, rains and the inundation of riverbanks, the fertility of the soil and of domesticated animals—took on a preponderant importance. Changing functions meant changed relations and symbols: whatever libation men might still make to animistic beings, they were on the way to supplanting the reality of a holistic environment with the narrower one of the human element and to recognizing that there was a human nature beside and apart from that of the physical world.

When we put the culture of the Pueblo Indians or the Hurons beside that of the Pennsylvania Germans, we are at once aware how different the animistic emphasis is from the dominantly social. It is the difference between deriving power from supernatural forces with whom the tribesman is kin and drawing it from the potentialities inherent in a particular social pattern. Animistic thinking runs all through Pennsylvania "knowledge," but the *Heimat* and *Freindschaft* that symbolized the social bond testify to the oneness, the wholeness, the all-inclusive reality of the clan. The physical universe—known and used through the weather lore of moon, birds, and animals and through the lore of planting—was "fenced in" like the farms, oriented to a social microcosm. The Indians were members of a great cosmic family; among the Pennsylvania Germans this situation was almost reversed: natural forces, like horses and cattle, were part of everyday family life.[3] It was the *Familienkreis* that was ultimately real.

In the complex of social realities in the Middle Ages the most typical and expressive myth is that contained in the famous analogy between society and the human organism, each of whose organs or members plays its own peculiar role.[4] Few villeins of an English manor, few craftsmen of a guild, could paint so graphic and symmetrical a picture of society; but the customary rule and communal ceremonies of the village and the ritualized code of the crafts reflected in unconscious fidelity "the moral fusion of men physically associated in labor."[5] "Each man, each act, was part of a total life drama, the plot of which was known and in which the part allotted to each was prescribed."[6]

The Industrial Revolution paradoxically gave tremendous impetus to the primacy of social interests in workers' communities. "The symbolic universe that had patterned the ways of men across the ages in village, manor, or gild"[7] vanished in the upheaval, but the basic need to recreate traditional social values found new symbols in the trade unions. In the United States the mechanic, starting (like the farmer) with a view of human nature to which the Declaration of Independence had given dynamic novelty and from the farmer's conviction that the producer was the germinal core of society, transformed a political creed into a social and economic one.[8] From the crusade for the Holy City of Equality through public education and social reform he turned to joust with the barons besetting his own castle for equal access to credit and equal bargaining power.[9] But whether the struggle was ideological or opportunistic, through the Knights of Labor or through craft unions, men were moving toward a new expression, a new myth, of social reality—a myth which assumed that the trade union was a natural and enduring form of democracy.

The creed of the new society of workingmen was articulated (in the Middle West) by crusading editors of labor periodicals in Cleveland, Cincinnati, Chicago, and Milwaukee. The language and locale might vary, but not the essential articles of the myth —the foundation concepts of what was basic in human and social nature, the superstructure of the "natural" forms of society built upon it, the girders of power, and atop the roof its golden cross of divine approval. Excerpted from typical labor periodicals, the myth ran thus:

It is inherent in man and nature to be socially combined.[10]

We hold that an inherent right, a living, fundamental, tangible principle, underlies the superstructure of every properly organized Union in the country . . . applicable alike in adversity or success.[11]

There are certain moral forces, certain ideas at work, which will compel the workers to unite in groups.[12]

We hold the labor . . . employed in useful occupations of industry to be the one true source of national wealth.[13]

We workingmen have discovered the architectural plan of the industrial structure of the future.[14]

There is no institution so democratic as the centre in which a group of workmen exercise their activity, be it a factory, forge, or field . . . .[15]

Co-operation is one of the new social forces of the age. It is without doubt a new power of industry.[16]

UNION. Talismanic word, the principle old, the doctrine divine. It
is now in our power to inaugurate a new epoch, a new social faith.[17]
Trade unions are the teachers and saviors of the world . . . destined
to be the levellers of caste . . . the fore-runners of cosmopolitan
society—the harbingers of universal happiness . . . . They are the
voice of God.[18]

To infer that the Cleveland coopers, the iron molders of Pittsburgh, or Chicago's meat packers lived and breathed the faith
these spokesmen professed would be to ignore the disillusioned
cries of the editors themselves. Laboring men, they charged, were
filled with "apathy" and "ingratitude"; [19] in dark seasons of depression their membership cards dropped like autumn leaves. But
if for common workingmen the craft unions were not yet the
expression of that fundamental principle applicable in adversity
or success, if the architectural plan of the future was still vague
in their minds, there were many thousands of them—immigrants
from Czechoslovakia, Germany, and elsewhere—whose patterns
of social reality gave unsuspected support to the myth.

Schooled in benevolent and social organizations like the Czech
sokols and the German Turnvereine, where they reaped daily the
satisfactions inherent in the compass of intimate activities, these
workingmen transferred ideas of co-operation, interdependence,
and freedom from their *ethnic* media to the larger *occupational*
communities. Their influence is a revealing chapter in the story
of industry; as early as the 1850's the influx of German immigrants
"gave new life to the American labor movement, and new unions
were speedily formed in the larger cities, the majority of whose
members were German workmen"; [20] as late as the 1880's the
distinguishing feature of the trade union movement was the
predominance of the foreign-born.[21] For the emerging ideology of
labor power these men helped to provide the vital base of social
reality.

"The foundation-stone of modern philosophy is power," af-
firmed the *Workingman's Advocate* in 1866.[22] This was the symbol in which men had wrapped their aspirations for equality a

half-century before; now it was acquiring a new content and a new direction. Labor editors were still crying "Illumine the mind of labor" [23]—still persuaded that an educated workingman could meet his problems and his employer on equal terms; but they were beginning to realize that the new society of labor was itself a pregnant source of power. "Co-operation possesses a power and an elevating influence," the *Advocate* told its readers; "a greater degree of equality will be established in society." [24] Before such prevailing winds M. A. Foran launched the coopers' magazine upon its maiden voyage: "We must make our organization a social power capable of controlling and influencing the general arrangement of society in our behalf." [25] And in this spirit—kindled by the levelling principle of man's brotherhood and of a new machine technology that promised to obliterate the distinction between the skilled and the unskilled [26]—the Knights of Labor formulated a co-operative creed that won almost three-quarters of a million converts to a common faith.

For a few years it seemed as if the new society had in fact emerged: the reality of labor organization and the power of united action appeared as the natural expression of democracy.[27] But as suddenly as it had gathered steam the juggernaut of the Knights of Labor, sidetracked by Jay Gould and stalled in the stockyards of Chicago, had been rolled off the main line of labor development. The failure of strikes seemed proof enough that the train would never reach its destination: workingmen by tens of thousands abandoned the coaches, troubled by the bitterness of the opposition outside the organization and the conflict of principles within.[28] And yet these troubles, catastrophic as they were, only accent the basic fault—that the Knights were attempting to organize the workers' "elemental protest against oppression and degradation" [29] on a system that had neither occupational nor ethnic group consciousness, that lacked both the physical bond and the "moral fusion" of men working together. If the Knights lost power so suddenly, it was because they never actually possessed it: they could not—at least at this stage of labor development—reduce a heterogeneous membership to a social melt and cast it in molds of reality from which the instruments of power might be forged. It was not they but their rivals, the young American Federation of Labor, who—using a melt long since refined in the tradition of craft autonomy—provided the "identifications, expectations, and demands [that] render power authoritative" [30] and channelled the current within a social core. [31] To the Federation, no less than to the Pennsylvania Germans, this nuclear core seemed the natural center, the enduring pattern, of reality.

17 · THE INDIVIDUAL IN SEARCH OF
THE RATIONAL ONE

*T*he American Federation of Labor, for all its success in supplying cohesion in the final quarter of the nineteenth century, and in hammering policy into contract provisions, was relying upon a formula of reality that looked largely to the past. By the same token the ideology of the Knights of Labor looked to the future, to the time when craft would mean less than equality, and community more than skill. But quite apart from this effort to find common cause for the whole body of workingmen, the Knights' brief successes had brought into the foreground, both for labor leaders and industrialists, an idea charged with momentous potentialities. This was the realization that strength was inherent in organization itself,[1] that a system of organization, unencumbered with the immemorial trappings of race, geography, or craft, could be the prime base of power.

The feeling that lay beneath this realization is one of the oldest and most deeply ingrained of any folk attitude. The dream of freeing one's social universe from the immediate and local limitations that enclose it and then of freezing it into a pattern of enduring, automatic equilibrium recurs millennially—from the Brahmin's quest for the One to rational designs for ideal republics and the rule of natural law. But it was the fluidity of American life that brought the idea of transcending these limitations into focus now.[2] Everywhere Americans could see democracy dissolving racial bonds, railroads cutting through economic mountains and prairies, machines carving up craft techniques, and credit—impersonal and intangible—lifting the horizons of corporate growth. These were the historical projections of an outlook radically different from the urge for group identification. They were the expressions of a frame of mind that looked upon things and people, upon human as well as natural resources, not as organic components of a cohesive social reality, but as the means of organization, as interchangeable parts of a planned pattern.[3] To men with such an outlook the inherent strength of organization suggested by the experience of the Knights of Labor eventuated, not in any of the usual patterns of human equation, but in the manipulation of rational symbols to achieve a structural hierarchy.

The salt breeze of rationalism had been rising for some time, a breeze that had fanned revolt against the restrictive corporate life of the Middle Ages and that filled the nostrils of generations of New England individualists. At the level of the mackerel sky, Transcendentalists and Deists elaborated the creed that "mind is the only reality,"[4] that man was endowed with a spark of divine reason, and so reason could lead him most truly to comprehend God and the universe. On the plane of Yankee folk thought, there was a prevailing confidence in the efficacy of the written and spoken word—in the identification of word and deed ("sayin' is doin'"), and in the power of rational symbols (bonds and figures, statutes and constitutions, maps and blueprints) to measure, chart, and exploit nature, or to build society—in the image of the individual. For the individual "sumtotalized" society. Romanticists, like rationalists, protested against an over-regimented or corrupt civilization: the Jesuits in Canada had hoped to re-create a "terrestrial paradise" on a model of primitive innocence and simplicity—the tribal oneness of the Hurons or the original Christian communities in Palestine.[5] The symbol of French Canadian settlements was the priest; the symbol of Yankee towns in the Middle West was a composite of speculator, lawyer, and engineer. The Yankee was in search of a social unity, a rational cosmos, constructed by social engineering—a mechanistic, not an organic, community.[6]

The New England entrepreneurs, lumber barons, promoters, and manufacturers, and the industrial leaders who followed in their trail were involved in mythical thinking quite as deeply as their Pennsylvania German or Southern Appalachian neighbors. The rational myth that underlay their basic assumptions reveals all the familiar phenomena and techniques of animistic and social myths.[7] The Yankee, too, wrapped up reality in symbols—abstractions defined by metaphors as truly as were the emotional pleas of a Methodist circuit rider.[8] He narrowed reality to workable analogies or equations, which are "reciprocally related, refer to one another, illumine and explain each other."[9] He reduced everything to human terms—not animistic or dominantly social, but those that appeared to be basically human, to the rational, the man-in-man. He had to find in himself the values he repudiated as "outworn disguises" of society; like Plato and Emerson, he had to re-create the universe and society in his own mental image. And having extended the symbols of empirical reality to all other aspects of life, he reached the idea that the cosmos is a rational whole and mankind one—a unity admitting of reciprocal relations in politics and ethics as in mathematical equations.[10] But for all its basic similarity to other types of myth, there is one vital—and historically significant—difference: rational symbols show a "tremendous readiness to enter into *combinations*";[11] and reason is not content (as are other approaches to reality) with being caught up and absorbed by what it touches but takes it "only as a point of departure, from which it can run the whole gamut of impressions in various directions, until these impressions are fitted together into one unified conception, one closed system."[12]

This is the approach that rational individualism brought to the problem of social co-ordination—more specifically, that industrial leaders brought to the establishment of the corporation.

It was the kind of abstractive thinking that would create society on a contractual basis and would take the contractual word, the manufacturing process, the economic principle as entities, the more real and the more permanent in proportion as they were made independent of the shifting claims of personalities, economic cycles, or politics. Plato, discouraged in the hope of putting his scheme of a rationally constructed society into practice, would be astonished to see how completely the corporate system has characterized the history of an epoch. He would be amazed to see the actualization of a pattern which, "having once sprung the old restraints of ownership," [13] has its own inner coherence and perfects its own law. But what must intrigue any apostle of permanence is the autonomous character of corporate enterprise, a device with a hydromatic pulse capable of flourishing, without change of skeletal structure, under any type of government or society.[14]

The most obvious base of corporate power is, of course, property ownership, including control of raw materials, patents, and production facilities. But on that base has been built a super-structure of power—the power inherent in the organization itself. This is the pattern of remarkably integrated combinations of abstract, anonymous symbols that eventuate in processes of production, arrangements of distribution, pyramids of management, and relations of ownership. The hierarchal framework of the corporation feeds power vertically through the plant community; its interlocking directorates disseminate power horizontally through several such communities. Like a state within a state, the corporation assumes the functions of government—not only its three divisions but also the prerogative of imposing coercive sanctions.[15]

Industry had sprung not only the old restraints of ownership; it was emancipated as well from most of the rules of custom. No skeletal structure could be more cleanly stripped of the flesh of social mores (whether ethnic, political, or religious) or less dependent upon the heartbeat of traditional folk myth. But as industry, and especially corporate enterprise, became the dominant force in the national economy, as its aims were socialized and extended to society as a whole, it necessarily took on the flesh and blood of American folk assumptions. It equated its purposes with the ideals of the American heritage; it took a new interest in the nature of man and in the ideological undergirdings of its power; and in so doing it drew upon the age-old processes of myth.

In the elaboration of the industrial myth, theorists set out resolutely to retrace the well-worn folkways to social and economic equilibrium. The starting point was the laissez-faire persuasion of an era competing for the spoils of natural abundance; along the pilgrimage the economic world picked up analogies with natural law: "Competition is to economics," asserted Joseph A. Labadie, "what gravitation is to physics." "Economic life," wrote Frank Fetter, "is like physical life, a constant adjustment." [16] To prevent competition was to interfere with the "law" of supply and demand, "the grand regulator of wages for the best interests of all," the only "permanent equilibrium." [17] Competition was but one aspect, of course, of the rhythm in the ebb and flow of business, "natural tides" [18] that ran too deep for legislation to affect. [19] Once again, as it had been in the golden scale of the Mean and in other equilibrial myths, the point of balance in society seemed to have been revealed: competition, said Julian W. Sturtevant, was the foundation of all free society. [20]

From this patrimony of rational individualism an emerging industrial ideology reaped a high rate of interest. As the idea that nature's laws should not be tampered with (what Nature hath wrought man may not change!) was used to justify the autonomy of an enterprise that operated by them, so competition by natural selection automatically sifted the leaders, the elite. And as Andrew Carnegie's Gospel of Wealth had formulated a folk philosophy [21] to justify the great personal fortunes to which the elite were supposedly entitled as essential to the progress of society and their possessors as the trustees of the public interest, so the industrial myth found the idea of stewardship useful in supporting both "the concentration of power within the several forms of pyramidal authority, and the specific use of this power as it is brought to bear upon the interests of different classes of the population." [22] This individualistic ideology is the measure of the change from regarding the corporate system as a technique for organizing materials, men, and management to considering it as the blueprint for the social structure itself. But it could go no further in clothing the bare bones of rational reality and power: to make headway in equating itself with "the American way" it would need the strong heart of basic folk assumptions, especially those long since naturalized by the farmer.

It was Jefferson who articulated the agrarian myth [23] and propagandists of the Middle West who painted it with the sunlight of the Mississippi, but its focal symbol was mirrored in the Homestead Bill and in pastoral idylls circulated in the advertisements of the railroad companies. As we have suggested, the homestead symbol was highly complex—a rich compound of the legacy of individualism and an animistic belief in the personal action of Providence to realize an agrarian millennium. But its pervasive power for over a century and for millions of settlers and immigrants arose largely from the way in which it came, through traditional folk processes of thought, to image the American dream. It symbolized, in its frontier reminiscences, the doctrine of the unique origin of this new democratic society—a part of the age-old absorption with "first beginnings"—which gave rise to the doctrine of America's unique mission. [24] It imaged those half-conscious equations of the farmer's "natural goodness" with the virgin land, of success with merit, or of local with national values—identifications that exchanged their cargoes, like two railway lines, once the tracks were laid in the same gauge. [25] These reciprocal identifications over the years helped to make up the grand equation of democracy with the farmer's way of life and his "conscious identification with the success of democracy" [26] —a cumulative permutation of agricultural folkways with free-

dom, equality, and individual worth. The agrarian myth simplified society into producers and non-producers and, by absorbing
into a pregnant image the associated symbols of school bell,
steeple, and courthouse and regarding everything as derivative of
agriculture, it made the homestead "the stronghold of democracy
on the continent," [27] the genuine pattern of American life.

This image, in the hands of men who saw in it not the core of
reality but an objective, utilitarian symbol, became the catchword
of promotional propaganda. Speculators everywhere in the
growth of the great Mississippi Valley—not least Stephen A.
Douglas, political godfather of railway land grants and homestead sovereignty—minted the native ore of "homestead" into the
currency of commerce and industry. Middle Western promoters
were not the first, to be sure, who clothed their business ideology
with homespun: spokesmen for Eastern enterprise had long since
developed a "pastoral mythology" about the laboring classes, and
Harrison's log-cabin campaign merely focused the political
magic which the conservative Whig party had found in the common man's values.[28] But it was in the Middle West, where agricultural power had been preserved, that conservatives first assimilated the new democratic moods; [29] and it was here that industry
took over from the farmer the notion that railways and factories
were the natural and inevitable enlargement of the homestead.

In the agricultural economy of the 1850's, the idea that industry was the farmer's great new hired man worked conspicuously
to the advantage of both—especially in the development of the
interior, where industry's stake in the Great Lakes region was
the natural complement of the promise of the Mississippi Valley.[30]
But before the century had ended, the hired man, who was now
accounting for more of the nation's wealth than the farmer,[31]
had come to realize that if he were to win the support of an
agriculturally-minded nation in the development of industrial
power, he would need to challenge the farmer's hold upon the
national myth.

To displace the myth itself would have been as unwise as it

was impracticable: its symbols had all the magic of folk belief and religious sanctions. It was the farmer who had to be displaced—*within* the myth. And so the agrarian images in the national gallery of myth were painted over, in one panel after another, with corresponding idylls of industry.[32] Natural resources and productive processes replaced the virgin soil as "given," and as the chief source of the national wealth. It was now the industrial leader, not the farmer, who sat in the throne of "producer," and the old bifurcation of society into producers and nonproducers took on a different color. The nation's institutions were no longer derivatives of agriculture; they now owed their support and well-being to corporate enterprise. There was less emphasis on equality as the guarantee of social equilibrium and more on the automatic operation of economic "laws" like that of supply and demand. As industry—now the balance wheel of society—fared, so fared the nation. The homestead, in a word, had become Homestead, Incorporated.

The combination of rational and agrarian myths gave this symbol an extraordinary vitality. It blended the reality of an environment conceived in subjective human terms—that of "God's free man, treading upon a land which Heaven had bestowed upon him" [33]—with the reality of an impersonal, automatic system of organization that interchanged men and materials according to economic hypotheses. It made it possible to personify the corporation and reduce human motives to mathematical formulae, to draw at convenience upon the equilibrial symbols of natural law and social equality, and to identify industrial expansion with national progress [34] and industrial civilization with the American way of life.

*W*here there is organization, there is power." [1] In this century no organization has become so powerful as the state; through its development and integration of the various kinds of power and its absorption of individual and group values,[2] it has become a social cosmos. As a focal medium in which fundamental assumptions are socialized, the nation symbolizes reality; and the myth which expresses that reality and its power relations is "the pattern of basic political symbols current in a society . . . the political symbols most firmly accepted." [3] Political myths, then, may be regarded as justifications or rationalizations, based on some generally assumed reality, of groups in power or seeking to supplant power, myths that not only lead men to act, as Sorel believed,[4] but to accept a leader's program of action.

The modern Faust has wandered in quest of Truth through one political myth after another—through the German *Walpurgisnacht* of Spirit, Will, and the Master Race, the steppes of Dialectic Materialism, and the English and American high seas of Reason and Liberty. And at the end of each quest he has said: "This is all in all. Here foothold is! Realities here center!" So Pericles might have spoken in the agora of Athens, where the pattern of city-state democracy took the place of, or rather became, a religion of the state. Why each "truth" was espoused is familiar history; what we need to consider is how each became Truth, the master myth.

The lively interest within the last few years in political myth-making [5] might create the impression that we are confronted with formidable new developments in social neuroses—that we are on the threshold of startlingly new insights into mass psychology; and yet the analysts themselves are quick to point out our reversions to elemental reactions.[6] Modern mythmakers, of course, no longer subscribe to primitive realities; but the need for restoring simplicity and order to a bewildering social universe was as pressing in Nazi Germany and in the Soviet Union as among American Indians; and the need was met in much the same way—by personifying great impersonal forces, attributing the causes of failure, evil, and frustration to other classes, races, or nations.[7] Here, too, were the all-embracing dichotomies of good and evil into which primitive men ordered their animistic world, a bi-polar world created out of uncritical analogies and contrasts. Facile equations innocent of fact produced the identification of what is with what ought to be, of "purity" of race with inherent superiority, of industrialism with *the* American way of life, and of "the welfare of the community and the progress of mankind . . . with an abstract entity, called . . . the dialectic of history and . . . the totalitarian state." [8]

But the gamut of techniques of simplification in political myth had not yet been run. The common folk habit of accepting the new only as it can be assimilated to folk memory [9] is repeated in an ideology that "maintains its prestige by associating chiefly with venerable but outmoded value judgments, and by recognizing with difficulty any fact that it does not recall in its youth." [10] Of four reactions to new ideas—rejection of the new, discarding of the old, arrangement in thought-tight compartments, and harmonizing of the new with the old [11]—myth almost invariably follows the last, as in industry's adaptation of the agrarian myth. And constant repetition of political symbols tends to limit the alternatives to which the rising generation can become emotionally attached.[12] The net effect of these simplifying techniques is to channel belief into an emotionally satisfying Truth, a "magnet, which draws men into the central focus of the leader group and fuses them with the others there." [13]

Once the seed of Truth is formed, it luxuriates into neighboring gardens. Political myths, like the rest, are susceptible to symbolic extension "upon situations which have no actual resemblance to the experience on which they were based." [14] "Groups produce value-systems," says Laski, which "will always claim universality; they will represent themselves as valid for persons beyond the group," for "the nation," "all right thinking men," or "mankind." [15] Myths seem, moreover, to follow what Tannenbaum calls the inner logic of institutions, each of which "tends to be all-embracing, laying claim to the entire man, and showing an impelling tendency to assume all responsibility for the governance of society." [16]

But political myths, like Jack's beanstalk, reach "up" as well as out, until they curl their tendrils round the pillars of eternal verity. The same urge that elevated Roman values like Reason and Faith to godhead impels modern mythmakers to some ideology or symbol that will have ultimate validity. "Every national and cultural myth is created in the same way," wrote Jaeger,[17] "by narrowing the field of vision and extolling one particular nation's achievements to the pinnacle of the absolute." From a slightly different point of view Marie Swabey supports this conclusion: "The commonest device of myths today is that of selecting some single contributory factor to social life (such as race, culture, or economic class) and magnifying it into a sweeping explanation of history." [18]

Each of these myths resembles the one magic formula for which primitive men were always searching; but in another sense —in the attempt to set up something automatic and self-perpetuating—each is a resumption of the immemorial quest for an equilibrium in society like that of the physical universe. As

Homer's Moira, a principle both of the balance of cosmic forces and of the power regulating the affairs of men,[19] lay behind the classical concept of justice as a balancing of accounts and behind the golden mean, so today "political philosophy can claim no exemption from the doctrine of the golden mean," [20] or (to put it in the larger perspective) from the myth of equilibrium.

When Swabey spoke of the magnifying of a single contributory factor to social life, when she remarked that dialectic is for Communists "a new means of universal knowledge, pre-eminent in its explanatory and predictive power," [21] she was referring to what may be called "point of balance" equilibrium—the central formula on which all else must pivot.[22] Of this kind also are the Nazi myth of Race and early American political philosophy. "Liberty thus turned out to be," said Becker, "not only an inherent natural right of the individual, but also a preordained and natural mechanism for bringing about the material and moral progress of mankind." [23] For a time American theory has been moving away from the "Newtonian scheme of government," [24] away from a point of balance center to another equilibrial myth—that of "constant adjustment." "Though perfect equilibrium is not achievable," Tannenbaum believes, "a working equilibrium is possible; and attainment of that might well be considered the great task of statesmanship, the true purpose of government, and the major problem of political theory and social ethics." [25] This adaptation "lies at the heart of the power problem," wrote Merriam, "under all forms of political and other social organization— the staple of their activities." [26] Behind this way of thinking lies an assumption historically rooted in American ideology—that the checks and balances of democratic politics "are natural not artificial; that they are flexible rather than rigid." [27] The credo "all men are created free and equal" was once (to give our own interpretation to Becker) a point-of-balance myth; but freedom was soon taken for granted, whereas equality—under many forms and names—became a crucial and continuing issue in American history, a myth of constant adjustment.[28] The strength of the myth today is due in great part to the conviction that there are muliple forms of power in America that must somehow be kept in equilibrium.

But the notion of the multiplicity of power, derived from the obvious fact that there are multiple power groups, is in some respects illusory. These groups utilize much the same elements of power in differing proportions; and, like labor unions and corporations, they are in many issues more often facing one another as opposing teams on the same power field than engaging in separate sports. If power is, as Riesman says, situational, mercurial, and amorphous, it has also been concentrated through the decline of older separations—"between those who sought power through wealth and wealth through power; between those locally oriented and those nationally oriented; between those who looked to business models and those who looked to agrarian ones." [29] The multiple forms of power which most major groups use—organization, property, reserve funds, coercive sanctions, and "public relations"—converge to an unprecedented degree in industry: so highly developed and so thoroughly integrated are they that industry, more than any other power group, symbolizes the nation's strength and values. The interlocking of these vast powers not only within industry but with those of the state as well portends an increasingly monolithic power structure, whose productive functions image (through the equation with Americanism) the "American way of life." [30]

"The American Creed," says Gunnar Myrdal, "is itself one of the dominant 'social trends.'" [31] It is that, and more: it is a significant movement away from the equilibrial myth of constant adjustment to that of a point of balance. As it did once when Liberty was the natural mechanism for promoting progress, the American creed now again occupies a pivotal center, confronting totalitarian myth with its own crystallization of opinion. For the American way of life—as it has come to be defined in current ideology—is no longer a working equilibrium, an adaptation of value systems, a flexible process, but a social canon, an orthodoxy descriptive of social "reality" and justifying the kinds of power utilized to create it.

The realities, the forms of power, and the myths of contemporary society are literally "worlds" remote from those of primitive animism, the clan structure of the Roman gens, or the medieval social organism. Nature is no longer a psychological phenomenon, as it was in a Huron Indian ritual, but a system of empirical observations and theoretical postulates; society is no longer kinship with the descendants of Mars nor a hierarchical order analogous to the human body but a complex of group relations. The objective, rational symbols into which both physical and social reality have been abstracted have long since begun to replace the old cosmogonies.

These enormous differences in "realities" should not, however, obscure the fact that we are concerned with the same basic needs as men have had for many thousands of years, and that our prevailing assumptions, like theirs, are produced through the interaction of reality, power, and myth. And our conception of reality, our mental environment, despite the revolutionary impact of science and mass education, is still shaped and fitted as it was in primitive, classical, and medieval times—by the folk "logic" of analogy, contrast, and reciprocity; by personification and stereotyping; by the use of symbols; and by simplifying problems and issues to a single factor and then magnifying it to an absolute. Reality systems and forms of power change, and with them the myths; but back of the myths are ceaseless quests like the search for equilibrium on the cosmic and social plane, a search for the automatic, permanent, self-renewing that varies in content with each culture but has not changed in character or in intensity. The conclusion is difficult to avoid that the manner in which people today account for their role in the universe and in society is essentially the same as it has been for millennia.

*T*here are some things that even a historian might be expected to take for granted. One of these is the relative constancy and the unpredictable character of human nature; another is the broad base of reality, "so translucent, and so pervading, and seemingly necessary, that only by extreme effort can we become aware of it." [1] But if he is to avoid swinging constantly round in the eddy of events he is describing, if he is to escape the presuppositions of the culture he is attempting to interpret, he must take this reality, this basic mental environment, into account.[2] He must recognize that the materials of history are "value-charged," [3] that even "the ideology of . . . any society is only half the story; the other half . . . lies below the surface"; [4] and that "no one," as Lecky said, "can be truly said to understand any great system of belief, if he has not in some degree realized the point of view from which its arguments assume an appearance of plausibility and cogency." [5]

But his general perspective becomes local and specific only when it is concretely expressed in power relations and current myths. This is the point at which it becomes characteristic of a particular people or period and so reveals cultural differentiation; it is also the point at which reality enters the arena of action and so becomes historically important. The American Indians and the Lower Middle Westerners translated a community of essence, a kinship with the physical universe, into a personal dynamic continually renewed in ritual, folklore, and revivals—emotionally impregnated forms that focus the stimuli of action.[6] The early American farmer's faith in an agricultural millennium, the conviction that he most truly represented democracy, concretely symbolized in the homestead and elaborated in "the myth of the garden," left its impact upon the economics of westward expansion and the politics of industrialism. The naked reality of industrial organization—itself a source of technological and social power—by replacing the farmer's "genuine democracy" with folk symbols of "the American way of life," succeeded in changing the emphasis from an equilibrium of adjustment to a focal point of balance. And at the center of modern political systems lie symbols that bind people together, instruments of power that facilitate action at a distance,[7] symbols that today deify the absolute state and its leader as the "personification of a collective wish." [8] In each case typical patterns of belief and behavior appear which make possible historical treatment in the full perspective of folk psychology and in line with processes of folk logic that recur in each era.

Folklore and other symbolic folk expressions are not alone the product of some quaint vestigial culture; they are constantly coming into being among *all* classes of people because they are immemorial techniques of reducing broad presuppositions to the human equation. Each generation, rephrasing its outlook on the universe and society, finds characteristic modes of symbolizing that outlook in ways that will have the widest and soundest currency. The myth that articulates these assumptions is, then, an expression of the whole people; [9] it may be truly said: "the civilization of an epoch is its myth in action." [10]

Reference Matter

NOTES

Abbreviations Used in the Notes:

J.R.   The Jesuit Relations and Allied Documents
TISAS   Transactions of the Illinois State Agricultural Society
Ia. Home.   Iowa Homestead and Western Farm Journal
Pr. Farm.   Prairie Farmer

In addition, works that are listed in the Bibliography will be cited in shortened form in the Notes.

Chapter 2

1 Bourne, *The Voyages and Explorations of Samuel de Champlain*, II, 227–28.
2 *Ibid.*, pp. 198–99.
3 Grant, *Voyages of Samuel de Champlain*, p. 269.
4 Bishop, *Champlain*, p. 182.
5 Bourne, *The Voyages and Explorations of Samuel de Champlain*, II, 7–8.
6 Wrong and Langton, *Sagard's Long Journey*, p. 254.
7 Bourne, *The Voyages and Explorations of Samuel de Champlain*, II, 8–9.
8 Barbeau, *Huron and Wyandot Mythology*, pp. 45–46.
9 Wrong and Langton, *Sagard's Long Journey*, p. 260.
10 Grant, *Voyages of Samuel de Champlain*, pp. 255–56.
11 *Ibid.*, pp. 243, 245.
12 *J.R.*, X, 219.
13 Bourne, *The Voyages and Explorations of Samuel de Champlain*, I, 208.
14 *Ibid.*, p. 178.

15 *Ibid.*, p. 209.
16 François du Peron, *J.R.*, XV, 177.
17 Grant, *Voyages of Samuel de Champlain*, p. 322. Cf. Jean de Brébeuf, *J.R.*, X, 49: " . . . these Peoples admire and esteem highly those persons who have anything that elevates them above the crowd. Such persons they call oki . . . ." Cf. also *J.R.*, XII, 243, and Sagard's comment on the *oki* "which does and knows something out of the ordinary" (Wrong and Langton, *Sagard's Long Journey*, p. 170).
18 *J.R.*, XXXIX, 25.
19 Kenton, *The Indians of North America*, I, 513.
20 Champlain, *Voyages and Discoveries*, III, 144, as quoted in Kinietz, *The Indians of the Western Great Lakes*, p. 140.
21 Bourne, *The Voyages and Explorations of Samuel de Champlain*, II, 28.
22 *Ibid.*, pp. 29–30.
23 Grant, *Voyages of Samuel de Champlain*, pp. 250–51.
24 *Ibid.*, p. 250.
25 *Ibid.*, p. 251.
26 Bishop, *Champlain*, p. 251.

Chapter 3
1 *J.R.*, XXIII, 277.
2 *Ibid.*
3 Jean de Brébeuf, *J.R.*, VIII, 99, and Barthelemy Vimont, *J.R.*, XXIII, 277.
4 Jones, *A History of the Ojibwa Indians*, p. 255.
5 Crouse, *Contributions of the Canadian Jesuits*, p. 81. On the vitality of the dream of a Northwest Passage to the East, cf. Landon, *Lake Huron*, p. 29 (Cartwright's new clerical gown to impress the Chinese when he entered Hudson Bay in 1602; Thomas James' letter, on leaving England in 1631, to the Emperor of Japan), and Smith, *Virgin Land*, p. 22: "So rich and compelling was the notion that it remained for decades one of the ruling conceptions of American thought about the West."
6 Butterfield, *History of Brulé's Discoveries*, p. 37.
7 Barbeau, *Huron and Wyandot Mythology*, pp. 408–9.
8 *J.R.*, X, 127–29.
9 W. E. Connelly, "Wyandot Folk-Lore," *Twentieth Century Classics and School Readings* (Topeka, Kansas, 1899), pp. 67 ff., as quoted in Barbeau, *Huron and Wyandot Mythology*, p. 304.
10 Barthelemy Vimont, *J.R.*, XXIII, 277–79.

11 *Ibid.*, p. 279.

12 Blair, *Indian Tribes of the Upper Mississippi*, I, 293.

13 Cf. Paul Radin, *Journal of American Folklore*, XXII(1909), 308–10.

14 *J.R.*, XXIII, 279.

Chapter 4

1 *J.R.*, VIII, 97.

2 *J.R.*, X, 49.

3 *J.R.*, X, 37.

4 *J.R.*, X, 39.

5 *Ibid.*

6 *Ibid.*

7 Paul le Jeune, *J.R.*, XI, 41.

8 Paul le Jeune, *J.R.*, XII, 143.

9 *J.R.*, X, 95.

10 *J.R.*, VIII, 121.

11 *Ibid.*, p. 123.

12 They looked upon these remedies, Father François le Mercier observed, "with the same eye with which we in France regard our most common remedies" (*J.R.*, XIII, 33).

13 François le Mercier, *J.R.*, XIII, 213. Aenons, a Huron chieftain, went farther afield: the epidemic, he said, had come from the Mohawks through the Andastes (Le Mercier, *J.R.*, XIV, 9).

14 Brébeuf, *J.R.*, X, 109.

15 Le Mercier, *J.R.*, XIV, 53.

16 Le Mercier, *J.R.*, XIII, 159.

17 Le Mercier, *J.R.*, XIII, 147. Cf. Le Jeune, *J.R.*, XII, 237: "I opened the letters of our Fathers who are with the Hurons, and learned therefrom that the contagion continued in that country, that calumnies were multiplying, that the demons were making open war against us. These tribes believe that we poison and bewitch them, carrying this so far that some of them no longer use the kettles of the French. They say that we have infected the waters, and that the mists which issue thence kill them; that our houses are fatal to them; that we have with us a dead body, which serves us as black magic; that, to kill their children, some Frenchmen penetrated the horrid depths of the woods, taking with them the picture of a little child which we had pricked with the points of awls, and that therein lay the exact cause of their death." In the representation of the last

judgment that the Fathers had shown the Hurons at the village of Ouenrio, the serpents and the fire tormenting the heaps of the damned were intended, the Indians thought, to poison themselves and to consume them with "the heats of this pestilential fever" (Le Mercier, *J.R.*, XIV, 103).

18 Le Mercier, *J.R.*, XIV, 51.

19 *Rationalism in Europe*, I, 102.

20 "The end of the sixteenth century and the beginning of the seventeenth, a period noted for religious chaos and conflict, marked the height of the witchcraft prosecutions" (Thomas Wertenbacker, *The First Americans* [New York: Macmillan, 1927], p. 142).

21 Lecky, *Rationalism in Europe*, I, 85.

22 "The main cause of the dreadful tightening up of witch-hunting in the sixteenth century seems to have been the gradual acceptance in most countries . . . of the theory that dealings with the supernatural were direct dealings with the devil . . . when popular superstition came to the conclusion that all spirits were devils in disguise . . ." (Oman, *The Sixteenth Century*, p. 228).

23 Brébeuf's comments (*J.R.*, X, 193–95) form a continuous paragraph; Le Jeune's are taken from *J.R.*, IX, 119, and XII, 17. Le Jeune had spoken scornfully of the Algonquin medicine man in 1636: "Now whether they really have some secret communication with the Devil, *which I greatly doubt*, or whether they have not,—having taken issue with one of these two Sorcerers, I defied him to kill me with his magic . . ." (*J.R.*, IX, 17). By the following year, however, he is ready to admit that "there is no doubt they have communication with the Devil" (*J.R.*, XII, 15). "Not that the Devil communicates with them as obviously as he does with the Sorcerers and Magicians of Europe" (*J.R.*, XII, 7).

24 It is interesting to compare Le Jeune's views with those of the sixteenth-century skeptic Reginald Scott who "was of opinion that Satan and his crew were a reality, but worked by mental temptation to make unscrupulous people commit crimes . . . . In that way men might be said to be inspired by a devil—who put into their brains ingenious and horrible ideas, when they were already contemplating sin" (Oman, *The Sixteenth Century*, pp. 222–23).

25 Le Jeune, *J.R.*, IX, 113–15; XI, 255–57; XIII, 17.

26 Le Jeune, *J.R.*, XIV, 155. After early doubts (*J.R.*, IX, 119), Le Jeune admits: "All this makes me conjecture that the devil en-

ters into them and causes this throbbing, to more firmly bind them to himself . . ." (*J.R.*, XII, 229). Cf. also Brébeuf, *J.R.*, VIII, 123: the medicine men were "true Sorcerers, having access to the Devil."

27 Le Jeune, *J.R.*, XI, 239. Cf. also Le Jeune, *J.R.*, XI, 197, and XII, 169: "The devil worries and frightens them, every year causing evil reports to be circulated among them."

28 *J.R.*, XIII, 105.

29 *J.R.*, X, 177. Brébeuf's comment follows his brief description of the *Ononhwaroia*.

30 Fox, *Saint Ignace*, pp. 22–23.

31 Jerome Lalemant, *J.R.*, XVII, 167.

32 *Ibid.*, p. 165.

33 *Ibid.*, pp. 165–67.

34 *Ibid.*, p. 167.

35 *Ibid.*, X, 171.

36 *Ibid.*, p. 169.

37 *Ibid.*, XVII, 169.

38 *Ibid.*

39 *Ibid.*, p. 171.

40 *Ibid.*, p. 173.

41 *Ibid.*

42 Wrong and Langton, *Sagard's Long Journey*, p. 264. Cf. Lalemant, *J.R.*, XXIII, 53: "But, as among Christians, after each Saint has had his own day, there is a more solemn Festival in which all the Saints are honored in Company, so likewise in this Country, after each Demon has been honored in his town, there is a public celebration during Winter, at which all the Demons are honored on the same day. This celebration is called Ononhouaroia, or 'upsetting of brain' . . . ."

43 *J.R.*, XI, 251.

44 The *Lonouoyroya* (*Ononhwaroia*) is, says Sagard, "their great contrivance and the most fitting means, as they say, of driving out of their town or village the devils and evil spirits which cause or procure and bring all the diseases and infirmities they bear and suffer in body and in mind" (Wrong and Langton, *Sagard's Long Journey*, p. 264).

45 *J.R.*, XVII, 207.

46 *Ibid.*, pp. 177–79.

47 *Ibid.*, X, 201; cf. X, 175.

48 *Ibid.*, XVII, 181.

49   *Ibid.*, p. 182.
50   *Ibid.*, p. 185.
51   Brébeuf: *J.R.*, X, 183: ". . . after having recommended to them war feasts, *Ononhwaroia* . . . he [a monster wounded by one of the tribe] buried himself in the earth, and disappeared. Might this indeed have been some infernal spirit?" Lalemant: *J.R.*, XVII, 193–95: "A ceremony so solemn prompted us to search for its source and origin; and we have found, through the accounts of the old men, both of this village and that of St. Joseph, that the authors of this feast . . . are no others than the Demons." Cf. also *J.R.*, XVII, 153.
52   Lalemant, *J.R.*, XVII, 185.
53   *Ibid.*, p. 113.
54   For blankets to satisfy the desires of the sick and so complete the ritual (*Ibid.*, pp. 171–73).
55   *Ibid.*, pp. 193–97.
56   *Ibid.*, pp. 195–97.
57   *J.R.*, X, 169.
58   "The commonest device of myths today is that of selecting some single contributory factor to social life (such as race, culture, or economic class) and magnifying it into a sweeping explanation of history" (Marie Swabey, "The Leading Myths of Our Time," *Ethics*, XLIX [1939], p. 170). So also Werner Jaeger: "Every national and cultural myth is created in the same way—by narrowing the field of vision and extolling one particular nation's achievements to the pinnacle of the absolute" (*Paideia*, III, 77).
59   *J.R.*, VIII, 121.
60   For Sagard's observations, see ch. 5, "Cemeteries Preach Powerfully"; for Champlain's, see Grant, *Voyages of Samuel de Champlain*, p. 329.
61   Claude Dablon, *J.R.*, LV, 35. Similar comments by Dablon may be found in LIV, 297; LVI, 25; LVIII, 81; LX, 277. These passages, however, refer to Christian Hurons; tribal "charity and union" appear more clearly in Paul Ragueneau, *J.R.*, XXXV, 209.
62   Before Lady Montagu's championship of inoculation in the first quarter of the eighteenth century, specifics for smallpox (as for other diseases) were a witches' paradise: powdered toads were recommended in a letter of 1643 from a London doctor to Governor Winthrop of Connecticut (O. W. Holmes, "Receipts to Cure Various Disorders," *Mass. Hist. Soc., Proceeds.*, V [1860–1862], 381, quoted in Wertenbaker, *The First Americans*, p. 167, n. 2).

63 Cf. John H. Kennedy, *Jesuit and Savage in New France* (New Haven: Yale University Press, 1950), p. 159: "Later missionaries willingly recognized the tribal spirit of the Indians as their highest expression of group consciousness."

Chapter 5

1 *J.R.*, XXXIII, 203–9.
2 Wrong and Langton, *Sagard's Long Journey*, p. 281.
3 *J.R.*, X, 197–99.
4 Wrong and Langton, *Sagard's Long Journey*, p. 86.
5 *La vie admirable de Ste. Brigide* (1652), quoted in Henri Bremond, *A Literary History of Religious Thought in France*, trans. R. L. Montgomery (N.Y.: Macmillan, 1928), p. 194.
6 Campbell, *Pioneer Priests of North America*, II, 44–45.
7 Kenton, *The Indians of North America*, I, 378.
8 Wrong and Langton, *Sagard's Long Journey*, p. 85.
9 *J.R.*, XXII, 31.
10 *J.R.*, X, 281.
11 *Ibid.*, p. 283.
12 *Ibid.*
13 Kenton, *The Indians of North America*, p. 123, n. 1.
14 *Ibid.*, p. 287.
15 *Ibid.*, p. 293.
16 Wrong and Langton, *Sagard's Long Journey*, p. 295.
17 *Ibid.*
18 *Ibid.*, p. 297.
19 *Ibid.*, pp. 297–99.
20 *Ibid.*, p. 297.
21 Wrong and Langton, *Sagard's Long Journey*, p. 295.
22 *Ibid.*, p. 131.
23 *Ibid.*, p. 73.
24 *Ibid.*, p. 12.
25 *J.R.*, X, 215.
26 *Ibid.*, p. 265.
27 Wrong and Langton, *Sagard's Long Journey*, p. 264.
28 *J.R.*, III, ch. viii.
29 Kenton, *The Indians of North America*, I, 131.
30 *J.R.*, VI, 231.
31 *J.R.*, XXXII, 283.
32 Chinard, *L'Amérique et le rêve exotique*, pp. 140–41.
33 Wynne, *The Jesuit Martyrs of North America*, p. 66.
34 Quoted by Gilbert Chinard, "La Philosophie de J. J. Rousseau,"

Publications of the Modern Language Association, XXVI (1911), 488. Chinard adds: "Cette fois il y a plus que du dépit dans le ton de l'écrivain, c'est déjà tout le *Contrat Social,* et Rousseau ne dira rien de plus fort."

35 Chinard, *L'Amérique et le rêve exotique,* p. 143; cf. Introduction, p. vii: "L'apogée de ce mouvement (trouver le bonheur en se mettant à l'école des sauvages) est marqué par le Discours sur l'Inégalité, résultat de deux siècles et demi de discussions, de révoltes et de rêves utopiques."

Chapter 6

1 Bressani, *J.R.,* XXXIX, 25.

Chapter 7

1 It may well be that mass movements in the last decade—of Americans to the West coast and of English and French into central Africa—rival in volume and significance those of the nineteenth century into the Middle West, but the figures for this area are impressive by any comparison. To the nearly 5,000,000 living north of the Ohio River in 1850 (Hubbart, *The Older Middle West,* p. 5) there were added, for example, a large majority of the 1,250,000 Germans who came to the United States from 1856 to 1861; the 10,000 Norwegians settled about Chicago in 1860; most of the 105,326 Swedes who came in a single year (1882); and considerable numbers of the 236,000 Poles who migrated to America 1880–90 (Wittke, *We Who Built America,* pp. 188, 287, 262, and 420). These movements together with those of the Irish, Czechs, Slovaks and other peoples, offer unparalleled opportunities to investigate the impact of folk beliefs upon the historical development of a specific area.

2 The North Central area may be considered more precisely as three distinct zones: that drained by the Ohio River, the Great Lakes Basin, and the intervening prairies (Avery Craven, "The Advance of Civilization into the Middle West in the Period of Settlement," *Sources of Culture in the Middle West,* ed. Dixon Ryan Fox [N.Y. and London: D. Appleton Century Co., 1934], pp. 43–44).

3 Faulkner, *American Economic History,* pp. 297–98: "Two-fifths of the inhabitants of South Carolina . . . emigrated west of the mountains to form . . . the predominating element of the Old Northwest." Cf. also Hubbart, *The Older Middle West,* p. 4:

"There is every evidence that the West at that day [1833] was an appendage of the upland South, with Pennsylvania population influences a very important factor"; and Rusk, *The Literature of the Middle Western Frontier*, I, 16: " . . . the racial stock of early Kentucky . . . was to determine to no small extent the character of the frontier until after 1840."

4 Augmenting initial settlements, 90,000 from New England and 220,000 from New York moved into the Middle West in the decade of the 1850's (Billington, *Westward Expansion*, p. 599).

5 For the Pennsylvania Dutch infiltration into the Middle West, cf. G. M. Ludwig, "The Influence of the Pennsylvania Dutch in the Middle West," *Publications of the Pennsylvania Folklore Society*, X (1945), 14–56; Faust, *The German Element in the United States*, I, 129, 422, 427, 458; and Wittke, *We Who Built America*, p. 200, who mentions notable settlements in the Ohio counties of Stark, Tuscarawas, Wayne, and Holmes. Gustave Koerner (*Memoirs*, ed. Thomas J. McCormack [Cedar Rapids, Ia.: The Torch Press, Publishers, 1909], I, 322) comments in passing on the Pennsylvania Germans in Missouri.

6 Gates, *The Illinois Central Railroad*, pp. 176–77.

7 By 1850 the population center of the United States had moved to the western part of Ohio; from 1850 to 1855 the population of Michigan and Illinois had doubled, Wisconsin's had more than doubled, and Iowa's had trebled, largely because of immigration from abroad that reached its peak in 1854 (Hubbart, *The Older Middle West*, p. 91). In 1853 New York and Chicago were linked for the first time by rail. The six million acres sold by the government in Iowa, Wisconsin, and Michigan in 1855 (*ibid.*, p. 92) and the ten thousand McCormick reapers in use that year (Faulkner, *American Economic History*, p. 221) helped to make the Middle West the leading wheat producing area by 1859 (Shannon, *The Farmer's Last Frontier*, p. 163).

8 E.g., "If it rains on Monday, it will rain all the week." Folk beliefs mentioned here have been drawn chiefly from Thomas, *Kentucky Superstitions*.

9 The idealization of the farmer in the Middle West has been almost continuous from Crèvecœur to the present (cf. Dorothy A. Dondore, *The Prairie and the Making of Middle America* [Cedar Rapids, Ia.: The Torch Press, 1926]).

"The Western farmer had been told that he was not a peasant but a peer of the realm; that his contribution to society was basic, all others derivative and even parasitic in comparison . . . " (Smith, *Virgin Land*, p. 192). Representative of such sentiments is John Wentworth's assertion that "to [agriculture] we are indebted for the . . . development and welfare of the human species in every respect" (*Pr. Farm.*, III [1843], 113).

10 Except for sporadic eruptions, as in sixteenth- and seventeenth-century witchcraft, folk belief has only recently emerged from the subliminal realm of social consciousness. The peasantry, says Aubrey F. G. Bell (*Cervantes* [Norman: Univ. of Oklahoma Press, 1947], p. 130), has had "its individualism welded by the pressure of necessity into a discreet *consonancia* . . . "; it is doubtful if folk belief has hitherto enjoyed the opportunity afforded by the nineteenth-century Middle West of articulating its goals in ideological myth, applying its characteristic patterns of thought to social developments, and becoming sufficiently dominant to affect historical event.

11 Kardiner, *The Psychological Frontiers of Society*, p. 39.

12 The loves and sorrows of lords and ladies appear frequently, of course, in these ballads from the Southern Appalachians, but the people who sang and heard them must have identified themselves completely with the characters. "When I sing these songs," said Mrs. Carrie Grover, "it seems like I'm the feller it's all happening to" (Wells, *The Ballad Tree*, p. 307).

13 Before the development of well-established controls, the circuit-riding preacher was no ordinary stabilizing force; and the fear of hell which he excited at the camp meetings was a fear of social disruption as well as of personal torment. Cf. Eggleston, *The Circuit Rider*, p. 104: "The terribleness of Indian warfare, the relentlessness of their own revengefulness, the sudden lynchings, the abandoned wickedness of the lawless, and the ruthlessness of mobs of 'regulators' were a background upon which they founded the most materialistic conception of hell . . . ."

14 The significance of these well-known reactions for folk belief and for mythmaking processes is what contemporary psychoanalytical theory calls "the tendency for individuals to associate all aggressive and hate feelings with one object . . . and all love feelings with another . . ." (T. Maling, "Psycho-Analysis and the Study of Politics," *The Sociological Review* [April, 1939], quoted in Snyder and Wilson, *Roots of Political Behavior*, p. 7).

15 "The Fourth of July, in the Middle Period, was both a gala day and a national sabbath. The celebration of 'the Glorious Fourth'

manifested in some aspects the boisterous extravagances of the camp meetings of evangelical Protestantism and in others the austere dignity of a Calvinist service of worship" (Gabriel, *The Course of American Democratic Thought*, p. 94).

16 Hubbart, *The Older Middle West*, p. 76.

17 Billington, *Westward Expansion*, p. 609 and Cole, *The Irrepressible Conflict*, p. 129.

18 An extreme illustration is Timothy Flint's report of a Western preacher's exclamation: " . . . heaven is a Kentuck of a place" (Clark, *The West in American History*, p. 380).

19 Circulars were widely distributed, and agents attended county fairs and public meetings (Gates, *The Illinois Central Railroad*, p. 178).

20 Karl T. Griesinger, *Lebende Bilder aus Amerika* (1858), in Handlin, *This Was America*, p. 264.

21 *Ibid.*

22 Gates, *The Illinois Central Railroad*, p. 103. In 1856, nine million acres were in the hands of small businessmen, professional speculators, or Eastern capitalists (pp. 110–11). The Swedes, too, were fearful of Yankee speculators in Illinois (Benson and Hedin, *Americans From Sweden*, p. 84).

23 Cf. Shannon, *The Farmer's Last Frontier*, p. 9: "In the best farming regions of Europe the tendency is to cherish old soils because the family, through generations, has learned to understand them. This also helps to account for the greater acreage production of those areas."

24 *Hosianna, ein Liederbuch für Sonntagschulen*, . . . (published with *Inbeltöne, eine Sammlung von Liedern und Melodien*, . . . [Cleveland: Thomas & Mattill, 1896] p. 26). The couplet refers to *die himmlische Heimath*—a significant concept though a familiar one, e.g., in such hymnbooks as *Silberklänge* (Cleveland, 1899), *Lieder-Perlen* (St. Louis, 1894), or *Die Perle* (Cincinnati, 1894). Social and religious connotations attach to the word "home" in every language, of course; but among immigrants it had a special force.

25 *Hosianna*, pp. 39, 167; *Inbeltöne*, p. 162.

26 Faust, *The German Element*, II, 55.

27 This is not to minimize the subtle and pervasive effects of language in culture, the untranslatable words carrying with them centuries of development, nor to disparage the influence of the immigrant press as a "halfway house" to Americanization (cf.

Blegen, *Grass Roots History*, p. 110; Park, *The Immigrant Press and Its Control*, p. 79, and Benson and Hedin, *Americans From Sweden*, p. 319), nor again to underestimate the importance of the immigrant societies and brotherhoods—the Sokols, Turnverein, Svea Society, Gymanfa Ganu, etc. These cultural concomitants, however, were less fundamental for immigrant farmers than their agricultural way of life. So long, moreover, as church services were conducted in the native tongue, the use of English in other activities was generally encouraged.

28 Gates, *The Illinois Central Railroad*, pp. 189–90, and Wittke, *We Who Built America*, p. 268. Agents were stationed in Norway and Sweden by David A. Neal, a director of the railroad to promote immigration. The railroad's interest in the Swedes is further illustrated by the sale of lands to Rev. Nilsson Hasselquist as a site for the Illinois State University.

29 Perhaps because native and immigrant folk reactions to the homestead appear on the surface so obvious or so closely involved with more significant developments, no special study has been made on the subject from the very extensive materials in state historical collections, foreign-language newspapers, county histories, etc.

30 The summary Faust (*The German Element*, II, 28–30) gives of the qualities of the Pennsylvania Dutch and later German immigrant farmers may with equal truth be applied to, say, the Swedes, Norwegians, or Bohemians. "In farming the Pennsylvania Dutch could always outlast the English or the Scotch-Irish, but not the Bohemians. The thrift, industry, and devotion to the soil of these Europeans are just as pronounced as those attributed to the Pennsylvania Dutch" (G. M. Ludwig, "The Influence of the Pennsylvania Dutch in the Middle West," *Publications of the Pennsylvania Folklore Society*, X [1945], 30).

31 III (1843), 16, 99, 4, 175, and 6.

32 *Ibid.*, III, 113; IV (1844), 83, 148–49.

33 Gates, *The Illinois Central Railroad*, p. 112.

34 Among Yankee lumbermen David Whitney and Orrin W. Robinson prospered in Michigan and Moses Strong and Philetus Sawyer in Wisconsin; William Austin Burt in the Superior region and Samuel L. Mather, organizer of the Cleveland Iron Mining Company, promoted the exploitation of the newly developed ore resources (Holbrook, *The Yankee Exodus, passim*).

35 *Pr. Farm.*, III (1843), 175.

36 Dillaway, *The Gospel of Emerson*, pp. 73–74.
37 Eleven major lines helped to give Illinois more railroad mileage than any other state except Ohio (Gates, *The Illinois Central Railroad*, pp. 88–89).
38 Faulkner, *American Economic History*, pp. 220–21.
39 Shannon (*The Farmer's Last Frontier*, p. 182) gives 1863 as the date on which Chicago may be said to have wrested the lead from Cincinnati.
40 Quoted in Sandburg, *Abraham Lincoln: The Prairie Years*, p. 288.
41 By 1860 "the Great Valley" had been extended to include the industrial North. Milburn (*Pioneers, Preachers and People*, p. 449) after commenting on the rapid growth of cities and marts in the Old Northwest, speaks of "the Nation of the Valley"; Wright (*Chicago: Past, Present, Future*, foreword) sums up current thinking in the phrase "the Great Interior." With regard to national unity, ". . . on the eve of the crisis of 1860, the agrarian myth of the garden and the newer calculus of technological change led to the same conclusion" (Smith, *The Virgin Land*, p. 162).
42 Hubbart, *The Older Middle West*, p. 116.
43 Douglas's support of the homestead measures, a free-soil angle of popular sovereignty, and of railroad land grants were planks in his typically Western platform of promoting the unity of North and South, developing the interior, and encouraging expansion westward.
44 Milburn, *Pioneers, Preachers and People*, pp. 451, 459, 460.
45 The railroad's advertising became, in the hands of Lieutenant-Governor Francis Hoffman (who had come to America in 1839), extremely effective: in four years he sold 80,000 acres to Germans from other Middle Western States and from abroad. As a result, the Illinois counties of Washington, Marion, Effingham, Shelby, and Cumberland were largely German (Gates, *The Illinois Central Railroad*, pp. 201–5).
46 Cole, *The Irrepressible Conflict*, p. 112
47 Hubbart, *The Older Middle West*, p. 110.
48 Cole, *The Irrepressible Conflict*, p. 252.
49 Cf. Buck, *The Granger Movement*, p. 74.
50 Quoted in Cole, *The Irrepressible Conflict*, p. 112. Italics mine.
51 Koerner, *Memoirs*, I, 417; cf. p. 483; Faust, *The German Element in the United States*, II, 128–29; Hubbart, *The Older Middle West*, p. 144.

52 *Ten Years of Preacher-Life*, pp. 41–42.
53 Carl Sandburg, *Abraham Lincoln: The Prairie Years*, pp. 216–17.
54 Strickland, *Peter Cartwright*, p. 172.
55 Letter to H. L. Pierce and others, April 6, 1859 (Basler, *Abraham Lincoln*, p. 489).
56 Speech in Reply to Douglas at Chicago, July 19, 1858 (Basler, *Abraham Lincoln*, pp. 390, 401–2).
57 "But I believe, with our most excellent Discipline, that we should 'be ashamed of nothing but sin' " (Strickland, *Peter Cartwright*, p. 280).
58 Basler, *Abraham Lincoln*, pp. 84, 140.
59 *Ibid.*, pp. 401–2.
60 *Ibid.*, pp. 274–75.
61 Speech at Peoria in Reply to Senator Douglas, October 16, 1854 (*Ibid.*, p. 312).
62 *Ibid.*, p. 308.
63 Speech in Reply to Douglas at Springfield, Ill., July 17, 1858 (*Ibid.*, p. 420).
64 Speech at Peoria in Reply to Senator Douglas, October 16, 1854 (*Ibid.*, p. 309), and "A House Divided," Speech Delivered at Springfield, Ill., June 16, 1858 (*Ibid.*, p. 373).
65 E.g., Lincoln "likened a man's character [in a law case at Concord] . . . to a piece of white cloth, which . . . could be washed . . . ; whereas the character of the girl . . . was like a broken and shattered bottle . . . which could not be restored . . . " (Sandburg, *Abraham Lincoln: The Prairie Years*, p. 105).
66 Basler, *Abraham Lincoln*, pp. 76–81.
67 "The doctrine of self-government is right—absolutely and eternally right—but it has no just application . . . " in Douglas's interpretation (Speech at Peoria, October 16, 1854 [Basler, *Abraham Lincoln*, p. 303]).
68 Strickland, *Peter Cartwright*, pp. 376, 487.
69 " . . . my ancient faith teaches me that 'all men are created equal' . . . " (Basler, *Abraham Lincoln*, p. 303).
70 *Children of the Market Place*, p. 433 (quoted in Hubbart, *The Older Middle West*, p. 141).
71 Republicans emphasized the similarity in the doubtful counties of Indiana and Illinois (Hubbart, *Older Middle West*, p. 143).

Chapter 8

1 Such amulets and other forms of white magic were commonly used by powwow doctors among the Pennsylvania Germans during much of the nineteenth century and occasionally in the twentieth, although often "the sick man turned to the powwow doctor as a drowning man clutches at a straw" and was careful not to publicize it (Klees, *The Pennsylvania Dutch,* pp. 302–3).

2 The comments of the editor, Robert B. Thomas, in the *Farmer's Almanack,* Calendar of March, 1830 (as quoted in Kittredge, *The Old Farmer,* p. 206) aptly illustrate both the growing skepticism and the prevalence of rural folk belief: "Signs and omens and prognostics continually fill the minds of some . . . . A silly old woman . . . happened to get a first sight of the new moon over her left shoulder, and it made her sad and glum through the month . . . . Farmer Bluejoint has nailed an Ass's shoe to his hogsty to keep the evil spirit from his herd of swine . . . . What power has superstition!"

3 "The chief logical principle in folklore is analogy," Archer Taylor observes. "In folk medicine, it is called the principle of sympathetic magic . . . . Analogy is a very old method of reasoning . . . . It underlies much of our own thinking . . . " ("The Problems of Folklore," *Journal of American Folklore,* LIX [1946], 104). Perhaps the earliest analogy was the belief that the universe, like man, had a soul; in recent history the principle appears in homeopathy, for example, or in the notion of a society evolving like Darwin's species.

4 The force of analogy is apparent also in Pennsylvania German folk medicine, which included the belief that dogwood bark acted either as an emetic or as a purgative depending upon whether the bark were stripped up or down (W. F. Hoffman, "Folklore of the Pennsylvania Germans," *Journal of American Folklore,* II [1889], 29).

5 *Farmer's Almanack,* Calendar of May, 1804, as quoted by Kittredge, *The Old Farmer,* p. 85.

6 Cobwebs to foretell rain is a bit of almanac weather-lore (Klees, *The Pennsylvania Dutch,* p. 310). The hoot of an owl at dusk, the cry of a peacock, whippoorwill, killdeer, cuckoo, turtledove —all these were signs of rain (William J. Rupp, *Bird Names and Bird Lore Among the Pennsylvania Germans,* Part IV: "Beliefs,

Superstitions and Sayings," in Pennsylvania German Society, *Proceedings and Addresses* [Norristown, Pa., 1946], LII, 245).

7 *Farmer's Almanack* for 1836, as quoted by Kittredge, *The Old Farmer,* p. 248: Jonathan Timbertoes to his old Dutch hostess, "who had agreed to entertain him under the roof of her log cottage, for and in consideration of a bran new tin milk-pan."

8 *New-England Almanack* for 1836. Echoes appear in the *Agricultural Almanac* for 1854: "Who dainties love, shall beggars prove."

9 Berks County, Pennsylvania, newspaper, 1841–63.

10 Where Cutler and Generals Rufus Putnam and Benjamin Tupper organized (1786) the Ohio Company of Associates.

11 The attractions of Indiana and Illinois were glowingly advertised in Henry W. Ellsworth's *Valley of the Upper Wabash* (N.Y.: Pratt, Robinson and Co., 1838).

12 Green Bay (Wis.) *Intelligencer,* April 9, 1835, No. 13, p. 3: "Coming from the south, the 'yankees,' anticipating the day of sale, have penetrated as far north as the Mannitowock River . . . seizing upon the choice and commanding sites, and 'making claims.'"

13 Paul W. Gates, "The Role of the Land Speculator in Western Development," *Pennsylvania Magazine of History and Biography,* LXVI (1942), 321.

14 Jared Elliot, *Essays Upon Field-Husbandry in New-England* (Boston, 1760), pp. 123–24, as quoted in Kittredge, *The Old Farmer,* p. 312.

15 "And Moses sent them to spy out the land of Canaan" (in the considerations for locating a colony drawn up by the Union Colony of E. Poultney, Vermont, quoted in Holbrook, *The Yankee Exodus,* p. 79). Yankee notions peddlers "surveyed the possibilities of various regions and, on returning home, reported their findings. They were the scouts for that great migration . . . of the hardy New England stock which first peopled the frontiers . . . . Scarcely a town in New England but was represented on the road by one or more itinerants . . . . Such were the young men who brought back to their New England homes news of the land Manasseh Cutler led his people to in the Marietta region of the Northwest Territory" (Wright, *Hawkers and Walkers in Early America,* p. 27).

16 *Agricultural Almanac, for the Year 1840* (Lancaster, Penna., Printed and Sold by John Bear).

17 Wood, *The Pennsylvania Germans,* p. 52.

18 W. F. Hoffman, "Folklore of the Pennsylvania Germans," *Journal of American Folklore*, I (1888), 198.

19 Dorson, *Jonathan Draws the Long Bow*, pp. 257–58.

20 C. Grant Loomis, "Sylvester Judd's New England Lore," *Journal of American Folklore*, LX (1947), 155, quoted from Judd's novel, *Margaret* (Boston: Jordan and Wiley, 1845), II, 97.

21 "This practical expression of mutual aid must not be overlooked in accounts which try to explain the stability of these people in their farming activities" (Wood, *The Pennsylvania Germans*, p. 45).

22 From Sylvester Judd's novel *Margaret*, quoted in C. Grant Loomis, "Sylvester Judd's New England Lore," *Journal of American Folklore*, LX (1947), 154. A fuller quotation will suggest the skeptical tone of the mid-nineteenth century: "There are no fairies in our meadows, and no elves to spirit away our children . . . . Our rivers harbor no nereids, they run on the Sabbath, are all sacred alike, Mill Brook as the Ganges . . . . We have no resorts for pilgrims . . . no summits looking into paradise. We have no traditions, legends, fables, and scarcely a history . . . . The Devil haunts our theology, not our houses . . . . No hideous ghosts appear at cock-crowing. Witches have quite vanished, and omens from sneezing and itching must soon follow . . . . Astrology, Alchemy, Physiognomy, and Necromancy are fast dying out, and Animal Magnetism has not ventured across the sea . . . . In our churchyards, bodies are buried on the North as well as on the South side" (*Margaret*, II, 39–40).

23 Cf. Paul W. Gates, "The Role of the Land Speculator in Western Development," *Pennsylvania Magazine of History and Biography*, LXVI (1942), 332: "The successful land dealer of one generation became the banker, the local political oracle and office holder or the country squire of the next. Scarcely a city or country town in the West but had its first family whose fortune had been made by shrewd selection of lands and their subsequent sale or rental to later comers."

24 *The Pennsylvania Dutch*, p. 315.

25 Cf. Ralph Wood, *The Pennsylvania Germans*, p. 33: "[The German farmer] looked upon his calling as a preferred way of life and not primarily as a commercial occupation . . . "; and p. 44: "He preferred his agricultural way of life because he felt that it had divine approval."

26 "Seemingly, the 'Milch Cow' possessed rights, too, according to a

York county will of 1766: 'The above Menshioned Cow is to goo [go] in the Same pasture that my Sons Cows goos in' " (Russell W. Gilbert, "The Pennsylvania German in His Will," *The American-German Review*, XVII [1951], 25–26).

27 Rupp, *Bird Names*, pp. 241–42.

28 "To Pastorius, and to most of his Pennsylvania German contemporaries, the moral fiber of human society depended upon man's relationship to the earth" (E. Gordon Alderfer, "Pastorius and the Origins of Pennsylvania German Culture," *The American-German Review*, XVII [1951], 10).

29 In philosophies and myths of protest against the *status quo* it is difficult to draw a sharp distinction between the rational and the romantic. The articulated protest may stem, of course, either from an emotional reaction to, or a reasoned analysis of, social ills; it turns to an idealized, romantic past generally when there is small anticipation of reform in the near future. But when nothing seems to stand in the way of making plans and bringing them to realization—of drawing blueprints and seeing them take shape in bridges, canals, or cities, the myth looks ahead, "justified" pragmatically (for the early American) by the certainty of accomplishment assured by political freedom and a wealth of national resources.

30 The view of the *Republic* as a synthesis of the four cardinal virtues, each of which had prevailed in a particular era of Greek history, has been developed by Jaeger, *Paideia*. The *Republic* may be a rational *tour de force*, but its frame of reference is romantic.

31 Haliburton, *Sam Slick's Wise Saws*, II, 168.

32 *Ibid.*, p. 2.

33 *Ibid.*, I, 304.

34 *Ibid.*, II, 34.

35 "Remarks on National Literature," *The Works of William E. Channing, D.D.* (Boston: American Unitarian Association, 1878), p. 131.

36 Lucy, Wife of Ethan Allen, *The History of the White Mountains from the First Settlement of Upper Coos and Pequaket*, as quoted in Botkin, *A Treasury of New England Folklore*, pp. 166–67.

37 The culture hero of the Pennsylvania German, in contrast, was the farmer whose land grew richer year by year, whose sons raised huge barns in the valley about him, or whose horses drew cargo from Philadelphia to Pittsburgh.

38 R. W. B. Lewis, "The Danger of Innocence," *Yale Review,* XXXIX (1950), 474.

39 Cf. Emerson's comment: "Time and space are but physiological colors which the eye makes . . ." (Dillaway, *The Gospel of Emerson,* p. 17).

40 "Speculation in real estate . . . has been the ruling idea and occupation of the Western mind . . . . The people of the West became dealers in land, rather than its cultivators. Scorning cheap clocks, wooden nutmegs, and apple-parers, the Yankee, stepping from the almost ridiculous to the decidedly sublime, went out West, and traded in the progress of the country" (D. W. Mitchell, *Ten Years in the United States: Being an English-man's View of Men and Things in the North and South* [London, 1862], p. 325, quoted in Harold U. Faulkner, *American Economic History* [6th ed., N.Y. and London: Harper & Bros., 1949], pp. 205–6).

41 Cf. Emerson: "As the granite comes to the surface and towers into the highest mountains, and, if we dig down, we find it below the superficial strata, so in all the details of our domestic or civil life is hidden the elemental reality . . ." (Dillaway, *The Gospel of Emerson,* p. 24).

42 "The true man, the 'man in man,' as Plato beautifully expresses the new idea, is the intellectual part of the soul" (Jaeger, *Paideia,* II, 353).

43 "Emerson, like the commercial drummer, made his living by travelling . . . vending his intellectual wares" (Gabriel, *The Course of American Democratic Thought,* p. 41).

44 Harriet Beecher Stowe's well-known comment bears repeating: "If there is a golden calf worshipped in our sanctified New England, its name is Logic . . . and I must say there is no trap for the Yankee like the logic-trap" (*Oldtown Folks* [Boston, 1897], p. 224, quoted in Perry Miller, *The New England Mind* [N.Y.: Macmillan, 1939], p. 115).

45 Emerson was referring to Nature rather than to the transcendental One, but the larger concept was anticipated in the essay "Nature."

46 "There, in the West, he [Emerson] thought, lay nature sleeping . . . . But there, where stars and woods and hills abounded, with all things still untried, could one not foresee a society . . . that . . . lived by the law of love and justice?" (Brooks, *The Flowering of New England, 1815–1865,* p. 537).

47 The first quotation is from "Over-Soul" (Dillaway, *The Gospel of*

Emerson, p. 11). Cf. also Perry Miller: ". . . Protestantism in its Calvinistic form encouraged the shift of emphasis in theology and philosophy from contemplation to action, from beatitude to utility" (*The New England Mind,* p. 173). The second and third quotations are from Dillaway, *The Gospel of Emerson,* pp. 21, 57.

48 "Self-Reliance" (*Ibid.,* pp. 49–50). Cf. also "Intellect": "He in whom the love of truth predominates will keep himself aloof from all moorings, and afloat"; and "Love": "He does not longer appertain to his family and society: *he* is somewhat; *he* is a person; *he* is a soul" (*Ibid.,* pp. 53–54).

49 *Ibid.,* p. 41.

50 "Circles" (*Ibid.,* p. 9).

51 *Ibid.,* pp. 73–74. Cf. also *ibid.,* p. 56: "We esteem nations important, until we discover that a few individuals much more concern us; then, later, that it is not at last a few individuals, or any sacred heroes, but the lowliness, the outpouring, the large equality to truth of a single mind,—as if in the narrow walls of a human heart the whole realm of truth, the world of morals, the tribunal by which the universe is judged, found room to exist."

52 "Emerson, evolving a philosophical description of the universe, drew upon the railroad for evidence and illustration to uphold his transcendentalist views of a benevolent World-Soul" (G. Ferris Cronkhite, "The Transcendental Railroad," *The New England Quarterly,* XXIV, 328). Cf. also p. 311: "In developing an independent and integrated American culture, the West would play a crucial role—and so would the railroad . . . ." For Walt Whitman, too, the railroad was a symbol: among other inventions, it would restore man's lost harmony with nature (Smith, *Virgin Land,* p. 47).

53 To the Transcendentalist, "the doctrine of the moral order was, in effect, a doctrine of cosmic constitutionalism" (Ralph H. Gabriel, *The Course of American Democratic Thought,* p. 18). "The Constitution was increasingly regarded as an incarnation of that law and order so essential to the counting-house, the factory, and the mercantile establishment" (Curti, *Growth of American Thought,* p. 405).

54 Cf. Klees, *The Pennsylvania Dutch,* p. 59: "One cannot help wishing that they [the Amish] had for the country as a whole some of the same feeling of responsibility they have for the members of their own sect." In contrast with the Yankees' "private

enterprise and public service," the Pennsylvania Germans practiced "private service and public enterprise."

Chapter 9

1 J. A. Wight's suggestion for a motto in an address before the Union Society at the annual Cattle Show at Plainfield, Ill., Oct. 17, 1844, published in the *Pr. Farm.*, IV (Dec., 1844), 279.

2 Milburn, *Ten Years of Preacher-Life*, p. 54: ". . . many a hymn have I sung, and many a sermon have I preached to him [the horse]."

3 Strickland, *Peter Cartwright*, p. 84. Cartwright rode the Scioto Circuit in 1805–6.

4 Havighurst, *Land of Promise*, p. 40.

5 Milburn, *Ten Years of Preacher-Life*, p. 58.

6 *Ibid.*, p. 78; cf. Boatright, *Folk Laughter*, p. 130, who quotes Henry Fowler, *The American Pulpit* (N.Y., 1856): "All the varied experiences with nature, with people, in conversation, by anecdote, on the road, in the cabin, through the field, are made to contribute to [the sermon's] life."

7 Strickland, *Peter Cartwright*, p. 145.

8 Milburn, *Pioneers, Preachers and People*, p. 403.

9 Strickland, *Peter Cartwright*, p. 465.

10 Boatright, *Folk Laughter*, pp. 152, 157.

11 Milburn, *Ten Years of Preacher-Life*, pp. 42, 91.

12 Milburn, *Pioneers, Preachers and People*, p. 404.

13 Thomas, *Kentucky Superstitions:* p. 34 (#292), communion table; p. 66 (#653), snow; p. 10 (#13), green veil; p. 11 (#23), heavy hair; p. 73 (#754), casket.

14 Cf. Eggleston, *The Circuit Rider*, p. 204.

15 Strickland, *Peter Cartwright*, p. 486.

16 Milburn, *Ten Years of Preacher-Life*, p. 72.

17 Eggleston, *The Circuit Rider*, p. 259.

18 Thomas, *Kentucky Superstitions:* p. 155 (#1924), dream of the dead; p. 78 (#92), clear eyes; cf. p. 153 (#1889), "Dreams go by contraries."

19 *Ibid.:* p. 187 (#2397), cold winter; p. 188 (#2419), March lamb; p. 188 (#2422), March mists.

20 *Ibid.:* p. 187 (#2408), February days; p. 188 (#2411), February thunder; cf. p. 190 (#2453), "The number of fogs in summer indicates the number of snows in winter."

21 *Ibid.:* p. 190 (#2460) and 214 (#2825); cf. p. 199 (#2592), "The number of days old the moon is when it snows for the first time is the number of times it will snow that year," and p. 189 (#2440), "If it rains on July first, it will rain seventeen days in the month."

22 Strickland, *Peter Cartwright,* p. 99.

23 Milburn, *Ten Years of Preacher-Life,* p. 197.

24 Strickland, *Peter Cartwright,* p. 442.

25 *Ibid.,* p. 393.

26 Wells, *The Ballad Tree,* p. 275.

27 Eddy, *Ballads and Songs From Ohio:* pp. 135–36 (#43), "Old Grumble" (or "Further Grumble"); p. 146 (#48), "No, Sir"; and p. 50 (#15), "Little Musgrave and Lady Barnard."

28 Gardner and Chickering, *Ballads and Songs of Southern Michigan,* p. 94, "The Sailor Boy."

29 Eggleston, *The Circuit Rider,* p. 330.

30 Eddy, *Ballads and Songs From Ohio:* p. 305 (# 140), "Wicked Polly"; and p. 159 (#56), "Pretty Polly."

31 Cf. *ibid.:* p. 34 (#12), "Sweet William"; p. 227 (#102), "The Green Fields and Meadows"; and p. 120 (#39), "The Keys of Heaven."

32 Wells, *The Ballad Tree,* p. 84.

33 Philbrick, *Understanding English,* p. 66.

34 For descriptions of typical camp meetings, cf. Milburn, *Ten Years of Preacher-Life,* pp. 62–63; Strickland, *Peter Cartwright,* pp. 37, 45; Eggleston, *The Circuit Rider,* p. 256; Sweet, *Circuit-Rider Days,* p. 34; Clark, *The West in American History,* pp. 389–90; Charles A. Johnson, "Frontier Camp Meeting: Contemporary and Historical Appraisals, 1805–1840," *Mississippi Valley Historical Review,* XXXVII (June, 1950), 101; and Davenport, *Primitive Traits in Religious Revivals,* pp. 76–77.

35 Cf. Thomas, *Kentucky Superstitions,* p. 27 (#225): "If you sleep with a Bible under your head three successive nights, you will dream whom you shall marry."

36 *Ibid.,* p. 191 (#2465).

37 Sweet, *Circuit-Rider Days,* p. 266.

38 Eggleston, *The Circuit Rider,* p. 192.

39 Cf. Sweet, *Circuit-Rider Days,* p. 82: ". . . it was thought by many that more devils lurked in catgut and horsehair than Luther ever dreamed of."

40 The last four hymns are from Eggleston, *The Circuit Rider*, pp. 109, 107, 117, and 166.
41 Rourke, *American Humor*, p. 21.
42 Eggleston, *The Circuit Rider*, p. 162.
43 *Ibid.*, p. 117.
44 Cf. Sweet, *Circuit-Rider Days*, p. 34.
45 Strickland, *Peter Cartwright*, pp. 467, 145, and 400.
46 Thomas, *Kentucky Superstitions:* p. 96 (#1096), "For nose-bleeding, hold a Bible over the sufferer's head and read Ezekiel 16:6 three times"; and p. 24 (#195).
47 Strickland, *Peter Cartwright*, p. 451.
48 *Ibid.*, p. 181.
49 Milburn, *Pioneers, Preachers and People*, p. 418.
50 Eggleston, *The Circuit Rider*, pp. 74, 262.
51 Louise Pound, *American Ballads and Songs* (N.Y.: Scribner's, 1922), p. xviii.
52 Strickland, *Peter Cartwright*, pp. 192, 121, 400, 236, 444.
53 *Ibid.*, pp. 324, 448.
54 *Ibid.*, pp. 318, 447–48.
55 *Ibid.*, pp. 313, 31.
56 *Ibid.*, p. 218 ("to tie the puckering strings of their mouths"—i.e., to make them cry) and p. 400; Eggleston, *The Circuit Rider*, p. 163.
57 Wells, *The Ballad Tree*, p. 87.
58 Rourke, *American Humor*, p. 56.
59 Strickland, *Peter Cartwright*, pp. 223, 519, 494; cf. Rourke, *American Humor*, p. 135: "'New, new . . . make all things new.' The enchanting cry resounded through all this ecstasy of faith."
60 Eggleston, *The Circuit Rider*, p. 272.
61 Strickland, *Peter Cartwright*, p. 63.
62 Milburn, *Pioneers, Preachers and People*, p. 449; cf. p. 452, ". . . that mighty Hand which guides the fates of the Valley"; and p. 461, "So far as human foresight can discern, a future of marvellous grandeur and power awaits the Nation of the Valley."

Chapter 10

1 Fifth Annual Fair of the Tazewell County Agricultural Society, on September 29–30, 1854 (*Peoria Daily Press*, September 25, 1854). All details of the fair, including the names of persons

mentioned in the following pages, have been taken from *TISAS*, I, 242–65.

2   *TISAS*, I, 432, in a communication (Dec. 21, 1853) addressed to Bronson Murray, Corresponding Secretary, Illinois State Agricultural Society.

3   Pease, *The Frontier State, 1818–1848*, p. 178.

4   Adapted from Harry E. Pratt, ed., *Illinois as Lincoln Knew It: A Boston Reporter's Record of a Trip in 1847* (Springfield, Ill., 1938), p. 31.

5   Richard L. Power comments on the Yankee innovation of planting shade and fruit trees at Tremont (*Planting Corn Belt Culture*, p. 97).

6   Sandburg, *Abraham Lincoln: The Prairie Years*, p. 309. This was McCormick's estimate.

7   August, 1851, p. 355.

8   August 18, 1854: editorial addressed "To the Farmers of Peoria, Tazewell, Woodford, Marshall, Bureau, Stark, Henry, Knox and Fulton Counties" entitled "The State Fair."

9   *Illinois: A Descriptive and Historical Guide* (American Guide Series), p. 571.

10 Pro-Douglas slogans appeared in the *Peoria Daily Press*, August 23 and 24, and September 20, 23, and 25, 1854; the criticism of Douglas is from the *Peoria Weekly Republican*, September 29, 1854; here too is an instance of German opposition to the Nebraska Bill, September 16. Arthur C. Cole notes (*The Era of the Civil War, 1848–1870*, pp. 123–24) German activity in Tazewell (Pekin) and the appeal of the *Illinois Staats-Zeitung* for an American "liberty party."

11 Settlers in the bottomlands ("Egypt") of southern Illinois. Egypt was satirized as a land of "rich sile, an' big swamps, of tall corn and snortin' muskeeters, of human men and big turnips, of wild oxen and all-fired gals" (*Yankee Notions*, VI [March, 1857], 84–85, quoted in Power, *Planting Corn Belt Culture*, p. 86).

12 Cf. the editorial in the *Pr. Farm.*, August, 1855, pp. 233–34.

13 Edward Bates, in a speech to the Missouri Agricultural Society in the *National Intelligencer*, October 13, 1855.

14 *TISAS*, I, 252–65, carries Wight's address. Punctuation has been simplified and modernized.

15 Bruno Snell finds much the same kind of contrast between mythical and logical thought: ". . . the truth of logical thought . . . requires to be sought, to be investigated, pondered . . . ; mythi-

cal images, on the other hand, reveal to us of themselves their full context and significance . . . . Mythical thought requires receptivity; logic cannot exist without activity" (*The Discovery of the Mind*, p. 224).

16 *TISAS*, I, 54–55. Jonathan B. Turner speaks again (p. 58) of "the great locomotive power of science—mind."

17 Cf. the article of December, 1854, "Our Homes," by T. Mc-Whorter, Millersburg, Ill. (*TISAS*, I, 452). The low value farmers placed on their homesteads was a constant complaint; cf., e.g. (*ibid.* p. 458), J. P. Kirtland, "On the Development and Cultivation of an Elevated and Correct Taste Among the Farming Community": "the old home has no hold on their affections—or at least not enough to overcome the novelty of a new one." Cf. also Suel Foster: "It is a crying evil among our western farmers that they value their Homesteads too low" (*Pr. Farm.*, September, 1854, p. 325).

18 These quotations, in order, are from *TISAS*, I, 304 (Wight's address to the North-Western Fruit Growers' Association, October 4, 1853); *ibid.*, p. 452 (McWhorter, "Our Homes"); *ibid.*, p. 305 (address to the Fruit Growers); *Pr. Farm.*, June, 1850, p. 187 ("The Vignette," by J. H., Athens, Ill.); *TISAS*, I, 267 (Gooding, address at the Will Co. Fair, October 6, 1853); *ibid.*, p. 304 (address to the Fruit Growers. Wight added that "horticulture fosters a naturalness and simplicity of character").

19 Cf. J. B. Turner, *TISAS*, I, 59: ". . . a hard-handed able-bodied, strong-minded, whole-souled, all-knowing, all-conquering man, worthy of himself and of the God who made him such . . . ."

20 "Knowledge is happiness," said Wight; "the farmer who best understands his business and gives most intelligent thought to it is happiest in it" (*TISAS*, I, 257).

21 *Ibid.*, p. 59.

22 *Ibid.*, p. 56: shall the laborer "not here . . . begin to wield the powers of education and intellect for his INDUSTRIAL and SOCIAL salvation?"

23 *Ibid.*, p. 401: address to the League on Industrial Education.

24 Becker, *Modern Democracy*, p. 38.

25 J. B. Turner (*TISAS*, I, 58).

26 *Ibid.*, p. 59.

27 *Pr. Farm.*, October, 1854, p. 361.

Chapter 11

1 The Chaplain's prayer at the opening of the Grange meeting, from Kelley, *Manual of Subordinate Granges*, p. 3.

2 *Ia. Home.*, Mar. 13, 1874, p. 85: "The Grange is certainly a very proper place for the faint hearted to enter in search of life partners." Unless otherwise noted, all references to the *Ia. Home* are to Vol. XIX (1874).

3 All business meetings were confined to the fourth degree: cf. *Constitutions of the Patrons of Husbandry*, issued by the National Grange and the Iowa State Grange (Des Moines: Carter, Hussey, and Curl, 1873), and the *Pr. Farm.*, Feb. 14, 1874, p. 51. Unless otherwise noted, all references to the *Pr. Farm.* are to Vol. XLV (1874).

4 For reports of the plight of Osceola, Lyon, Sioux, and O'Brien Counties, see *Pr. Farm.*, Jan. 10, p. 1. Cf. also Jan. 24, p. 32, Weaver, *Past and Present of Jasper County*, I, 108, and *Ia. Home.*, Jan. 23, p. 29.

5 On co-operative enterprises in Jasper Co., see *History of Jasper County* (Chicago: Western Historical Co., 1878), p. 443, and Weaver, *Past and Present of Jasper County*, I, 108. For Murphy's connections with such enterprises and with the Grange, see Weaver, *ibid.*, II, 926 and *Ia. Home.*, Jan. 10, p. 21.

6 *Ia. Home.*, Jan. 9, p. 13.

7 "G. F. Foster, Son & McFarren, Flags and Banners, Society and Grange Regalias, No. 4 South Market St., Chic." (*Ia. Home.*, June 5, p. 183).

8 For savings of 20%–50% on groceries, sewing machines, implements, etc. effected by state agents of the Grange and gains in the sale of farm produce and stock, see *Pr. Farm.*, Jan. 10, p. 11, *Ia. Home.*, June 5, p. 179, Mildred Throne, "The Grange in Iowa, 1868–1875," *Iowa Journal of History*, XLVII (Oct., 1949), 305, W. A. Anderson, "The Granger Movement in the Middle West With Especial Reference to Iowa," *Iowa Journal of History and Politics*, XXII (Jan., 1924), 35–37, and Buck, *The Granger Movement*, p. 241. So successful was the co-ordination of buying that Dudley Adams of Iowa, National Master of the Grange, said (in Throne, "The Grange in Iowa," p. 307): "Now middlemen fear, manufacturers court, and politicians *love* us." Wholesale grocers (e.g., Z. M. Hall of Chicago) advertised extensively in the *Pr. Farm.* as supply houses for Grangers. Co-operative manufacturing, particularly in the case of the Werner Harvester, was far less successful.

9   The half-amused interest in spiritualist seances is well illustrated
    in the diary of Sarah Jane Kimball (Merrill E. Jarchow, "Social
    Life of an Iowa Farm Family, 1873–1912," *Iowa Journal of His-
    tory*, L [April, 1952], 148–50); for the other items see *Pr. Farm.*,
    Jan. 3, p. 5, and Jan. 19, p. 16, and *Ia. Home.*, June 5, p.
    178.

10 Cf. the Farmers' Declaration of Independence (*Ia. Home.*, June
    20, 1873): " . . . we hereby declare ourselves absolutely free and
    independent of all past political connections . . . "; cf. also *Pr.
    Farm.*, Jan. 17, p. 19, and Jan. 3, p. 7 (advertisement for the
    Chicago Times), Merrill, *Bourbon Democracy of the Middle
    West*, p. 57, and Taylor, *The Farmers' Movement, 1620–1920*,
    pp. 104–5.

11 " . . . the Fourth of July promises to be very generally cele-
    brated under the auspices of the Order" (*Ia. Home.*, June 5, p.
    184); cf. also Buck, *The Granger Movement*, pp. 76, 86, and
    Throne, "The Grange in Iowa," p. 305, who notes that as many as
    eighty Granges would celebrate together with parades, speeches,
    and feasting.

12 Meetings were held in Jasper County in 1873 prior to the conven-
    tion in August at Des Moines which resulted in the formation of
    the Anti-Monopoly party. The vote was divided between Anti-
    Monopoly candidates and Republicans in several other Iowa
    counties also in that year (Throne, "The Grange in Iowa," pp. 315,
    317).
        Most of the following slogans are taken from Stephe Smith,
    Grains For the Grangers (San Francisco: Union Publishing Co.,
    1873), pp. 237–38, quoted in Taylor, *The Farmers' Movement*,
    pp. 2–3. At a Patrons' celebration at Nauvoo, Ill., banners were
    carried reading: "Justice to all"; "We will have our rights"; "Hon-
    esty and capability the qualifications for office"; "We mean busi-
    ness" (*Pr. Farm.*, Jan. 17, p. 19). Cf. also the speech of John
    P. Irish: "UP with the good old Jefferson maxim 'THE GREAT-
    EST GOOD TO THE GREATEST NUMBER' " (in Throne, "The
    Grange in Iowa," p. 294).

13 "We must fight fire with fire, as one, who, surrounded with a
    prairie fire, sets fire to the grass at his feet, to stay the approach-
    ing flames and save himself" (address of M. M. Morrill, Nauvoo,
    Ill., in *Pr. Farm.*, Jan. 17, p. 19). The need for better organization
    had, of course, been urged long before 1874; cf., e.g., *ibid.*, Mar.
    20, 1870: "The great need of the producers always has been in
    Organization."

14 *Pr. Farm.*, Feb. 7, p. 1; cf. Jan. 17, p. 19, and Jan. 24, p. 28.

Such phrases as "unjust and excessive discriminations" (Jan. 24, p. 1), "extortion" (Jan. 10, p. 15), and "soulless corporations" (Feb. 7, p. 43) became stereotyped reactions to monopolistic practices. It was discriminatory (even more than excessive) rates that, according to George H. Miller ("Origins of the Iowa Granger Law," *The Mississippi Valley Historical Review*, XL [March, 1954], 678), lay at the root of the Iowa movement to restrict intrastate railroad rates. Railroad agitation was a primary factor in the development of agricultural organizations in 1873; the Grange, which was only part of the wider movement, became its chief mouthpiece (Taylor, *The Farmers' Movement*, p. 139).

15 *Pr. Farm.*, Jan. 3, p. 3, and Feb. 14, p. 1. Figures cited were those of Francis A. Walker, Superintendent of the Census. For opposition to middlemen, cf. also *Ia. Home.*, June 5, p. 181, and the "Declaration of Purpose of the National Grange" adopted at the Seventh Session of the National Grange at St. Louis, Mo., Feb. 4, 1784 (conveniently reprinted in Greer, *American Social Reform Movements*, p. 88).

16 J. A. Patterson, addressing the Farmer's Club at Decatur, Ill., expressed a common view: "There is a combination existing between railroad corporations and Wall street brokers, and they . . . hold the whole country at their mercy" (*Pr. Farm.*, Jan. 17, p. 19). On matching combination with co-operation, see *ibid.*, Jan. 31, p. 35 ("Taught by capital the power of combination, labor presents its solid masses . . . . The term co-operation . . . carries with it . . . an outlook to secure justice and equity, as opposed to encroachment of sinister combination among men" —Osborne's address to the Wis. State Grange on Jan. 20), Feb. 7, p. 1 (J. B. Turner's characterization of corporations as having "instantaneous power of combination and co-operation"), and Jan. 24, p. 27, and *Ia. Home.*, Apr. 24, p. 133. Cf. also the statement of the Bloomington, Ill., Convention of Jan. 15–16: "If railway autocrats conspire to rob producers and consumers then the producers and consumers must organize for the protection of their interests." The power of organization soon made itself felt in the reduction of freight rates and in boycotts against plow and corn-planter manufacturers (cf., e.g., *Ia. Home.*, June 5, p. 184, and Mar. 27, p. 101, and *Pr. Farm.*, Jan. 10, p. 11, and Jan. 17, p. 19).

17 In September, 1874, Iowa led the nation in the number of

Granges, 1,999 (Throne, "Grange in Iowa," p. 299); the greatest strength was centered in Jasper County, with 61 Granges
(Weaver, *Past and Present of Jasper County*, I, 106), where the
first Grange in Iowa was organized, at Newton, April, 1868. The
Grange took root in the Middle West: more than three-fourths of
all local organizations were in Iowa and Minnesota, and their
viewpoint exercised a predominant influence in the National
Grange (Taylor, *The Farmers' Movement*, pp. 124, 130–31).

18 Spoken at a Grange installation, June, 1870 (*Ia. Home.*, Mar. 10,
1871). O. H. Kelley, founder of the Grange, had in 1867 set it
squarely on this Jeffersonian principle: the Grange "is based upon
the axioms that the products of the soil comprise the basis of all
wealth" (in a letter to Anson Bartlett in Taylor, *The Farmers'
Movement*, p. 151). Cf. *Ia. Home.*, May 8, p. 149: " . . . feeding and clothing the nation, and producing the raw material that
has built up our prosperous manufactories and flourishing commerce . . . ," and Throne ("Grange in Iowa, p. 315): "Farmers' conventions, many of them Grange-inspired, began calling for
nominations of 'producers' for state affairs." As for non-producers,
the Patrons' "desire is simply to exterminate the drones and parasites of society" (*Pr. Farm.*, Feb. 28, p. 1).

19 Farmers complained that double profits were made at their expense (see, e.g., *Ia. Home.*, June 5, p. 179).

20 "If rates were a guide, Omaha was situated between Chicago
and Iowa, Denver was on the Mississippi, and San Francisco on
the Missouri, while the interior towns of Iowa and Nebraska were
located on Behring Strait" (N. B. Ashby, *The Riddle of the Sphinx*
[Des Moines, 1890], p. 130, as quoted in Throne, "The Grange in
Iowa," p. 311). Carpenter's comment is printed in the Ia. State
Agric. Soc. *Report*, 1872, pp. 194–95 (in Throne, "The Grange
in Iowa," p. 291).

21 Reprinted in *Ia. Home.*, June 20, 1873, p. 195, *Pr. Farm.*, July
12, 1873, and *Chicago Tribune*, June 17, 1873.

22 *Pr. Farm.*, Jan. 24, p. 27. On patents, cf. *Ia. Home.*, Apr. 24, p.
132, and *Pr. Farm.*, Feb. 7, p. 44. By 1872 an estimated one-
third of elevators and warehouses were controlled by Grangers
(Ross, *Iowa Agriculture*, pp. 98–99); in 1874, however, all mar-
keted wheat of seven or eight states passed through the hands of
a monopoly (some thirty owners and nine controlling firms)
operating fourteen elevators (Shannon, *The Farmer's Last Frontier, Agriculture 1860–1897*, p. 181).

23 *Pr. Farm.*, Feb. 7, p. 43: "The privileges which the people have granted to railroad corporations have become instruments of oppression" (from the meeting of the Wis. State Grange at Watertown). For reactions against land grants to railroads, see *ibid.*, Jan. 3, p. 3, and Taylor, *The Farmers' Movement*, pp. 141, 178. When railroads first came in, public sentiment in Iowa, as elsewhere, opposed restrictions on rates and fares (e.g., Miller, "Origins of the Iowa Granger Law," *The Mississippi Valley Historical Review*, XL [March, 1954], 660, and Buck, *The Granger Movement*, p. 11).

24 Throne, "The Grange in Iowa," p. 292.

25 There was some awareness, however, that over-inflated railroad bonds, discriminatory rates, etc., were not the sole factors in the farmer's plight. The *Ia. Home.* noted (June 5, p. 179) that the West had overdone by overproduction and by buying from distant manufacturers. On the rapid increase of farm surplus during the 1870's, see Throne, "The Grange in Iowa," p. 292.

26 Lottie M. Rose, "The Pioneer Railroad," in *Pr. Farm.*, July 2, 1870.

27 Cf. Buck, *The Granger Movement*, pp. 11–14.

28 Rose, "The Pioneer Railroad," in *Pr. Farm.*, July 2, 1870. The simplifying technique that shaped the symbol "Monopoly" is well illustrated by the shading of complaints, e.g., about financial exaction into accusations of power (McConnell, *The Decline of Agrarian Democracy*, p. 10).

29 On painting issues in moral colors, see Greer, *American Social Reform Movements*, p. 84. "Monopoly" had many an alias, e.g., "ring" (the Harvester Ring, the Plow Ring, etc.) and "corner": *Pr. Farm.*, Feb. 14, p. 51 *et passim*, *Ia. Home.*, Mar. 27, p. 101 *et passim*.

30 Cf. Throne, "The Grange in Iowa," p. 293, Taylor, *The Farmers' Movement*, pp. 9–10, 142–43, and Merrill, *Bourbon Democracy of the Middle West*, pp. 80–81.

31 Lasswell and Kaplan (*Power and Society*, p. 123) utilize terms from Mannheim to distinguish the two types of myth: "The *ideology* is the political myth functioning to preserve the social structure; the *utopia*, to supplant it."

32 *Ia. Home.*, Jan. 9, p. 13; cf. Jan. 23, p. 29: " . . . every basket has a copy of the Homestead spread over it." The editor, General W. P. Wilson, was a crusading proponent of the Grange. Farm newspapers were passed around from family to family (Buck, *The Granger Movement*, p. 287).

33 *Ia. Home.*, July 10, p. 211, and Jan. 30, p. 38. Cf. June 5, p. 179, for violation of the "great law of compensation."

34 *Ia. Home.*, Feb. 13, p. 50. Another recurring theme appears in Mrs. E. H. Coltrin's "Battle Cry of Freedom" (*Pr. Farm.*, Feb. 7, p. 43).

35 The best example of the attempt through the courts to establish fixed schedules of maximum rates is the Iowa Railroad Act of March, 1874 (Buck, *The Granger Movement*, p. 171, Ross, *Iowa Agriculture*, p. 103, and Miller, "Origins of the Iowa Grange Law," *The Mississippi Valley Historical Review*, XL [March, 1954], 677); equally notable are the Potter law of Wisconsin and the case of *Munn* v. *Illinois* (in which Illinois was upheld by the United States Supreme Court). These "granger laws" are significant as marking the shift from laissez faire.

36 The details and order of the initiation ceremony are taken from Kelley, *Manual of Subordinate Granges*, pp. 3–52.

37 "Ceres, the goddess of grain, comes from the sweet literature of the past, and lives once more in the Grange . . . . These offices are not simply honorary, but remind woman of part of her duties as a good Patroness of Husbandry" (Mrs. Hathaway, in *Pr. Farm.*, Jan. 17, p. 19). In the National Grange in 1874, Mrs. Dudley Adams held the office of Ceres and Mrs. O. H. Kelley that of Pomona (*Pr. Farm.*, Jan. 3, p. 3).

38 *Pr. Farm.*, Jan. 17, p. 19.

39 *Ibid.* and *Ia. Home.*, May 1, pp. 138, 141. On educational aims, cf. *ibid.*, Mar. 6, p. 74, and Jan. 30, p. 38. That a pragmatic purpose mingled with the more idealistic is apparent from *Pr. Farm.* (Jan. 24, p. 1): "The sons and daughters of farmers need the best education that can be given them, in order that they may battle successfully with the hydra-headed monopolies that will everywhere rise up against them."

What Iowans conceived the aims of the Grange to be is well attested in *Ia. Home.*: as a medium for the equality of women (Mar. 20, p. 90); "mutuality of interest and congeniality of taste" (June 5, p. 181); "Order is Heaven's first law" (June 12, p. 189); social advantages (May 22, p. 164); elevation of the farmer's calling (Mar. 13, p. 83); "live and let live" (May 8, p. 149); "reform, advancement, progress" (May 22, p. 165); promotion of libraries (Feb. 20, p. 64).

40 Names of the songs are from *Ia. Home.*, Mar. 13, p. 82.

41 The ballads are taken from "The Old Album of William A. Larkin," by Ann Musick, *Journal of American Folklore*, LX (July–

Sept., 1947), 201–35. Larkin moved from Ohio to Pekin, Ill., and then to Mahaska Co., Ia., where he was in great demand at Grange "play parties."

42 The Grange reaction is an excellent illustration of Chapple and Coon's comment on ritual as "a symbolic configuration used to restore equilibrium after a crisis" (Eliot D. Chapple and Carleton S. Coon, *Principles of Anthropology* [N.Y.: Henry Hall & Co., 1942], p. 706).

43 There was no doubt that the association between agrarianism and democracy was still real; yet the ratio of the farm population in the nation had dropped to one-half and the farmer's income to one-fifth of the total. The issue of power, therefore, was inevitable (cf. McConnell, *The Decline of Agrarian Democracy*, p. 1: "Agrarianism spoke in the name of all. The enemy which it challenged was power").

44 Cf. Dudley Adams' address before the National Grange (*Pr. Farm.*, Feb. 14, p. 51: "While we readily assent to the proposition that railroads . . . add immensely to the development of the country . . . , still in our inmost soul we feel deeply wronged at the return made for the kind and liberal spirit we have shown them."

45 " . . . we are the slaves of those whom we created" (*Pr. Farm.*, Feb. 14, p. 51); cf. *ibid.*, Jan. 31, p. 35: " . . . labor is subjected to a condition very much akin to that of vassalage." The phrase "Slave-power of monopoly" appeared on the title-page of Smith's *Grains for the Grangers* (Taylor, *The Farmers' Movement*, p. 166).

46 Cf. *Pr. Farm.*, Jan. 31, p. 35, "power of combinations"; Feb. 14, p. 51, "gigantic combination"; Jan. 17, p. 19, "There is a combination existing between railroad corporations and Wall street brokers; [these] hold the whole country at their mercy." Cf. also *Pr. Farm.*, Feb. 28, p. 67: "Look at the reaper combination, the sewing machine combination, the wood screw combination, the hoe farming combination . . . . Who forms and sustains these combinations and rings?"

47 *Ibid.*, Jan. 17, p. 19.

48 *Ibid.*, Jan. 31, p. 35.

49 *Ia. Home.*, May 8, p. 149.

50 *Ibid.*, June 5, p. 181.

51 William P. Lippincott, Vernon, Ia., in *Ia. Home.*, Sept. 11, p. 293. Lippincott was referring to the proportion of the farm population.

52 *Pr. Farm.*, Jan. 3, p. 3. Cf. *Ia. Home.*, June 5, pp. 181, 184 (quoting the *Rural World*): " . . . the farmers will attain once more their proud eminence, peace and plenty will fill their measure of happiness"; and July 10, p. 221.

53 *Pr. Farm.*, Jan. 31, p. 35.

54 *Ibid.*

55 *Ibid.*, Feb. 28, p. 67.

56 Cf. *ibid.*, Jan. 3, p. 1: "[There was hope of promise in] free institutions, free schools, free religion, free speech, free press, free labor . . . . They [Grangers] abhor anarchy . . . . They know and respect the rights of man." Emerson had done much to popularize the application to the farmer of "natural man" (see Douglas C. Stenerson, "Emerson and the Agrarian Tradition," *Journal of the History of Ideas*, XIV [January, 1953], 109). Farmers, like most Americans, saw no difference in the meaning of natural in "natural man" and "natural rights."

57 Cf. Taylor, *The Farmers' Movement*, p. 282: "So crude a reaction as a movement operates upon obvious comparisons and contrasts and is most subtly tuned to general trends, but it is never capable of detailed analysis of intricate facts."

58 The extension of the myth to all society is apparent in the "Declaration of Purpose" (in Greer, *American Social Reform Movements*, p. 88): " . . . we mutually resolve to labor for the good of our Order, our country, and mankind." The absolutizing of the myth is illustrated in the motto of the Grange—"Esto perpetua." Cf. also *Ia. Home.*, Jan. 30, p. 38: "[The Grange] will raise the standard of social culture to a height never before reached by any people in any nation . . . ."

59 Metaphorical thinking, by emphasizing the purity or intensity of attributes, was a means of adjusting facts to accepted beliefs. If many metaphors were "adjectival"—simply descriptive of external appearances (Snell, *The Discovery of the Mind*, p. 197)— there were more that revealed what Cassirer (*An Essay on Man*, p. 105) calls "immediate qualitativeness" and a synthetic view of life (p. 108). On "depth" symbols, see Wheelwright, *The Burning Fountain*, p. 26 *et passim*. Grangers' metaphorical symbols were more useful for impulse control than for control of the outer world—a natural phenomenon in this instance, considering that group culture when challenged seems to become highly personal and subjective.

60 *Pr. Farm.*, Feb. 14, p. 51: "The Order has become recognized as

one of the great powers in the land, and the gates are besieged, from ocean to ocean, by hordes . . . who suddenly discover that they are interested in 'agricultural pursuits,' but only as hawks are interested in the sparrow." Cf. *Ia. Home.*, May 8, p. 149, on the Grange as "the most powerful organization in the world."

61 *Ia. Home.*, June 5, p. 184.

62 *Ibid.*, Apr. 10, p. 117.

Chapter 12

1 Cleveland *Plain Dealer*, Mar. 27, 1886.

2 *Ibid.*

3 *Ibid.*, Mar. 28, 1886.

4 Cf. James H. Kennedy, *A History of the City of Cleveland*, p. 459.

5 *Journal of United Labor*, VI (Mar. 10, 1886), 2019. The *Journal* was the official publication of the Knights of Labor. On Terence V. Powderly's attitude toward the eight-hour-day movement (in a "secret circular" issued on Mar. 13, 1886, Knights were advised not to rush into the movement), cf. Gerald N. Grob, "Terence V. Powderly and the Knights of Labor," *Mid-America*, XXXIX, New Series, XXVIII (Jan., 1957), 44, and Commons *et al.*, *History of Labour*, II, 378–79.

6 *Journal of United Labor*, VI (Apr. 10, 1886), 2038. Cleveland assemblies were among the more than four hundred organized during the month.

7 Rose, *Cleveland*, p. 389.

8 *Plain Dealer*, Apr. 11, 1886.

9 *A Half Century's Progress, 1836–1886* (Wis. Hist. Coll.), pp. 57–59. Oil refineries (90 establishments) employed 10,000 men; capital invested amounted to $30,000,000. Iron and steel (160 establishments) employed 17,000 men; capital invested (together with the products) was $25,000,000.

10 *Journal of United Labor*, VI (Feb. 25, 1886), 2012: "How little of the grand improvements of the age can the great masses of people enjoy in this country . . ." (letter to the editor from Oregon, Mo.); cf. also June 10, p. 2085: "Why does he who produces all enjoy nothing?" For discharge of workers because they were Knights, cf. *ibid.*, June 25, 1886 (Champion Machine Co., Springfield, Ohio), *Plain Dealer*, Apr. 2 and 4, 1886 (Gould's Southwest System), and Cleveland *Weekly Leader and Herald*, Mar. 13 and 20, 1886 (Gould).

11 Kennedy, *History of the City of Cleveland*, pp. 458–60. On Cleveland shipping, cf. Hatcher, *Lake Erie*, pp. 305–7.
12 Robison, *History of the City of Cleveland*, pp. 217–18, and *Plain Dealer*, Apr. 10 and 15, 1886.
13 The *Journal of United Labor*, e.g., printed an address by Rev. S. C. Eby of St. Louis asserting that "all the evidences of development among workingmen and workingwomen tell of a prophetic day when their voice shall be heard in the land not as a clamor of the masses, but as the distinct expression of the mighty union of rational and intelligent men and women" (Jan. 10, 1886, p. 1168). Sessions of the general assembly of the Knights of Labor were closed with the song "If We Will, We Can Be Free:"

> Hark! uncounted, countless numbers
> Swell the peal of agony;
>
> .   .   .   .
>
> Like the rush of many waters,
> Comes the cry "We will be free!"

> Greenway, *American Folksongs of Protest*, p. 46.

14 All items are from the *Plain Dealer*, Apr. 15, 1886.
15 Lomax, *American Ballads and Folksongs*, p. 22 (from "Paddy Works on the Erie").
16 Korson, *Pennsylvania Songs and Legends*, pp. 360–61.
17 *Plain Dealer*, Apr. 15, 1886.
18 Lomax, *American Ballads and Folksongs*, pp. 478–79 (from "Red Iron Ore").
19 Lomax, *Folk Song USA*, p. 167 (from "Once More a-Lumb'ring Go").
20 In Franz Rickaby (ed.), *Ballads and Songs of the Shanty-Boy* (Cambridge, Mass.: Harvard Univ. Press, 1926), pp. 11–14.
21 Lomax, *American Ballads and Folksongs*, p. 438 (from "The Hard-Working Miner").
22 The report of James M. Brady, District Master Workman, is published in full in the *Journal of United Labor*, VII (Aug. 25, 1886), 2154.
23 Eleanor E. Ledbetter, *The Czechs of Cleveland* (Cleveland: Americanization Committee, 1919), pp. 9, 35; cf. also Rose, *Cleveland*, p. 362.
24 Čapek, *The Čechs in Amercia*, p. 54: "The archbishop claimed a prior lien on the peasant's soul; the emperor held a chattel mortgage on his body; the lord usurped the fruits of his labor."

25 According to Mrs. Eva (Chyba) Bock of Bowling Green, Ohio, who lived in Prague until her marriage, the Communist government of Czechoslovakia regarded this song as subversive.

26 All Czechoslovakian folksongs have been taken from Botsford, *Folk Songs of Many Peoples*, pp. 137–44. Mrs. Bock, who learned these songs when she was a child, assures me that they are an important part of the living heritage of Czechoslovakia today. Recordings of many of them were secured in August, 1956, from Mrs. Frank Lukas, who migrated to the United States in her girlhood. Mrs. Lukas testifies to the continuing popularity of the songs among Czechoslovakians in the United States, not least in her own community, Friendship, Wisconsin.

27 For "association by emotive congruity," cf. Wheelwright, *The Burning Fountain*, pp. 98–99.

28 Cf. *ibid.*, pp. 25–29, 48–51 *et passim*, for an analysis of "depth language" as opposed to steno-language (the language, e.g., of science and mathematics).

29 Botsford, *Folk Songs of Many Peoples*, p. 131, translated from the Czech of Josef Tyl by F. B. Zdrůbek.

30 *Plain Dealer*, Apr. 28, 1886.

31 *Ibid.*, Apr. 27, 1886.

32 *Ibid.*, Apr. 29, 1886.

33 *Ibid.*, Apr. 27, 1886.

34 *Ibid.*, Apr. 29, 1886.

35 For figures (1885) on ore and the Cleveland Rolling Mills, cf. Hatcher, *Lake Erie*, pp. 312, 299. On immigration, cf. *Plain Dealer*, Apr. 25, 1886, Commons *et al*, *History of Labour*, II, 381, and Selig Perlman, *A History of Trade Unionism*, p. 86.

36 Rose, *Cleveland*, pp. 428–29. Charles M. Hall developed an electrolytic process for the reduction of aluminum ore; Alfred and Eugene Cowles patented an electric furnace for smelting ores (p. 429).

37 "Knowledge is Power" in *Coopers' Monthly Journal*, I (July, 1870), 3. "Politics is Bread," *ibid.*, VI (Jan., 1875), 19; cf. also June, 1875, p. 163.

38 *Plain Dealer*, Apr. 27, 1886.

39 *Journal of United Labor*, VI (Mar. 25, 1886), 2020. The context of this phrase is the complaint that workers are no longer on a plane of equality (equity) with their bosses: "This sentiment of equity is wounded, crushed and destroyed by the present industrial organization . . . ."

40 *Plain Dealer,* May 1, 1886; cf. also *Journal of United Labor,* Feb. 25, 1886 (machines bring a divorce between capital and labor), and Commons *et al, History of Labour,* II, 358: "The dominant feature was the introduction of machinery upon an unprecedented scale."

41 Feb. 25, 1886, p. 2012: " . . . great masses of people cannot enjoy the bounties of their country"; May 25, p. 2079: " . . . labor which alone produces the wealth of society . . . "; June 10, p. 2085: "Is it not we who feed the rich, the idle and the useless? Is it not to our labor that they owe their palaces, their brownstone fronts . . . their luxuries . . ."; cf. also Mar. 25. On loss of equilibrium, cf. June 25, p. 2098.

42 On Gould's alleged lack of faith, cf. *Plain Dealer,* May 3, 1886; on discrimination against Knights in employment, cf. *Journal of United Labor,* May 25, 1886, p. 2077, and June 25, 1886, p. 2102; cf. also note 10.

43 *Plain Dealer,* Apr. 29, 1886.

44 *Ibid.,* Apr. 26, 1886.

45 *Ibid.,* Apr. 28 and 30, 1886.

46 *Ibid.,* Apr. 26 and 30, 1886.

47 *Ibid.,* May 2, 1886. Gompers added: " . . . the workingman's habits improve, his ideas are more expansive, the exercise of his privileges are more sacred in his eyes . . . . [This measure] is to the best interests of . . . the perpetuation of our institutions . . . ." Spokesmen (*ibid.*) generally elaborated the above themes: the eight-hour day is a moral and economic elevator (John Swinton); it is "a proposition for the increase of popular intelligence" (Henry George); it would increase "the general consumption and therefore production of wealth"; it would advance the "moral progress of the laboring classes"; "democratic institutions can only be sustained by the increasing intelligence of the people which can be most easily . . . accomplished by a general reduction in the hours of labor" (George Gunton, quoted from the April *Forum*). The Cleveland *Weekly Leader and Herald* believed that the eight-hour day would stimulate workingmen "to a finer patriotism" (Feb. 27, 1886).

48 The movement for the eight-hour day had gained force as early as 1872 (Samuel Gompers, cited in the *Plain Dealer,* May 2, 1886, p. 9), it was revived in 1881 at the session of the Federation of Trades and Labor Unions of the United States and Canada, the resolution to establish the eight-hour day on May 1, 1886,

was adopted by the 1884 Convention of the Federation of Organized Trades and Labor Unions and a program outlined at its 1885 meeting for the 1886 demonstration (Gompers, *Seventy Years*, p. 290).

49 *Plain Dealer*, May 2, 1886. Gompers asserted later (*Seventy Years*, p. 291): "[The eight-hour day] was a slogan which concentrated the united attention of workers upon the achievement of a decisive forward movement in their own interests and in the interests of industry."

50 See notes 61–63.

51 *Plain Dealer*, May 3, 1886.

52 *Ibid.*

53 *Ibid.*, May 6 and 7, 1886.

54 *Ibid.*, May 4, 5, and 6, 1886, and Michael J. Schaack, *Anarchy and Anarchists* (Chicago: F. J. Schulte and Co.), p. 130, *et passim*.

55 *Plain Dealer*, May 8, 1886.

56 *Ibid.* The situation was accurately assessed, however, in the editorial "No Anarchism in Cleveland."

57 *Ibid.*, May 7, 1886.

58 *Ibid.*, May 8, 1886.

59 Clark, *Thomas Paine*, p. 34. Robert Ingersoll also appealed to Cleveland Bohemians. Cf. Ledbetter, *The Czechs of Cleveland*, p. 19 ("free thinking organizations by the end of the 80's included fully half of the Czechs of Cleveland"), and Čapek, *The Čecks in America*, pp. 135, 188, 196. Čapek (*Ibid.*, p. 119) estimates that at least half of the Czechs in America seceded from their old-country faith.

60 Clark, *Thomas Paine*, p. 165.

61 A Sokol was founded in 1879 on Wendell Ave. (Ledbetter, *The Czechs of Cleveland*, p. 30); the Tyl dramatic society was established in 1881 (*ibid.*, p. 14), and the Lumir musical society in 1867 (*ibid.*, p. 15).

62 On equality, cf. Mar. 25, p. 2026: "This sentiment of equality in nature is the political creed of our epoch . . . ," and Jan. 10, p. 1178: "the equity and solidarity of conditions." On harmony, cf. June 25, p. 2098: "Harmony cannot exist if man, in all his actions, is not in equilibrium—in harmony with nature, with himself and with his fellow-beings . . . ," and Feb. 25, p. 2007: "Men may fade and pass away [wrote Powderly], isolated labor societies may struggle and die, but that which was intended to

bar out sectional strife and bind all workers together must live on." Cf. also May 10, p. 2071, on balance of power between capital and labor.

63 Mar. 10, p. 2016, and June 25, p. 2098: "The cause of evolution is an incessant tendency toward equilibrium . . . ."

64 July 10, p. 2110.

65 These and other tales of Krakonos were secured in July, 1951, from Mrs. Eleanor E. Ledbetter, who translated them from the Czech of Ludmila Grossmaneva (*Krakonos, The King of the Mountains*).

66 *Journal of United Labor*, VII (Aug. 25, 1886), 2154.

67 *Plain Dealer*, May 25, 1886.

68 *Ibid.*, May 26, 27, and 30, 1886.

69 *Ibid.*, May 20 and 30, 1886, and Ware, *The Labor Movement in the United States*, p. 185. Half a year later (December 8) the cigarmakers joined with some twenty-four other national unions in Columbus, Ohio, to form the American Federation of Labor (cf. Dulles, *Labor in America*, p. 161).

70 Gompers, *Seventy Years*, p. 261.

71 *Ibid.*, pp. 223, 287. "In those early days," Gompers believed (p. 223), "not more than a dozen people had grasped the concept that economic organization and control over economic power were the fulcrum which made possible influence and power in all other fields."

72 "Strikes and Arbitration," *North American Review*, CXLIII (May, 1886), 505: "The workingman of the United States," Powderly asserted, "will soon realize that he possesses the power which kings once held—that he has the right to manage his own affairs."

73 Perlman, *A History of Trade Unionism*, p. 91.

Chapter 13

1 Nevins, *Ford*, p. 511.

2 A thorough treatment of most phases of the myth may be found in Sutton, *et al.*, *The American Business Creed*. An illuminating study of the myth as it is revealed in the attitudes of and toward national figures in business is Diamond's *The Reputation of the American Businessman*.

3 Nevins, *Ford*, pp. 463–64.

4 Ford, *My Life and Work*, p. 147.

5 *Ibid.*, p. 26. Cf. McCormick, *The Century of the Reaper*, p. 248:

"Machinery, itself a product of the free genius of liberated thought, rescued our national life . . . ."

6 W. J. Cameron, Ford public relations representative, in Richards, *The Last Billionaire*, pp. 277–78.

7 Garrett, *The Wild Wheel*, pp. 94–96.

8 *Ibid.*, pp. 96, 29.

9 Nevins, *Ford*, p. 491.

10 Cf. Burlingame, *Backgrounds of Power,* p. 109: "All mass production by machines and of machines may be traced to these two beginnings." Notable landmarks in mass production, of course, were Eli Whitney's production of interchangeable parts for guns, Oliver Evans' innovations in flour milling, and Cyrus McCormick's use of automatic sequence.

11 For the reality and power of Process, cf., e.g., my article, "Throne and Scepter: Greek Views of Reality and Power," *Kentucky Foreign Language Quarterly*, Vol. IV (1957).

12 Drucker, *The New Society*, p. 22. Drucker is referring to Ford.

13 Garrett, *The Wild Wheel*, p. 93.

14 The rate of speed of the chassis-assembly line by the end of 1914 (Nevins, *Ford*, p. 474).

15 It could stand for (i.e., have a value ratio to) assets, or earnings based on assets, or potentialities of growth based on earnings, or even "faith in the future" based on these potentialities.

16 Burlingame, *Backgrounds of Power*, p. 195.

17 J. P. Morgan died in March, 1913.

18 Ford, *My Life and Work*, p. 229.

19 Cf. Faulkner, *The Economic History of the United States*, p. 416.

20 Cf. Cochran and Miller, *The Age of Enterprise*, p. 355: "By 1914 most of the traditional areas for profitable enterprise were closed to all but those who had access to large amounts of investment capital, and the control of such capital had itself become concentrated in a very few hands." Major steps to check consolidation included: in 1913, legislation strengthening the ICC, the Pujo Committee's investigation of the "Money Trust," the Owen-Glass Act, and the creation of the Federal Reserve System; in 1914, the Federal Trade Commission Act and the Clayton Act.

21 Following Charles Adams (*North American Review*, Vol. CXII [Apr., 1871]) and Woodrow Wilson (in his address "The Lawyer and the Community," printed in *The Public Papers of Woodrow Wilson*, ed. Ray Stannard Baker and William E. Dodd [N.Y.:

Harper & Bros., 1926], II, 255), recent observers have stressed the autonomous character of corporate enterprise. Cf. Cochran and Miller (*The Age of Enterprise*, p. 308): "The great corporations had their own . . . internal diplomacy . . . their own hereditary offices and strategic marriages, their own ministerial cabinets . . . ." Brady (*Business as a System of Power*, p. 257) compares the modern economic "state" to the medieval guild economy and to agrarian states' rights doctrines of the planter aristocracy; Berle and Means (*The Modern Corporation*, p. 357) refer to a concentration of economic power "which can compete on equal terms with the modern state"; Wells (*Monopoly and Social Control*, p. 105) sees "the development of concentrated economic power in America" as "the action of a fatalistic force." Cf. also p. 157: ". . . the fatalistic drive of objective environmental forces."

22 Ford, *My Life and Work*, p. 191.

23 Ford summed up his position when he said of his procedure (*My Life and Work*, p. 32): "Nearly all of these various features had been planned in advance. That is the way I have always worked. I draw a plan and work out every detail on the plan before starting to build."

24 *Ibid.*, p. 270; cf. *seq.*: "The basis of all economic reasoning is the earth and its products."

25 *Ibid.*, p. 191.

26 *Ibid.*, p. 6.

27 *Ibid.*, p. 7: "The foundations of society are the men and means to *grow* things, to *make* things, and to *carry* things."

28 *Ibid.*, pp. 233, 204. On the analogy of Highland Park's processing of raw materials, Ford envisaged the farmer (the "greatest producer") as the greatest merchandiser once he could "change his grain into flour, his cattle into beef, and his hogs into ham and bacon" (p. 233).

29 *Ibid.*, p. 9.

30 *Ibid.*, p. 120. Cf. p. 9: "The economic fundamental is labour . . . . The moral fundamental is man's right in his labour."

31 *Ibid.*, pp. 53, 14. The phrase is "excess weight," but the omission accurately represents Ford's view.

32 Cf. *ibid.*, p. 113: "We measure on each job the exact amount of room that a man needs; he must not be cramped—that would be waste. But if he and his machine occupy more space than is required, that is also waste."

33 *Ibid.*, p. 83.

34 *Ibid.*, p. 111: "The organization is so highly specialized and one part is so dependent upon another that we could not for a moment consider allowing men to have their own way. Without the most rigid discipline we would have the utmost confusion. I think it should not be otherwise in industry." For the impersonality of workers' relations with one another and with their foremen, cf. p. 97: " . . . I want as little as possible of the personal element," and p. 112: "there is not much personal contact . . . a factory is not a drawing room."

35 *Ibid.*, p. 24: "Machines are to a mechanic what books are to a writer. He gets ideas from them . . . ."

36 Nevins, *Ford,* title of chap. xviii.

37 Ford, *My Life and Work,* p. 95.

38 *Ibid.*, p. 99: "This rating system simply forces a foreman to forget personalities—to forget everything other than the work in hand." Cf. also p. 98: "A department gets its standing on its rate of production."

39 *Ibid.*, pp. 55, 179, 40.

40 *Ibid.*, p. 104. For Ford's view of his own contribution to the good society, cf. p. 2: "I do not consider the machines which bear my name simply as machines . . . . I take them as concrete evidence of the working out of a theory of business—a theory that looks toward making this world a better place in which to live."

41 *Ibid.*, p. 134: "Progress is not made by pulling off a series of stunts. Each step has to be regulated."

42 *Ibid.*, p. 124: "Perfect the [wage] system and we may have universal justice."

43 Business ideology puts a high premium on rational control: the businessman, according to the creed, is necessarily the most rational figure in a generally rationalist nation—his actions are guided by rational norms; responsible for "realistic" decisions in a changing technology, he cannot afford to be moved by extraneous considerations of tradition and sentiment (cf. Sutton *et al., The American Business Creed,* pp. 259–60, 275, 348 *et passim.*

44 Ford, *My Life and Work,* p. 163. The emphasis on business responsibility for the public welfare in the business creed rests upon a series of equations—especially the assumed congruity between the ideals of free enterprise and those of the nation, and the link between business and progress, specifically between competition

and a richer standard of living (cf. Sutton *et al., The American Business Creed,* pp. 173, 180, 215).

45 Ford at times regards profit simply as a by-product of efficient, intelligent production. The business creed makes the profit motive central: the incentive of profit corresponds to the fundamental laws of human nature; identified with individual self-interest, it is the fundamental condition of human happiness (Ford, *My Life and Work,* pp. 170, 183, 284).

46 Ralph Waldo Emerson, in Richard D. Mosier, *The American Temper: Patterns of Our Intellectual Heritage* (Berkeley and Los Angeles: Univ. of California Press, 1952), p. 202.

47 Ford, *My Life and Work,* p. 163.

48 *Ibid.,* p. 264.

49 For contemporary industry's assumption of internally consistent economic laws and of the "integrated wholeness of society," cf. Sutton *et al., The American Business Creed,* pp. 30–31, 41. Diamond (*The Reputation of the American Businessman,* p. 171) notes business ideology's view of free enterprise and the American people as parts of a general unity.

50 Mosier, *The American Temper,* p. 203: ". . . the horological soul dreams of its chronometrical truth."

51 Ford, *My Life and Work,* p. 264.

52 Ford, *My Life and Work,* p. 158. In 1910 John Kirby, Jr., President of the National Association of Manufacturers, referred to "the natural law of economics, which, in the nature of things, is as irrevocable as the law of gravitation" (Sutton *et al., The American Business Creed,* p. 385). For similar views among economists, cf. Dorfman, *The Economic Mind,* III, 137, 362, 373–74.

53 Sutton *et al., The American Business Creed,* pp. 32, 35; cf. Diamond, *The Reputation of the American Businessman,* p. 171.

54 Their methods of reducing the world to a simple unit differed radically, of course, from one another. Cf., e.g., "Yankee Notions and Pennsylvania Knowledge."

55 On the important role in business ideology of "selectivity" and oversimplification, cf. Sutton *et al., The American Business Creed,* pp. 316–19. The prime factor of simplification was analogy—as in the assumed similarity between relations in the shop and those in the American family (part of the general picture presenting business and business leaders as "the people"), and in the persistent identification of free enterprise with the nation (with

reciprocal interchange of qualities); cf. *ibid.,* p. 63, and Diamond, *The Reputation of the American Businessman,* pp. 173–74. Cf. also p. 179: "The economic environment in which the businessman operates is presented as synonymous with the nation itself, and the nation and economic system are interchangeable parts of the same mechanism."

56 The pivotal point of balance (according to business ideology) is competition. Its economic foci (regulation of prices, guarantee of improved quality and economic opportunity, etc.) are broadened to include the equilibrial bases of society as a whole—e.g., through its supposed correspondence with human nature and its connotations of freedom. Although it has been repeatedly demstrated that competition does not lead to equilibrium (cf., e.g., Robinson, *Monopoly and Competition,* pp. 245–54), the modern creed endorses Sturtevant's contention that competition is the foundation of all free society (Dorfman, *The Economic Mind,* p. 73).

Competition, according to Lynch (*The Concentration of Economic Power,* pp. 108–9), is "a term which men have learned to employ with quite the same animistic and emotional content as certain mystical catch phrases . . . of less civilized ages." It "has become part of the folklore of the twentieth century, a heritage of the nineteenth."

Chapter 14

1 *Philosophy in a New Key,* p. 280. Cf. Collier, *Indians of the Americas,* p. 205: "Events and action are not the all; ideas, ideals and intentions are the master facts; they saturate events, and transsubstantiate their meanings; and they outlast."

2 "To understand a nation it is necessary to know not only its true history but also the history which its people believed" (Swain, *The Ancient World,* I, xix).

3 Kardiner, *The Psychological Frontiers of Society,* p. 36. Cf. also p. 39: "The empirical reality systems we found in the manipulation and making of tools, the knowledge of planting, and so forth; the projective systems in religion, folklore, and many other systems."

4 Feibleman, *The Theory of Human Culture,* p. 76.

5 Gabriel, *The Course of American Democratic Thought,* p. 26. Cf. also Whitehead, *Adventures of Ideals,* pp. 13–14: "In each age of the world distinguished by high activity there will be

found at its culmination, and among the agencies leading to that culmination, some profound cosmological outlook, implicitly accepted, impressing its own type upon the current springs of action."

6 Lasswell and Kaplan, *Power and Society*, p. 117.

7 *A Study of War* (Chicago: Univ. of Chicago Press, 1942), II, 936. Cf. also p. 1047: "Opinion has superseded custom and law as the unifying force in modern civilization and as the life-blood of the symbols whose possession and use constitutes political power." Wright is speaking of political power, but his remarks apply as well to other forms.

8 Riesman, *The Lonely Crowd*, p. 139. Cf. also p. 250: power "is founded on interpersonal expectations and attitudes."

9 R. H. Tawney, quoted in Lasswell and Kaplan, *Power and Society*, p. 86.

10 Frankfort, *The Intellectual Adventure of Ancient Man*, p. 8.

11 Malinowski, quoted in Jung and Kerenyi, *Essays on a Science of Mythology*, p. 7.

12 Frankfort, *The Intellectual Adventure of Ancient Man*, p. 25.

13 Lasswell and Kaplan, *Power and Society*, pp. 76, 104, 103. Cf. p. 117: "[The political myth] consists of the symbols invoked not only to explain but also to justify specific power practices."

14 *Ibid.*, p. 103.

15 Becker, *New Liberties for Old*, p. 42.

Chapter 15

1 *Religion in Primitive Society*, foreword.

2 In recent years a series of popular reactions has betrayed a reality of an animistic character: e.g., the widely circulated "picture" of Christ in the clouds over Korea (*Time*, Dec. 3, 1951, pp. 63–64); the broadcast of an invasion from Mars that created panic in parts of the United States and Canada and riot in Mexico; the mystical yearnings of the 80,000 people whom a Wisconsin woman's visions brought to her farm home at Necedah by highway, rail, and air (cf. e.g., *Life*, Vol. XXIX [Aug. 28, 1950]).

3 This account of primitive reality is drawn largely from Wallis, *Religion in Primitive Society;* Frankfort, *The Intellectual Adventure of Ancient Man;* and Cassirer, *Language and Myth.*

4 Symbolized in such deities as Mithra and Zeus.

5 Francis La Flesche, *The Osage Tribe: Rite of the Wa-xo'-be* (Bureau of American Ethnology, Annual Report, Washington,

D.C., 1928), quoted in Collier, *Indians of the Americas*, p. 184.

6   *Indians of the Americas*, pp. 184, 185.

7   *Ibid.*, pp. 187, 188.

8   *Ibid.*, pp. 35–36.

9   *Power and Society*, p. 98.

10 J. Hackin *et al.*, *Asiatic Mythology*, pp. 29–30, quoted in Ralph Turner, *The Great Cultural Traditions* (N.Y.: McGraw-Hill Book Co., Inc., 1941), II, 106–7.

11 Cf. Becker, *New Liberties for Old*, pp. 13–14: "Particular value judgments of this sort are related to, and partly determined by, particular matter-of-fact knowledge; but they are also related to, and partly determined by, other value judgments of wider scope that derive their validity from tradition and habit rather than from any connection with particular and current matter-of-fact knowledge."

12 An overwhelming proportion, for example, of the more than 4,000 folk sayings and beliefs collected by Daniel L. and Lucy B. Thomas (*Kentucky Superstitions*) fall into these categories.

13 Kardiner (*The Psychological Frontiers of Society*, p. 44) emphasizes this static character: "That a society which is dominated by projective techniques lacks adaptability can be amply illustrated by contrasts found in cultures described in this book." Cf. also p. 353: " . . . the patterns of a previous adaptation with all the relationships involved are elaborated in fantasy, at the expense of current adaptations demanded by the current reality."

14 Cassirer, *Language and Myth*, p. 93.

15 *Ibid.*, pp. 91 ff.

Chapter 16

1   "The human individual," says Mead (*Mind, Self, and Society*, p. 377), "thinks first of all entirely in social terms."

2   As it did, apparently, in the Neolithic Revolution.

3   The reality and power in a particular social pattern may also be illustrated in the Roman gens. The significance of the initiation rites, for example, among Romans of the early Republic is that by attaching a child formally to the clan through his gentile name, making him heir to his patrimony and able to enjoy the legal, economic, and religious prerogatives contained in the power of the paterfamilias, and finally, through his membership in the

clan, endowing him with national citizenship, they gave him a claim to existence in the reality of the gens. Whether it was a Cato censoring the mores of the nation, or a family like the Fabii utilizing the patriarchal structure of the college of augurs, the army, and the Senate to strengthen itself and the state, their power to coerce rested upon the general acceptance of values implicit in the gens. The power symbols which defined their authority (*patria potestas, auctoritas, imperium*) embodied assumptions regarding this social absolute of a kinship that provided an environment absorbing all aspects of private and corporate life.

4 Cf. Tawney, as quoted in Lasswell and Kaplan, *Power and Society*, p. 23.

5 Tannenbaum, *A Philosophy of Labor*, p. 31.

6 *Ibid.*, p. 30.

7 *Ibid.*, p. 8.

8 Perlman, *A History of Trade Unionism*, p. 280.

9 Cf., e.g., the publication of the Knights of Labor, *Journal of United Labor*, Mar. 25, 1886, p. 2026: "But in the face of our system of public education this argument [that the wealthy will always be better educated and therefore retain their power] does not hold good. It is not their superior knowledge that gives them their power; it is the methods of production and the instruments of labor . . . ."

10 *Coopers' Monthly Journal*, Sept., 1872, p. 550.

11 *Workingman's Advocate*, Nov. 5, 1864.

12 *Journal of United Labor*, Mar. 25, 1886, p. 2026.

13 *Workingman's Advocate*, May 18, 1866.

14 *Journal of United Labor*, Feb. 25, 1886, p. 2017.

15 *Ibid.*, Feb. 10, 1886, p. 1190.

16 *London Workingman*, quoted in *Workingman's Advocate*, Aug. 11, 1866.

17 *Coopers' Monthly Journal*, Nov., 1871, p. 423.

18 *Ibid.*, pp. 388–89.

19 Cf. *ibid.*, July, 1870, p. 30.

20 Wittke, *We Who Built America*, p. 237.

21 Perlman, *A History of Trade Unionism*, p. 82.

22 Aug. 18, p. 2.

23 *Coopers' Monthly Journal*, Nov. 1871, p. 387. Cf. also *Workingman's Advocate*, May 26, 1866, p. 2.

24 July 21, 1866.

25 July, 1870, p. 6. Spelling and punctuation have been slightly altered.
26 Cf. the *Journal of United Labor*, Feb. 25, 1886, p. 2011.
27 *Ibid.*, Jan. 10, 1886, p. 1166.
28 Cf. Dulles, *Labor in America*, p. 146.
29 Perlman, *A History of Trade Unionism*, p. 90.
30 Lasswell and Kaplan, *Power and Society*, p. 98.
31 Cf. Tannenbaum, *A Philosophy of Labor*, p. 10: "Institutionally the trade-union movement is an unconscious effort to harness the drift of our time and reorganize it around the cohesive identity that men working together always achieve."

Chapter 17

1 For the influence of the Knights of Labor, cf. Dulles, *Labor in America*, p. 148: " . . . the Noble and Holy Order had given a tremendous impetus to the organization of labor and both its successes and failures were to be of continuing significance for the growth of the labor movement as a whole. For the Knights had . . . created a solidarity among the workers that had been but dimly felt before their advent, and they offered a challenge to the power of industry that revealed as never before the inherent strength of organization."
2 Cf. William Ellery Channing, quoted in Curti, *The Growth of American Thought*, p. 249: "man unembarrassed by all the outworn disguises which in the Old World concealed those qualities which made him man, might . . . rise to communion with the Supreme Mind . . . ."
3 Cf. Tannenbaum, *A Philosophy of Labor*, p. 53: "Men became interchangeable, equal, unrelated, and subject to manipulation."
4 Ralph Waldo Emerson: "Mind is the only reality, of which men and all other natures are better or worse reflectors" (Dillaway, *The Gospel of Emerson*, p. 19).
5 The romantic individual, like the rational, builds his world upon himself; but his creed is *sentio, ergo sum* not *cogito, ergo sum.* To him nature is the macrocosm of the soul, the metaphor of self. The recreation of the simplicity, unity, and harmony of animistic reality is his goal, not mastery of nature; and he achieves it not through reason but through emotion and intuition. Romanticism is "fundamentally, a state of mind, a particular outlook on life, in which the human emotions and the human imagination act upon facts, either accepting them or leaving them alone . . . . It lays

the greatest stress on the individual—on his thoughts, feelings, and whole ego; it is the very essence of the subjective . . . . It may stand in awe of hoary tradition, yet in contradictory fashion it has small respect for established rules and regulations that happen to be inconvenient . . . . [It believes] with assurance that in [an] ivory tower it can create a new Heaven and a new earth fully as real and useful as the actual world of reality from which it may be seeking to escape" (editorial essay, Warnock and Anderson, *The World in Literature*, III, 279–80).

6 Cf. Popper, *The Open Society and Its Enemies*, p. 225: " . . . rationalism is closely linked up with the political demand for practical social engineering . . . ."

7 Cassirer (*Language and Myth*) sharply distinguishes the theoretical ("discursive" thinking) from the mythical. It is true that the "free ideality" of discursive thought, "which is the core of its *logical* nature, is necessarily lacking in the realm of mythic conception" (p. 32). The difference is, of course, that Cassirer does not use the term "myth" (as we do) to cover basic assumptions of a rational nature.

8 Cf. Philbrick, *Understanding English*, p. 72: "Abstractions are defined by metaphors. These metaphors involve other abstractions, which in turn must be defined by metaphor . . . ." Susanne Langer (*Philosophy in a New Key*, p. 59) refers to "an unconscious, spontaneous process of *abstraction*, which goes on all the time in the human mind . . . ."

9 Cassirer, *Language and Myth*, p. 32.

10 Von Ogden Vogt, *Cult and Culture* (N.Y.: Macmillan, 1951), p. 79, notes the mutual relations in ethics that are involved in rational oneness ("A philosophy of unity warrants an ethics of mutuality"), and John Locke comments on those in a state of equality "wherein all the power and jurisdiction is reciprocal" (*Social Contract*, ed. Ernest Barker [N.Y.: Oxford Univ. Press, 1948], p. 4).

11 Langer, *Philosophy in a New Key*, p. 76. The reference is to *verbal* symbols, but her comment applies as well to other rational symbols.

12 Cassirer, *Language and Myth*, p. 32. Cf. also p. 60: discursive thinking "even in apparently immediately 'given' data . . . recognizes an element of mental creation, and stresses this active ingredient."

13 Brady, *Business as a System of Power*, p. 230.

14 Cf. Drucker, *The New Society*, p. 27.

15 For a view of more extensive aspects of industrial power, Charles Adams' frequently quoted comment (*North American Review*, CXII [Apr., 1871], 244) is worth repeating: "These modern potentates have declared war, negotiated peace, reduced courts, legislatures, and sovereign States to . . . their will, disturbed trade, agitated the currency, imposed taxes, and . . . have freely exercised many other attributes of sovereignty . . . ."

16 Quoted in Dorfman, *The Economic Mind in American Civilization*, III, 137, 362. Cf. also Irving Fisher's comment on the quantity theory of money: " . . . practically . . . an exact law of proportion, as exact and as fundamental in economic science as the exact law of proportion between pressure and density gases in physics . . ." (Dorfman, *ibid.*, pp. 373–74). William Graham Sumner (quoted in the Amherst Series, *Democracy and the Gospel of Wealth* [Boston: D. C. Heath, 1949], p. vii) believed that "the social order is fixed by laws of nature precisely analogous to those of the physical order."

17 Aaron L. Chapin and Lyman H. Atwater, in Dorfman, *The Economic Mind in American Civilization*, pp. 70, 74. Irving Fisher considered his objective to be the undertaking of a "systematic representation in terms of mechanical interaction of that beautiful and intricate equilibrium which manifests itself on the 'exchanges' of a great city" (*ibid.*, p. 366).

18 Amasa Walker, quoted in Dorfman, *ibid.*, p. 54.

19 The analogy seemed so self-evident that monopolies, which affected the "natural" rhythm of business, had to be regarded as larger units within the competitive individualistic scheme, "persons" in the legal sense.

20 Quoted in Dorfman, *The Economic Mind in American Civilization*, p. 73.

21 Gabriel, *The Course of American Democratic Thought*, pp. 148, 153. Carnegie, says Gabriel, expressed a philosophy widely acted upon by the folk—farmers, laboring men, and millions in small enterprises. The Gospel of Wealth was "the result produced when the individualism of a simpler agricultural and commercial civilization was carried over into a society luxuriating in all essential natural resources" (p. 153).

22 Brady, *Business as a System of Power*, p. 259.

23 The development of "the myth of the garden" has been well traced in Smith, *Virgin Land*.

24 Cf. Gabriel, *Business as a System of Power*, pp. 170, 255–58.

25 Rev. William Lawrence gave classic expression to this folk equation of property ownership with morality in the well-known article "The Relation of Wealth to Morals," *World's Work*, Jan., 1901, reprinted in *Democracy and the Gospel of Wealth*. Cf. especially pp. 69, 70: " . . . it is only to the man of morality that wealth comes; . . . to seek for and earn wealth is a sign of a natural, vigorous, and strong character."

26 Alexander Mackay, *The Western World*, as quoted in Commager, *America in Perspective*, p. 114.

27 *Ibid.*, p. 116.

28 Schlesinger, *The Age of Jackson*, p. 271. Cf. p. 279: " . . . the revolution in political values forced the Whigs to talk as if they intended primarily to serve the common man." Cf. also pp. 293, 299, 305.

29 *Ibid.*, pp. 19, 283.

30 The idea lost nothing, moreover, from industry's sharing with agriculture the common store of American ideals—equality of opportunity and the rewards of individual enterprise together with faith in progress.

31 Cf. Shannon, *The Farmer's Last Frontier*, p. 349: "By 1850, the rising industrial structure was beginning to challenge the supremacy of agriculture, and before 1900, the farmer had taken a secondary position in the nation's economy."

32 Cf. Smith, *Virgin Land*, p. 195.

33 *Pr. Farm.*, III (1843), 175.

34 For the agricultural counterpart, cf. *ibid.*, p. 114: "It is an oft quoted saying that he who makes two ears of corn or two blades of grass grow where only one grew before performs more essential service to his country-men than the whole race of professional men."

Chapter 18

1 Randall MacIver, radio address, Columbia Bicentennial program, February 2, 1954. Cf. Robert S. Lynd (reprinted from Brady, *Business as a System of Power*) in Snyder and Wilson, *Roots of Political Behavior*, p. 370: "We live in an era in which only organization counts . . . ."

2 Martin Wight ("Power Politics," reprinted in Snyder and Wilson, *Roots of Political Behavior*, p. 135) notes the gravitation of loyalties since the Reformation to the nation-state and the fact that

modern history, in consequence, is a history of powers, forces, dynasties, and ideas.

3 Lasswell and Kaplan, *Power and Society*, pp. 116–17.

4 Sorel, *Reflections on Violence*, p. 32: " . . . the myths are not descriptions of things, but expressions of a determination to act." Cf. also p. 33: "Whilst contemporary myths lead men to prepare themselves for a combat which will destroy the existing state of things, the effect of Utopia has always been to direct men's minds towards reforms which can be brought about by patching up the existing system . . . ." Becker (*New Liberties for Old*, pp. 19–20) contrasts the activating function of myth with scientific understanding: "The function of a social ideology is . . . primarily moral rather than scientific: its primary function is to enable masses of men to act in the world rather than to contemplate it for understanding . . . . In order to enable masses of men to act with conviction, it must validate their activities by some more stable authority than can be derived from the incessant flux of immediate experience."

5 E.g., Cassirer (*The Myth of the State*, 1946), George Woodcock (*The Writer and Politics* [London: Porcupine Press, 1948]), and Popper (*The Open Society*).

6 Cf. Cassirer, *The Myth of the State*, p. 15: " . . . the processes themselves [of primitive thought] are very similar; they express the same desire of human nature to come to terms with reality, to live in an ordered universe, and to overcome the chaotic state in which things and thoughts have not yet assumed a definite shape and structure." Cf. also Daniel Katz, "Psychological Barriers to Communication" (reprinted in Snyder and Wilson, *Roots of Political Behavior*, p. 64): " . . . our thinking is so shot through with personification and analogy that the tendency is a serious impediment to . . . our intellectual handling of the important problems."

7 This tendency has been frequently noted, e.g., by E. F. M. Durbin, *The Politics of Democratic Socialism*, quoted in Snyder and Wilson, *Roots of Political Behavior*, pp. 32–33: "It is a universal tendency among the simpler people of all nations to attribute evil to some person or group of persons. It is present everywhere in party politics . . . . In each case what is noticeable and dangerous is that a vast power and a deep malignity is attributed to the inimical group."

8 Becker, *Modern Democracy*, p. 81.

9 Eddy (*Ballads and Songs From Ohio*, p. xvi) says of early English folk: "Whatever ideas were suggested to them from their masters in manor house or court or church, or whatever rumors came to them from the outside world, would find acceptance slowly, and only as they could be . . . assimilated to the common stock of materials which made their culture."

10 Becker, *New Liberties for Old*, p. 20.

11 Collier, *The Cosmogonies of Our Fathers*, pp. 13–14.

12 Lasswell and Kaplan, *Power and Society*, p. 20 (following Charles Merriam, *New Aspects of Politics* [Chicago: Univ. of Chicago Press, 2nd. ed., 1931]).

13 Charles Merriam, *Political Power*, 1934, reprinted in Lasswell, Merriam, and Smith, *A Study of Power*, p. 37.

14 Kardiner, *The Psychological Frontiers of Society*, p. 39.

15 The illustrations and the quotation from Laski are from Lasswell and Kaplan, *Power and Society*, p. 106.

16 In Snyder and Wilson, *Roots of Political Behavior*, p. 165. Cf. Von Ogden Vogt, *Cult and Culture* (N.Y.: Macmillan, 1951), p. 48: " . . . those elements of knowledge and taste and discipline which chiefly comprise personal or individual culture carry within themselves inescapable tendencies towards fulfilment in the social and the universal."

17 *Paideia*, III, 77.

18 "The Leading Myths of Our Time," *Ethics*, XLIX (Jan., 1939), 170.

19 William C. Greene, *Moira* (Cambridge, Mass.: Harvard Univ. Press, 1944), p. 17. For the Romans the ever-level ocean (*aequor*) symbolized what was fair and just (*aequum*). Cf. also the familiar symbol *Libra* (the Balance, the scales of justice) and our idiom "on the level."

20 Whitehead, *Adventures of Ideas*, p. 71.

21 "The Leading Myths of Our Time," *Ethics*, XLIX (Jan., 1939), 172. Cassirer (*The Myth of the State*, p. 289) emphasizes the role of prophecy as an essential element in the new technique of rulership.

22 The concept of a static golden age, which Miss Swabey ("The Leading Myths of Our Times," *Ethics*, XLIX [Jan., 1939] p. 171) finds characteristic of Communism ("an economic variant of the old myth of paradise lost and regained") belongs to the point-of-balance myth. Cf. also Quincy Wright, *A Study of War* (Chicago: Univ. of Chicago Press, 1942), II, 1028.

23 *New Liberties for Old*, p. 22.
24 Commager, *Living Ideas in America*, p. 193.
25 In Snyder and Wilson, *Roots of Political Behavior*, p. 170. "In-
    stitutional growth occurs only in a competitive institutional set-
    ting . . . . The concept . . . can only be made to mean move-
    ment toward equilibrium among social institutions . . . . The
    chief function of government is to help keep the balance" (pp.
    170, 172, 173).
26 In Snyder and Wilson, *ibid.*, p. 132. In the "need for some form
    of equilibrium, adjustment, *modus vivendi* between the various
    groups and individuals of the community," Merriam finds one
    aspect of the birth of power, and in the "adaptation of value
    systems . . . one of the great tasks of social control" (Lasswell
    et al., *A Study of Power*, pp. 21, 46).
27 Commager, *Living Ideas in America*, p. 226.
28 Cf., e.g., the *Journal of United Labor*, VI (Jan. 10, 1886), 1178:
    "The end which the true reformer should aim to reach is to se-
    cure an unimpeded oscillation which, while it is ever modifying
    society, shall not carry it from one extreme to the other. The
    devotees of industrial science believe that they have found this
    equilibrium of the oscillations of society, by eliminating all
    cracies and establishing a new industrial order, founded upon the
    equity and solidarity of conditions."
29 *The Lonely Crowd*, pp. 245, 252.
30 A random check of issues of *Time* magazine of a decade ago
    reveals how completely these functions have been equated with
    Americanism—e.g., the following advertisements: "America the
    Provider—Automobiles" (The National City Bank of New York,
    Nov. 17, 1947); "The American Way" (Inco Nickel, featuring
    big construction equipment, Nov. 10, 1952); "A Strong America
    is the Bulwark of Freedom!" (General Cable Corporation, Jan.
    7, 1952). Others—e.g., the Texas and Pacific Railway (Dec. 31,
    1951, and June 15, 1953) and Republic Steel (Dec. 31, 1951)—
    employ the religious motif.
31 *An American Dilemma*, in Snyder and Wilson, *Roots of Political
    Behavior*, p. 578.

Chapter 19

1 Whitehead, *Adventures of Ideas*, p. 14.
2 Cf. Ralph Turner, *The Great Cultural Traditions* (N.Y.: McGraw-
   Hill Book Co., 1941), I, ix: "By its nature history is a synthetic

subject; i.e., it studies the whole man and, ideally, all men in actions as they have been in the past. Such a study must employ whatever methods and concepts are available for the analyzing of the behavior of these men, for their actions cannot be comprehended, either in parts or as a whole, without a knowledge of the elements and the processes of human behavior."

3 Cf. Urban, *Beyond Realism and Idealism,* pp. 202 ff., for a discussion of values in history.

4 E. F. M. Durbin, in Snyder and Wilson, *Roots of Political Behavior,* p. 43.

5 Lecky, *History of the Rise and Influence of the Spirit of Rationalism in Europe,* I, 17.

6 "Man is essentially a role-taking animal," says Morris (introd. to Mead, *Mind, Self, and Society,* p. xxi). "Actually, our thinking always takes place by means of some sort of symbols" (*ibid.,* p. 146); "these symbols, instead of being a mere conditioning of reflexes, are ways of picking out the stimuli so that various responses can organize themselves into a form of action" (p. 123).

7 Lasswell and Kaplan, *Power and Society,* p. 136.

8 Cassirer, *The Myth of the State,* p. 280.

9 Feibleman, *The Theory of Human Culture,* p. 135; cf. also Jaeger, *Paideia,* I, 61.

10 Hermann Broch, introd. to *On the Iliad,* by Rachel Bespaloff (N.Y.: Pantheon Books, 1948), p. 17.

BIBLIOGRAPHY

Bibliographical Note

Historical and folk materials relating to folk groups in the Middle West are almost inexhaustible: supplementing general histories and monographs are extensive sources in, for example, the *Wisconsin Historical Collections,* the Newberry Library, and the Public Archives of Canada in Ottawa. There are numerous publications, however, of unusual interest or value which deserve special notice.

For the study of the Indians, French explorers and traders, and Jesuit missionaries in Canada in the seventeenth century, the seventy-three volumes of the *Jesuit Relations and Allied Documents* edited by Reuben Gold Thwaites and associates (Cleveland: Burrows Brothers, 1896–1901) are of paramount importance; much of this material, together with other sources, is available in Vernon W. Kinietz, *The Indians of the Western Great Lakes (1615–1760)* (Ann Arbor, Mich.: Univ. of Mich. Press, 1940). The writings of Champlain and Gabriel Sagard have been admirably translated and edited in H. P. Biggar, *The Works of Samuel de Champlain* (Toronto: Champlain Society, 1922–1936), 7 volumes; and George M. Wrong and H. H. Langton, *Sagard's Long Journey to the Country of the Hurons* (Toronto: Champlain Society, 1939). James H. Cranston's *Etienne Brûlé* (Toronto: The Ryerson Press, 1949) and Morris Bishop's *Champlain: The Life of Fortitude* (N.Y.: Alfred A. Knopf, 1948) are readable and perceptive interpretations of these intrepid *voyageurs.* An excellent general history of the early period is George M. Wrong, *Rise and Fall of New France* (N.Y.: Macmillan, 1938), 2 volumes. Drawing afresh upon the *Jesuit Relations,* John H. Kennedy in *Jesuit and Savage in New France* (New Haven: Yale Univ. Press, 1950) and Francis X. Talbot in *Saint Among the Hurons* (N.Y.: Harper, 1949) present a balanced view of the Jesuit mission in Canada.

The historian of Yankee folk beliefs is especially indebted to the compilers of folklore and ballads—to George Lyman Kittredge, *The Old Farmer and His Almanack* (Cambridge, Mass.: Harvard Univ. Press, 1920); Richard M. Dorson, *Jonathan Draws the Long Bow* (Cambridge, Mass.: Harvard Univ. Press, 1946); Thomas Chandler Haliburton, *Sam Slick's Wise Saws and Modern Instances* (London: Hurst and Blackett, 1853); Clifton Johnson, *What They Say in New England* (Boston: Lothrop, 1896); Emelyn E. Gardner, *Folklore From the Schoharie Hills*, New York (Ann Arbor: Univ. of Mich. Press, 1937); and Evelyn K. Wells, *The Ballad Tree* (N.Y.: Ronald Press, 1950). Old almanacs like the *New-England Almanack* are mines of early nineteenth-century folk belief. Yankee thought is illuminated in two well-known studies: Van Wyck Brooks' *The Flowering of New England, 1815–1865* (N.Y.: E. P. Dutton, 1936) and Perry Miller's *The New England Mind* (N.Y.: Macmillan, 1939); Richard D. Mosier essays an interpretation of the Yankee mind in *The American Temper: Patterns of Our Intellectual Heritage* (Berkeley: Univ. of Cal. Press, 1952). The Yankee peddler displays his wares once more in Richardson Wright's entertaining *Hawkers and Walkers in Early America* (Philadelphia: J. B. Lippincott, 1927); Stewart Holbrook's *The Yankee Exodus* (N.Y.: Macmillan, 1950) traces the migration of New Englanders westward.

Studies of the Pennsylvania Germans are legion: among the more scholarly are Albert B. Faust, *The German Element in the United States* (N.Y.: The Steuben Society of America, 1927; originally published by Houghton Mifflin, 1909); Jesse L. Rosenberger, *The Pennsylvania Germans* (Chicago: Univ. of Chicago Press, 1923): Edwin M. Fogel, *Beliefs and Superstitions of the Pennsylvania Germans* (Philadelphia: Americana Germanica Press, 1915); Ralph Wood, editor, *The Pennsylvania Germans* (Princeton: Princeton Univ. Press, 1942); George Korson, *Pennsylvania Songs and Legends* (Philadelphia: Univ. of Penn. Press, 1949); and Fredric Klees, *The Pennsylvania Dutch* (N.Y.: Macmillan, 1950).

The portrait of the itinerant preacher at the turn of the nineteenth century is vividly sketched by W. P. Strickland, editor, *Autobiography of Peter Cartwright* (N.Y.: Carlton and Porter, 1857); William Milburn, *Ten Years of Preacher-Life* (1859) and *The Pioneers, Preachers and People of the Mississippi Valley* (1860), both published by Derby and Jackson, New York; Edward Eggleston, *The Circuit Rider* (N.Y.: Scribner's, 1899); and William W. Sweet, *Circuit-Rider Days in Indiana* (Indianapolis: W. K. Steward, 1916). Frederick M. Davenport's significant are Robert A. Brady, *Business as a System of Power* (N.Y.: Columbia Univ. Press, 1943); Peter F. Drucker, *The New Society: The Anatomy of the Industrial Order* (N.Y.: Harper, 1949); Joseph Dorfman, *The Economic Mind in American Civilization, 1865–1918* (N.Y.: The Viking Press, 1949); Thomas C. Cochran and William Miller, *The Age of Enterprise* (N.Y.: Macmillan, 1951); and Francis X. Sutton *et al.*, *The American Business Creed* (Cambridge, Mass.: Harvard Univ. Press, 1956). Historical background of industrial ideology is supplied in A. A. Berle, Jr. and Gardiner C. Means, *The Modern Corporation and Private Property* (N.Y.: Macmillan, 1933); David Lynch, *The Concentration of Economic Power* (N.Y.: Columbia Univ. Press, 1946); Henry A. Wells, *Monopoly and Social Control* (Washington, D.C.: Public Affairs Press, 1952); and Harold U. Faulkner, *The Decline of Laissez Faire, 1897–1917*, Vol. 7 of *The Economic History of the United States* (N.Y.: Rinehart, 1951). Henry Ford's autobiography (in collaboration with Samuel Crowther), *My Life and Work* (Garden City, N.Y.: Doubleday, Page, 1922) is balanced by Allan Nevins' *Ford: The Times, the Man, the Company* (N.Y.: Scribner's, 1954).

In addition to collections of the folklore of the Yankees and the Pennsylvania Germans, there are regional and national compilations which have been particularly useful to this study. Of primary importance to the understanding of Canadian Indian folk belief are C. Marius Barbeau's *Huron and Wyandot Mythology*, Geological Survey of Canada, Memoir 80 (Ottawa, 1915) and Stith Thompson's *Tales of the North American Indians* (Cambridge, Mass.: Harvard Univ. Press, 1929). Stith Thompson's analysis of folktale motifs in *The Folktale* (N.Y.: The Dryden Press, 1946) is unsurpassed. The most thorough compilation of superstitions from the area of the Middle West is Daniel L. and Lucy B. Thomas, *Kentucky Superstitions* (Princeton: Princeton Univ. Press, 1920). Notable among collections of songs and ballads are Florence H. Botsford, editor, *Folk Songs of Many Peoples* (N.Y.: The Woman's Press, 1921); Mary O. Eddy, *Ballads and Songs From Ohio* (N.Y.: J. J. Augustin, 1939); John Greenway, *American Folksongs of Protest* (Philadelphia: Univ. of Penn. Press, 1953); and two anthologies of John A. and Alan Lomax, *Folk Song USA* (N.Y.: Duell, Sloan and Pearce, 1947) and *American Ballads and Folksongs* (N.Y.: Macmillan, 1955).

The recognition of the significance of mythopoeic thinking and of its relationship to reality and power is so recent that only a half dozen or so of pioneering studies have so far appeared. Of the first impor-

Primitive Traits in Religious Revivals (N.Y.: Macmillan, 19\
historical-psychological study of camp revival behavior.

The richest vein of agricultural folk belief runs through t
journals, notably the *Prairie Farmer* and the *Iowa Homeste*
Western Farm Journal. For historical perspective, three genera
ments of agriculture are particularly relevant: Carl C. Taylo
Farmers' Movement, 1620–1920 (N.Y.: American Book Co.,
Fred A. Shannon, *The Farmer's Last Frontier, Agriculture 1860*
(N.Y.: Rinehart, 1945); and Grant McConnell, *The Decline of A
ian Democracy* (Berkeley: Univ. of California Press, 1953).
Transactions of the Illinois State Agricultural Society, Vol. I (Spi
field, Ill.: Lanphier and Walker, Printers for the State, 1855) cont
detailed reporting of county fairs and of speeches delivered at farm
meetings. Of great value for an interpretation of the background a
beliefs of the Patrons of Husbandry are histories of Jasper Coun
Iowa; Stephe Smith, *Grains For the Grangers* (San Francisco: Unic
Publishing Co., 1873); Solon J. Buck, *The Granger Movement* (Cam
bridge, Mass.: Harvard Univ. Press, 1933); and Earle D. Ross, *Iowa*
Agriculture (Iowa City: The State Historical Society of Iowa, 1951).
Henry N. Smith has broken new ground in a fascinating study, *Virgin*
Land: The American West as Symbol and Myth (Cambridge, Mass.:
Harvard Univ. Press, 1950).

The *Journal of United Labor,* the official publication of the Knights
of Labor (Philadelphia); *Coopers' Monthly Journal* (Cleveland); and
the *Workingman's Advocate* (Chicago) are incomparable sources for
the articulation of labor issues and workers' creeds. Still indispensable
are John R. Commons *et al., History of Labour in the United States*
(N.Y.: Macmillan, 1918), 2 volumes; Selig Perlman, *A History of*
Trade Unionism in the United States (N.Y.: Macmillan, 1922); and
Norman Ware, *The Labor Movement in the United States, 1860–1895*
(N.Y.: D. Appleton, 1929). More recently attempts have been made
to formulate patterns of labor movements in such studies as Foster R.
Dulles's *Labor in America* (N.Y.: Thomas Y. Crowell, 1949); Thomas
H. Greer's *American Social Reform Movements: Their Pattern Since*
1865 (N.Y.: Prentice-Hall, 1949); and Frank Tannenbaum's *A Phi-*
losophy of Labor (N.Y.: Alfred A. Knopf, 1951). The reminiscences
of Samuel Gompers in *Seventy Years of Life and Labor* (N.Y.: E. P.
Dutton, 1925; reissued in 1943), 2 volumes, vividly reflect contemporary labor views.

Efforts to define and appraise the ideologies of economists, businessmen, and industrialists have proliferated since 1933; among the more

tance, however, are Ernst Cassirer, *Language and Myth,* translated by Susanne K. Langer (N.Y.: Harper, 1946) and Miss Langer's *Philosophy in a New Key* (Cambridge, Mass.: Harvard Univ. Press, 1942), which applies to certain areas Cassirer's researches on symbol. C. G. Jung and C. Kerenyi, *Essays on a Science of Mythology,* translated by R. F. C. Hull (N.Y.: Bollingen Foundation, Inc., published by Pantheon Books, 1949); Bruno Snell, *The Discovery of the Mind,* translated by T. G. Rosenmeyer (Cambridge, Mass.: Harvard Univ. Press, 1953); Katherine Collier, *Cosmogonies of Our Fathers* (N.Y.: Columbia Univ. Press, 1934); and Abram Kardiner *et al., The Psychological Frontiers of Society* (N.Y.: Columbia Univ. Press, 1945) contain in varying degrees materials bearing on the formulation of a theory of myth. The role of power in society is extensively explored by Harold Lasswell and Abraham Kaplan, *Power and Society* (New Haven: Yale Univ. Press, 1950) and by C. E. Merriam and T. V. Smith, *A Study of Power* (Glencoe, Ill.: The Free Press, 1950).

Selected Bibliography

COLLECTIONS

Wisconsin Historical Collections (1855———)
Michigan Pioneer and Historical Collections (1874–1929)
Canadian Archives Publications (1909———)

NEWSPAPERS AND JOURNALS

Cleveland *Plain Dealer*
Cleveland *Weekly Leader and Herald*
Coopers' Monthly Journal
Green Bay (Wis.) *Intelligencer*
Iowa Homestead and Western Farm Journal
Journal of United Labor
Peoria Daily Press
Peoria Weekly Republican
Prairie Farmer
Transactions of the Illinois State Agricultural Society
Workingman's Advocate

BOOKS

Barbeau, C. Marius. *Huron and Wyandot Mythology.* Geological Survey of Canada, Memoir 80. Ottawa: 1915.
Basler, Roy P. *Abraham Lincoln: His Speeches and Writings.* Cleveland and N.Y.: World Publishing Co., 1946.

Becker, Carl L. *Modern Democracy.* (3rd printing) New Haven: Yale Univ. Press, 1942.

———. *New Liberties for Old.* New Haven: Yale Univ. Press, 1941.

Benson, Adolph, and Naboth Hedin. *Americans From Sweden.* Philadelphia and N.Y.: J. B. Lippincott, 1950.

Berle, A. A., Jr., and Gardiner C. Means. *The Modern Corporation and Private Property.* N.Y.: Macmillan, 1933.

Biggar, H. D. *The Works of Samuel de Champlain.* Champlain Society of Toronto, 1922–36.

Billington, Ray A. *Westward Expansion.* N.Y.: Macmillan, 1949.

Bishop, Morris. *Champlain: The Life of Fortitude.* N.Y.: Alfred A. Knopf, 1948.

Blair, Emma H. *Indian Tribes of the Upper Mississippi and Great Lakes Regions.* Cleveland: The Arthur H. Clark Co., 1911.

Blegen, Theodore C. *Grass Roots History.* Minneapolis: Univ. of Minn. Press, 1947.

Boatright, Mody C. *Folk Laughter on the American Frontier.* N.Y.: Macmillan, 1949.

Botkin, Benjamin A. *A Treasury of New England Folklore.* N.Y.: Crown Publishers, 1947.

Botsford, Florence H. (ed.). *Folk Songs of Many Peoples.* N.Y.: The Woman's Press, 1921.

Bourne, Annie N. (trans.). *The Voyages and Explorations of Samuel de Champlain (1604–1616),* Vol. II. Toronto: The Courier Press, 1911.

Brady, Robert A. *Business as a System of Power.* Morningside Heights, N.Y.: Columbia Univ. Press, 1943.

Bremond, Henri. *A Literary History of Religious Thought in France.* Translated by R. L. Montgomery. N.Y.: Macmillan, 1928.

Brooks, Van Wyck. *The Flowering of New England, 1815–1865.* N.Y.: E. P. Dutton, 1936.

Buck, Solon J. *The Granger Movement.* Cambridge, Mass.: Harvard Univ. Press, 1933.

Burlingame, Roger. *Backgrounds of Power.* N.Y.: Scribner's, 1949.

Butterfield, C. W. *History of Brulé's Discoveries and Explorations.* Cleveland: Helman Taylor Co., 1898.

Campbell, T. J. *Pioneer Priests of North America,* Vol. II. N.Y.: The America Press, 1910.

Čapek, Thomas. *The Čechs in America.* Boston and N.Y.: Houghton Mifflin, 1920.

Cassirer, Ernst. *An Essay on Man.* Doubleday Anchor Bks., 1954.

————. *Language and Myth*. Translated by Susanne K. Langer. N.Y.: Harper, 1946.

————. *The Myth of the State*. New Haven: Yale Univ. Press, 1946.

Champlain, Samuel de. *Voyages and Discoveries*. Translated and edited by H. H. Langton and W. F. Ganong. Toronto: The Champlain Society, 1929.

Chinard, Gilbert. *L'Amérique et le rêve exotique dans la littérature française au XVIIe et au XVIIIe siècle*. Paris: Librairie Hachette et Cie, 1913.

Clark, Dan E. *The West in American History*. N.Y.: Thomas Y. Crowell, 1937.

Clark, Harry H. (ed.). *Thomas Paine*. N.Y.: American Book Co., 1944.

Cochran, Thomas C., and William Miller. *The Age of Enterprise*. N.Y.: Macmillan, 1951.

Cole, Arthur C. *The Irrepressible Conflict: 1850–1865*. N.Y.: Macmillan, 1934.

————. *The Era of the Civil War, 1848–1870*. Centennial History of Illinois, Vol. III. Springfield, Ill.: Illinois Centennial Commission, 1919.

Collier, John. *Indians of the Americas*. (2nd printing) N.Y.: The New American Library of World Literature, Inc., Nov., 1951.

Collier, Katherine. *Cosmogonies of Our Fathers*. Morningside Heights, N.Y.: Columbia Univ. Press, 1934.

Commager, Henry S. *America in Perspective*. N.Y.: Random House, 1947.

————. *Living Ideas in America*. N.Y.: Harper, 1951.

Commons, John R., *et al*. *History of Labour in the United States*, Vol. II. N.Y.: Macmillan, 1921.

Constitutions of the Patrons of Husbandry. Issued by the National Grange and the Iowa State Grange. Des Moines: Carter, Husey, and Curl, 1873.

Cranston, James H. *Etienne Brûlé*. Toronto: The Ryerson Press, 1949.

Crouse, Nellis M. *Contributions of the Canadian Jesuits to the Geographical Knowledge of New France (1632–1675)*. Ithaca, N.Y.: Cornell Publications Printing Co., 1924.

Curti, Merle. *The Growth of American Thought*. N.Y.: Harper, 1943.

Davenport, Frederick M. *Primitive Traits in Religious Revivals*. N.Y.: Macmillan, 1905.

Diamond, Sigmund. *The Reputation of the American Businessman*. Cambridge, Mass.: Harvard Univ. Press, 1955.

Dillaway, Newton (ed.). *The Gospel of Emerson*. Wakefield, Mass.: The Montrose Press, 6th edition, revised, 1949.

Dorfman, Joseph. *The Economic Mind in American Civilization, 1865–1918*, Vol. III. N.Y.: The Viking Press, 1949.

Dorson, Richard M. *Jonathan Draws the Long Bow*. Cambridge, Mass.: Harvard Univ. Press, 1946.

Drucker, Peter F. *The New Society: The Anatomy of the Industrial Order*. N.Y.: Harper, 1949.

Dulles, Foster R. *Labor in America*. N.Y.: Thomas Y. Crowell, 1949.

Eddy, Mary O. *Ballads and Songs From Ohio*. N.Y.: J. J. Augustin, 1939.

Eggleston, Edward. *The Circuit Rider*. N.Y.: Scribner's, 1899.

Faulkner, Harold U. *American Economic History*. N.Y.: Harper, 1949.

———. *The Decline of Laissez Faire, 1897–1917*. *The Economic History of the United States*, Vol. VII. N.Y.: Rinehart, 1951.

Faust, Albert B. *The German Element in the United States*. N.Y.: The Steuben Society of America, 1927.

Feibleman, James. *The Theory of Human Culture*. N.Y.: Duell, Sloan and Pearce, 1946.

Fogel, Edwin M. *Beliefs and Superstitions of the Pennsylvania Germans*. *Americana Germanica*, No. 18. Philadelphia, 1915.

Ford, Henry, in collaboration with Samuel Crowther. *My Life and Work*. Garden City, N.Y.: Doubleday, Page, 1922.

Fox, Dixon Ryan (ed.). *Sources of Culture in the Middle West*. N.Y.: D. Appleton-Century, 1934.

Fox, William S. *Saint Ignace*. Toronto: McClelland and Stewart, 1949.

Frankfort, H. and H. A., *et al. The Intellectual Adventure of Ancient Man*. (2nd impression) Chicago: Univ. of Chicago Press, 1948.

Gabriel, Ralph H. *The Course of American Democratic Thought*. N.Y.: The Ronald Press, 1940.

Gardner, Emelyn E. *Folklore From the Schoharie Hills*, New York. Ann Arbor: Univ. of Michigan Press, 1937.

———, and Geraldine J. Chickering (eds.). *Ballads and Songs of Southern Michigan*. Ann Arbor: Univ. of Michigan Press, 1939.

Garrett, Garet. *The Wild Wheel*. N.Y.: Pantheon Books, 1952.

Gates, Paul W. *The Illinois Central Railroad and its Colonization Work. Harvard Economic Studies*, XLII. Cambridge, Mass.: Harvard Univ. Press, 1934.

Gompers, Samuel. *Seventy Years of Life and Labor*. N.Y.: E. P. Dutton, 1925; reissued, 1943.

Grant, W. L. (ed.). *Voyages of Samuel de Champlain (1604–1618)*. N.Y.: Scribner's, 1907.

Greenway, John. *American Folksongs of Protest*. Philadelphia: Univ. of Pennsylvania Press, 1953.

Greer, Thomas H. *American Social Reform Movements: Their Pattern Since 1865*. N.Y.: Prentice-Hall, 1949.

Haliburton, Thomas Chandler. *Sam Slick's Wise Saws and Modern Instances*. London: Hurst and Blackett, 1853.

Handlin, Oscar. *This Was America*. Cambridge, Mass.: Harvard Univ. Press, 1949.

Hatcher, Harlan. *Lake Erie*. Indianapolis and N.Y.: The Bobbs-Merrill Co., 1949.

Havighurst, Walter. *Land of Promise*. N.Y.: Macmillan, 1946.

History of Jasper County. Chicago: Western Historical Co., 1878.

Holbrook, Stewart. *The Yankee Exodus*. N.Y.: Macmillan, 1950.

Hubbart, Henry C. *The Older Middle West, 1840–1880*. N.Y.: D. Appleton-Century, 1936.

Jaeger, Werner. *Paideia*, Vol. III. Translated by Gilbert Highet. N.Y.: Oxford Univ. Press, 1944.

Johnson, Clifton. *What They Say in New England*. Boston, 1896.

Jones, Rev. Peter. *A History of the Ojibwa Indians*. London, n.d.

Jung, C. G., and C. Kerenyi. *Essays on a Science of Mythology*. Translated by R. F. C. Hull. N.Y.: Bollingen Foundation, Inc., published by Pantheon Books, 1949.

Kardiner, Abram, *et al*. *The Psychological Frontiers of Society*. N.Y.: Columbia Univ. Press, 1945.

Kelley, O. H. *Manual of Subordinate Granges of the Patrons of Husbandry*. (4th edition) Washington, D.C.: Gibson Bros., 1872.

Kellogg, Louise F. *Early Narratives of the Northwest*. N.Y.: Scribner's, 1917.

Kennedy, James H. *A History of the City of Cleveland, 1796–1896*. Cleveland: The Imperial Press, 1896.

Kenton, Edna. *The Indians of North America*, Vol. I. Edited from *The Jesuit Relations and Allied Documents*. N.Y.: Harcourt, Brace, 1927.

Kinietz, W. Vernon. *The Indians of the Western Great Lakes (1615–1760)*. Ann Arbor: Univ. of Michigan Press, 1940.

Kittredge, George Lyman. *The Old Farmer and His Almanack*. Cambridge, Mass.: Harvard Univ. Press, 1920.

Klees, Fredric. *The Pennsylvania Dutch*. N.Y.: Macmillan, 1950.

Koerner, Gustave. *Memoirs*, Vol. I. Edited by Thomas J. McCormack. Cedar Rapids, Ia.: The Torch Press, 1909.

Korson, George. *Pennsylvania Songs and Legends*. Philadelphia: Univ. of Pennsylvania Press, 1949.

Landon, Fred. *Lake Huron*. Indianapolis and N.Y.: Bobbs-Merrill, 1944.

Langer, Susanne K. *Philosophy in a New Key*. Cambridge, Mass.: Harvard Univ. Press, 1942.

Lasswell, Harold, and Abraham Kaplan. *Power and Society*. New Haven: Yale Univ. Press, 1950.

————, C. E. Merriam, and T. V. Smith. *A Study of Power*. Glencoe, Ill.: The Free Press, 1950.

Lecky, W. E. H. *History of the Rise and Influence of the Spirit of Rationalism in Europe*, Vol. I. N.Y.: D. Appleton, 1873.

Ledbetter, Eleanor E. (trans. and ed.). *Krakonos, The King of the Mountains*. Bredska, 1930.

Lomax, John A. and Alan. *American Ballads and Folksongs*. N.Y.: Macmillan, 1955.

————. *Folk Song USA*. N.Y.: Duell, Sloan and Pearce, 1947.

Lynch, David. *The Concentration of Economic Power*. N.Y.: Columbia Univ. Press, 1946.

McConnell, Grant. *The Decline of Agrarian Democracy*. Berkeley and Los Angeles: Univ. of California Press, 1953.

McCormick, Cyrus. *The Century of the Reaper*. Boston: Houghton Mifflin, 1931.

Mead, George. *Mind, Self, and Society*. (3rd impression) Chicago: Univ. of Chicago Press, 1940.

Merrill, Horace S. *Bourbon Democracy of the Middle West, 1865–1896*. Baton Rouge: Louisiana State Univ. Press, 1953.

Milburn, William. *The Pioneers, Preachers and People of the Mississippi Valley*. N.Y.: Derby and Jackson, 1860.

————. *Ten Years of Preacher-Life*. N.Y.: Derby and Jackson, 1859.

Morris, Charles. *Signs, Language and Behavior*. N.Y.: Prentice-Hall, 1946.

Mosier, Richard D. *The American Temper: Patterns of Our Intellectual Heritage*. Berkeley and Los Angeles: Univ. of California Press, 1952.

Nevins, Allan. *Ford: The Times, the Man, the Company*. N.Y.: Scribner's, 1954.

Oman, Charles. *The Sixteenth Century*. N.Y.: E. P. Dutton, 1937.

Park, Robert E. *The Immigrant Press and its Control*. N.Y.: Harper, 1922.

Pease, Theodore C. *The Frontier State, 1818–1848*. *Centennial His-*

tory of Illinois, Vol. II. Springfield, Ill.: Illinois Centennial Commission, 1918.

Perlman, Selig. *A History of Trade Unionism in the United States.* N.Y.: Macmillan, 1922.

Philbrick, F. A. *Understanding English.* N.Y.: Macmillan, 1942.

Popper, K. R. *The Open Society and its Enemies.* (3rd impression) London: Routledge & Kegan Paul, 1949.

Power, Richard L. *Planting Corn Belt Culture.* Indianapolis: Indiana Historical Society, 1953.

Richards, William C. *The Last Billionaire.* N.Y.: Scribner's, 1948.

Riesman, David, *et al. The Lonely Crowd.* New Haven: Yale Univ. Press, 1950.

Robinson, Joan. *Monopoly and Competition and Their Regulation.* London: Macmillan, 1954.

Robison, W. Scott (ed.). *History of the City of Cleveland.* Cleveland: Robison and Crockett, 1887.

Rose, William G. *Cleveland: The Making of a City.* Cleveland and N.Y.: World Publishing Co., 1950.

Rosenberger, Jesse L. *The Pennsylvania Germans.* Chicago: Univ. of Chicago Press, 1923.

Ross, Earle D. *Iowa Agriculture.* Iowa City: The State Historical Society of Iowa, 1951.

Rourke, Constance. *American Humor.* N.Y.: Harcourt, Brace, 1931.

Rusk, Ralph L. *The Literature of the Middle Western Frontier.* N.Y.: Columbia Univ. Press, 1925.

Sandburg, Carl. *Abraham Lincoln: The Prairie Years.* N.Y.: Harcourt, Brace, 1926.

Schaack, Michael J. *Anarchy and Anarchists.* Chicago: F. J. Schulte, 1889.

Schlesinger, Arthur M., Jr. *The Age of Jackson.* Boston: Little, Brown, 1945.

Shannon, Fred A. *The Farmer's Last Frontier, Agriculture 1860–1897.* N.Y.: Rinehart, 1945.

Skinner, Constance L. *Beavers, Kings and Cabins.* N.Y.: Macmillan, 1935.

Smith, Henry N. *Virgin Land: The American West as Symbol and Myth.* Cambridge, Mass.: Harvard Univ. Press, 1950.

Smith, Stephe. *Grains For the Grangers.* San Francisco: Union Publishing Co., 1873.

Snell, Bruno. *The Discovery of the Mind.* Translated by T. G. Rosenmeyer. Cambridge, Mass.: Harvard Univ. Press, 1953.

Snyder, Richard C., and H. Hubert Willson. *Roots of Political Behavior.* N.Y.: American Book Co., 1949.

Sorel, Georges. *Reflections on Violence.* Translated by T. E. Hulme. N.Y.: Peter Smith, 1941.

Strickland, W. P. (ed.). *Autobiography of Peter Cartwright, the Backwoods Preacher.* N.Y.: Carlton and Porter, 1857.

Sutton, Francis X., et al. *The American Business Creed.* Cambridge, Mass.: Harvard Univ. Press, 1956.

Swain, Joseph W. *The Ancient World,* Vol. I. N.Y.: Harper, 1950.

Sweet, William W. *Circuit-Rider Days in Indiana.* Indianapolis: W. K. Steward, 1916.

Talbot, Francis X. *Saint Among the Hurons.* N.Y.: Harper, 1949.

Tannenbaum, Frank. *A Philosophy of Labor.* N.Y.: Alfred A. Knopf, 1951.

Taylor, Carl C. *The Farmers' Movement, 1620–1920.* N.Y.: American Book Co., 1953.

Thomas, D. L. and Lucy B. *Kentucky Superstitions.* Princeton: Princeton Univ. Press, 1920.

Thompson, Stith. *The Folktale.* N.Y.: The Dryden Press, 1946.

———. *Tales of the North American Indians.* Cambridge, Mass.: Harvard Univ. Press, 1928.

Thwaites, Reuben G. (ed.). *The Jesuit Relations and Allied Documents.* 73 vols. Cleveland: Burrows Brothers, 1896–1901.

Urban, Wilbur M. *Beyond Realism and Idealism.* London: George Allen and Unwin, 1949.

Wallis, Wilson D. *Religion in Primitive Society.* N.Y.: F. S. Crofts, 1939.

Ware, Norman. *The Labor Movement in the United States, 1860–1895.* N.Y.: D. Appleton, 1929.

Warnock, Robert, and George Anderson. *Tradition and Revolt. The World in Literature,* Vol. III. N.Y.: Scott, Foresman, 1950.

Weaver, James B. (ed.). *Past and Present of Jasper County,* Vols. I, II. Indianapolis. B. F. Bowen, 1912.

Wells, Evelyn K. *The Ballad Tree.* N.Y.: The Ronald Press, 1950.

Wells, Henry A. *Monopoly and Social Control.* Washington, D.C.: Public Affairs Press, 1952.

Wheelwright, Philip. *The Burning Fountain.* Bloomington: Indiana Univ. Press, 1954.

Whitehead, Alfred N. *Adventures of Ideas.* N.Y.: Macmillan Co., 1933; reprinted Nov., 1947.

Wittke, Carl. *We Who Built America.* N.Y.: Prentice-Hall, 1940.

Wood, Ralph (ed.). *The Pennsylvania Germans*. Princeton: Princeton Univ. Press, 1942.

Wright, John S. *Chicago: Past, Present, Future*. Chicago: Western News Co., 1868.

Wright, Richardson. *Hawkers and Walkers in Early America*. Philadelphia: J. B. Lippincott, 1927.

Wrong, George M., and H. H. Langton (ed. and trans.). *Sagard's Long Journey to the Country of the Hurons*. Toronto: The Champlain Society, 1939.

Wynne, John J. *The Jesuit Martyrs of North America*. N.Y.: The Universal Knowledge Foundation, 1925.

INDEX

283